Praise for *Cloud Devotion*

"A faithful and accessible version of a profound text that will nourish our spiritual journey throughout the year. Dr. Robinson invites us to explore how the wisdom of this unknown fourteenth-century mystic can guide and deepen our relationship with God."

—**The Rev. Dr. Jane Tomaine,** author of *St. Benedict's Toolbox* and *The Rule of Benedict: Christian Monastic Wisdom for Daily Living*

"Robinson's daily reflection questions helped me to slow down and ponder what I read and take it to heart. In addition, I find his Appendix B, where he offers basis for female authorship of *The Cloud*, compelling. Thanks to the spiritual direction of both authors, I expect this to be a tool that encourages a deeper life of prayer for years to come."

—**Dawn Taloyo, M.Div.,** Director of Pastoral and Congregational Health, Pacific Northwest Conference of the Evangelical Covenant Church

"David Robinson has given us a wonderful gift, bringing this classic to us in contemporary language and in small daily amounts with thought-provoking questions that provide us with a yearful of morsels that will nourish our souls. What a great way for those unfamiliar with *The Cloud of Unknowing* to savor its contents, and what a creative way for those who have read it to be reintroduced to it in a manner that demands deeply focused attention."

—**Dennis Okholm**, Azusa Pacific University; author of *Monk Habits for Everyday People*

"David Robinson's highly readable translation of *The Cloud of Unknowing* makes this classic text devotionally accessible. Designed for a year of daily use, Robinson's *Cloud Devotion* invites the reader into slow meditation on the profound themes of this fourteenth-century text. I commend *Cloud Devotion* with enthusiasm, not least for the pervasive call to a humble and dependent life in Christ."

—**Mark Labberton**, President, Fuller Theological Seminary

"The text of *Cloud Devotion* consists of deep and fascinating words and truth. It gets deeper the more one is living with it. It is helpful in the school of life for growing deeper in the glory of God to read and meditate each day of a year on these old words of trusting in God alone."

—**Sr. Dorothea Flandera, OSB**,
Abbess, St. Hildegard Abbey, Rüdesheim am Rhein, Germany

"*Cloud Devotion* provides awakening meditations for the year for those yearning for a new way of life. Each day offers thoughts from Scripture and wisdom reflections from *The Cloud*, stirring the person reading it with a desire to live and share God's love. It inspires one to continue living with purity of heart and with practical ways of persevering in humility. *Cloud Devotion* offers a person transformation from within."

—**Lucy Wynkoop, OSB**, co-author of *Lectio Divina: Contemplative Awakening and Awareness*

"My heart has yearned for this book. I wanted a guide to help me savor and reflect on the spiritual classic *The Cloud of Unknowing*. David has insightfully discerned how we might do this. The partnership of this unknown, ancient writer and this known, living pastor is masterful."

—**Dr. MaryKate Morse**, author of *A Guidebook to Prayer*,
Professor of Leadership and Spiritual Formation, Portland Seminary

"Marvelous. Simple. Profoundly rich. The loving grace of God breaks through and bubbles up, inviting the reader inward, upward, outward and onward, loving God, loving neighbor, and more fully finding oneself along the way. For anyone seeking to go deeper with God, *Cloud Devotion* is bountiful."

—**Rev. Prof. Marta Bennett,** pastor, professor, missionary,
living and serving in Kenya since 1994

"What a gift David Robinson has given us in *Cloud Devotion*, taking this ancient text in all its forbidding strangeness and rendering it into a plain yet vivid and accessible guide that makes good sense to the spiritually hungry living in the twenty-first century."

—**Richard Peace**, PhD, Senior Professor of Evangelism and Spiritual Formation, Fuller Theological Seminary; author of *Noticing God*

Cloud Devotion

THROUGH THE YEAR WITH

The Cloud of Unknowing

DAVID G. ROBINSON

PARACLETE PRESS
BREWSTER, MASSACHUSETTS

2020 First Printing

Cloud Devotion: Through the Year with The Cloud of Unknowing

Copyright © 2020 by David G. Robinson

ISBN 978-1-64060-433-9

Cover image: Thomas Robinson, photographer, "Cumulus Clouds Over Chapman Beach," www.zoomdak.com.

The Paraclete Press name and logo (dove on cross) are trademarks of Paraclete Press, Inc.

Library of Congress Cataloging-in-Publication Data
Names: Robinson, David, 1957- author.
Title: Cloud devotion : through the year with The cloud of unknowing /
    David Robinson.
Description: Brewster : Paraclete Press, 2020. | Includes bibliographical references. | Summary: "A
    year of daily devotionals based upon The Cloud of Unknowing, one of the great classics of Christian
    spirituality. It was written in the middle of England perhaps near Nottingham, in the middle of the
    fourteenth century. The anonymous author wrote in the language of common people, and describes
    spiritual life with God in down-to-earth, domestic language, with a holistic and humble vision of
    everyday spirituality. There are many scripture verses to guide you through the year"—Provided by
    publisher.
Identifiers: LCCN 2019031634 | ISBN 9781640604339 (paperback)
Subjects: LCSH: Cloud of unknowing. | Mysticism—History—Middle Ages,
    600-1500. | Devotional literature.
Classification: LCC BV5082.3 .R63 2020 | DDC 248.2/2—dc23
LC record available at https://lccn.loc.gov/2019031634

10 9 8 7 6 5 4 3 2 1

Published by Paraclete Press
Brewster, Massachusetts
www.paracletepress.com

Printed in the United States of America

To the women in my life
who have inspired me
to grow in my love for God

A voice came from the cloud, saying,
"This is my Son, whom I have chosen; listen to him."
LUKE 9:35

CONTENTS

Dear God,

open my heart and teach me to listen.

Nothing is hidden from You.

Cleanse the intent of my heart

with the unspeakable gift of Your grace,

that I may more perfectly love You,

more fully live in your presence,

and more worthily praise You.

Amen.

(A prayer of Alcuin, 735–804,
used as a frontispiece
in early manuscript editions of
The Cloud of Unknowing)

Living in a Land of Clouds

T he Bible is full of clouds. The word "cloud" shows up more than 150 times in Scripture, most often expressing the living presence of God. A rainbow appeared among the clouds in the time of Noah to express God's everlasting, loving commitment to humanity. A cloud guided the people of Israel for four decades through the wilderness before they entered the Promised Land. The glory of the Lord appeared to the people of Israel in a cloud in the wilderness. A cloud of God's presence came down upon Mount Sinai as Moses went up on the mountain to receive the Ten Commandments. A cloud hovered over the tabernacle, the holy place of worship for the wandering Israelites, as God's glory filled the place. The prayers of ancient Israel in the book of Psalms often describe God's presence in clouds. See Psalm 18:

> In my distress I called to the Lord; I cried to my God for help. . . .
> He parted the heavens and came down; dark clouds were under his feet.
> He mounted the cherubim and flew; he soared on the wings of the wind.
> He made darkness his covering, his canopy around him—the dark rain clouds of the sky.
> Out of the brightness of his presence clouds advanced. . . .
> The Lord thundered from heaven; the voice of the Most High resounded.

I am particularly moved by the phrase "out of the brightness of his presence clouds advanced."

God is often revealed in the Bible in radiant clouds. For example, God's presence came as a cloud, filling the temple of worship with the radiance of God's glory. The psalmist declares that God "makes the clouds his chariot and rides on the wings of the wind" (Psalm 104:3). Jesus went with his closest followers up to the top of a mountain where he was transfigured before them as the mountain was enveloped in a bright cloud. There, God spoke out of the radiance, declaring, "This is my Son, whom I love; with him I am well pleased. Listen to him!" Then, in the last days, Christ will return, "coming with the clouds of heaven," as foretold in the book of Daniel and declared by Jesus in the Gospels.[1]

This book of daily devotions is based upon *The Cloud of Unknowing*, one of the great classics of Christian spirituality. It was written in the middle of England perhaps near Nottingham, in the middle of the fourteenth century. The anonymous author wrote in the language of common people, not in Latin.[2] *The Cloud*—as it is often known—describes spiritual life with God in down-to-earth, domestic language, with a holistic and humble vision of everyday spirituality. Though very little is known about the author, what is known for certain is that she or he lived in a land of clouds.

I've lived most of my life in the Pacific Northwest, a land of clouds. Since 1993, my wife and I have lived on the north Oregon coast, a few minutes' walk from the beach. Our beach village averages over ninety inches of rain per year and 240 cloudy days per year. With such an abundance of clouds, we often enjoy weeks of mist, fog, and rain. When rain falls on my face, I feel as though my life has been blessed by God. No wonder I am drawn to devotional writing that focuses on clouds as a daily way into life with God.

In this edition of *The Cloud of Unknowing*, I've sought to remain as true as possible to the voice of this medieval classic. *Cloud Devotion* follows the original Middle English text sentence by sentence, with my own translation and paraphrase. I've divided the work into 366 small portions, adding a Scripture passage related to the theme from each daily reading.

I invite you to walk with God as you read this book. My hope is that you will hear Christ's personal and intimate invitation to come closer to God within the Cloud of Unknowing. As the writer of the book of Hebrews proclaims, "We are surrounded by such a great cloud of witnesses" (Hebrews 12:1). Along with the great cloud of witnesses across the centuries who have encountered God through *The Cloud of Unknowing*, may you also enter more fully into the brightness and glory of God's presence.

January

God's Way of Love

JANUARY 1

Follow God's example, therefore, as dearly loved children and walk in the way of love, just as Christ loved us and gave himself up for us as a fragrant offering and sacrifice to God.

EPHESIANS 5:1–2

In the name of the Father and of the Son and of the Holy Spirit, I encourage you and invite you, with as much strength as the bonds of love may support, to seek to live more fully in Christ's presence, growing daily as a follower of the way of love. No matter how this book came into your possession, as long as you've chosen to receive these words, do not merely read them on the page or write them down in a journal. Do more than merely tell a few others about this book. Read these words silently or aloud to someone. That is helpful. Better yet, learn to live these words not merely in your outward life, but deep within your heart, in the place where God desires to live within you. You are a dearly loved child of God. God invites you to walk in the way of love. This life with God is only possible by God's grace.

REFLECTION QUESTION: As you step into this year, what do you hope for in your life with God?

JANUARY 2

Therefore we do not lose heart. Though outwardly we are wasting away, yet inwardly we are being renewed day by day.

2 CORINTHIANS 4:16

In this present life, seek to grow into spiritual maturity. One of the very real challenges is that we live in mortal bodies that often become weary and eventually waste away. Knowing this about yourself, continue to seek to live more fully in Christ's presence, inwardly renewed by choosing to walk in the way of Jesus daily. Otherwise this book will amount to nothing. As you receive these words, I encourage you and any others who may read this book, by the power of love, to take your time through the year and read through the whole thing, from the opening pages to the end. Daily, take a little portion of time to reflect upon this way of life with God. Perhaps there are some insights in the beginning or in the middle that are left hanging, not fully understood until the end. If you pick and choose only what you like, you may inadvertently be misled. To avoid this trouble, I ask you, out of love, take your time to walk with God and perhaps also with a few others through these pages, from January all the way to the end of December.

REFLECTION QUESTION: What commitments are you making this year in your devotional life?

JANUARY 3

Then we will no longer be infants, tossed back and forth by the waves, and blown here and there by every wind of teaching and by the cunning and craftiness of people in their deceitful scheming. Instead, speaking the truth in love, we will grow to become in every respect the mature body of him who is the head, that is, Christ.

EPHESIANS 4:14–15

In the spiritual life, there will always be hawkers and gawkers, flatterers and tattlers, blamers and shamers, and every kind of wheeler and dealer who do not understand a life of devotion to God. Such people will not accept the invitation to draw near to God. There is little value in passing such a book as the one you are holding on to them, for they will merely meddle with what is written here or seek to peddle these words for profit. This book was not written for curiosity seekers, academics, or intellectuals. Although many such people may seek to live the good life, this book will not be of much help to those who read merely out of casual curiosity. Day by day, through the months ahead, do not let your life be tossed around by waves of fads and fashions, nor "blown here and there by every wind of teaching," but seek to grow and mature in your faith in Christ together with others, as you listen to the truth spoken with love.

REFLECTION QUESTION: What sources of truth do you listen to regularly?

JANUARY 4

Who may ascend the mountain of the LORD?
Who may stand in his holy place? . . .

They will receive blessing from the LORD
and vindication from God their Savior.
Such is the generation of those who seek him,
who seek your face, God of Jacob.

PSALM 24:3, 5–6

If you who currently live an active and external way of life, but also experience inner longings for God's Spirit, begin to follow these teachings; then, although Christ's ways are mostly hidden and secret, you will be given grace upon grace. Even if you are not devoutly seeking Jesus in the contemplative life, God's grace will be sufficient for you to invite you in closer. Now and then, through times of prayer and meditation you will perceive, through the mists of old ignorance, the heights of the mountains of life with the Lord. Even an occasional glimpse of these heights, by the grace of Christ's presence, will provide great comfort and encouragement to you.

REFLECTION QUESTION: How do you seek to be in God's presence?

JANUARY 5

You make known to me the path of life;
you will fill me with joy in your presence,
with eternal pleasures at your right hand.

PSALM 16:11

Friend of God, I ask you to look intently upon the pathway of life ahead, knowing God has called you and will equip you to walk in this way. Give thanks to God with all your heart so that you may continue, through the help of God's grace, to stand confidently in this way of life with good purpose and perseverance, even when many physical and spiritual enemies assail you. By the grace of our Lord Jesus Christ, walk in this way, fully in Christ's presence, and you will soon win the crown of everlasting life. As the ancient psalmist reminds us, God's intent is to make known to you the way upon which you are to walk. As you walk in this path of life, God will fill you with joy in Christ's presence, with eternal pleasures at God's right hand.

REFLECTION QUESTION: What brings you the most joy?

JANUARY 6

Oh, the depth of the riches of the wisdom and knowledge of God!
How unsearchable his judgments, and his paths beyond tracing out!

ROMANS 11:33

Friend of God, you do well to understand God's way by recognizing four distinct paths of the spiritual life: the ordinary path, the special path, the extraordinary path, and the perfect path. Three of these you begin and end in this life. The fourth you may begin in this life by God's grace, but it shall endure without end in the bliss of heaven. Notice how they are set here in order each one after the other; first ordinary, then special, then extraordinary, and finally, the perfect path. By this same order, God is calling to you by his great mercy, first in the ordinary places, then in special times, followed by extraordinary means, and finally stirring within your heart a desire for Jesus's life of perfection.

REFLECTION QUESTION: What are ordinary ways and special ways you walk with God?

JANUARY 7

Ask and it will be given to you; seek and you will find; knock and the
door will be opened to you. For everyone who asks receives; the one who
seeks finds; and to the one who knocks, the door will be opened.

MATTHEW 7:7–8

At first, you were living an ordinary way of life, among the company of your worldly friends. With everlasting love, God made you and formed you before you were born. By love, Jesus bought you with the price of his precious life while you were still lost in Adam's old ways. With love, Jesus opened the door for you to come near to God through an ordinary spiritual path, the path you walk through your daily life, now lived with God as your companion along the way.

REFLECTION QUESTION: When has a door opened to a new opportunity in your life with God?

JANUARY 8

For this reason I remind you to fan into flame the gift of God, which is in you through the laying on of my hands.

2 TIMOTHY 1:6

When the fire of your inner desire was kindled by God's grace, you began to place upon this fire the logs of longing. Jesus led you by the light and warmth of this fire into a special way of spiritual life, in which you learned to be a servant among Christ's followers. As Paul wrote to Timothy, fan the flames within you. The fire within is a gift from God. Learn to live more specially and devoutly in your service to God than you previously thought possible while you were still living in the ordinary path of spiritual life.

REFLECTION QUESTION: How is your inner fire burning?

JANUARY 9

For we are God's handiwork, created in Christ Jesus to do good works, which God prepared in advance for us to do.

EPHESIANS 2:10

Out of God's loving heart, you were known long before you were born. God has never given up on you. As Paul wrote long ago, you are God's creative masterpiece. You were created to do good works that will surprise and bless others. God has already prepared these wonders to come to life through you in the lives of others. Discover the mystery and grace of how secretly Jesus has been inviting you into the third path of spiritual living, the extraordinary path.

REFLECTION QUESTION: What extraordinary wonders is God doing in your life?

JANUARY 10

Be perfect, therefore, as your heavenly Father is perfect.

MATTHEW 5:48

The final and fullest way of living in God's presence is the way of perfection. People usually think perfection means living flawlessly, without ever making any mistakes. God alone makes no mistakes. Yet, God invites us to walk in the way of perfection. How can this be? Understand the ancient way of perfection, a journey into fullness, wholeness, and maturity in Christ. A person who walks in the way of perfection grows in maturity, becoming more and more complete. Be willing to walk along these four paths of spiritual life, going through many stages of growth, with God as the final goal. God will work within you, empowering you along the way to become more and more mature in Christ. God calls us to grow up, to become mature, to allow our life to be made whole again. Through this spiritual way of life, may we learn to lift up our feet and walk in love, stepping confidently forward into the perfect way.

REFLECTION QUESTION: What are some ways your faith life has grown recently?

JANUARY 11

He makes me lie down in green pastures,
he leads me beside quiet waters,
he refreshes my soul.
He guides me along the right paths
for his name's sake.

PSALM 23:2–3

I invite you to open your eyes and recognize your frailty. Ask yourself, *Who am I?* Pay attention to the vain ways you've been trying to win God's favor. God already loves you more than you know. As you lie down at night, look at the state of your weary, sleepy heart. Rest your soul in God's green pastures. Wake up in the morning, and drink deeply of Christ's love beside quiet waters. Let your life be refreshed and learn to listen to his voice calling to you along God's good paths. Try following Christ's example by humbling yourself and opening your heart to God's love. Though King of kings and Lord of lords, Jesus chose to humble himself to come live with us on earth. Among his flock of sheep, Jesus has graciously chosen you to be his beloved. As you learn to listen to the voice of the Good Shepherd, he will lead you to green meadows where you may be fed with the sweetness of his love as a token of the abundant heritage, which lies ahead in the kingdom of heaven.

REFLECTION QUESTION: Where do you find quiet waters and green pastures?

JANUARY 12

The hour has already come for you to wake up from your slumber, because our salvation is nearer now than when we first believed. The night is nearly over; the day is almost here. So let us put aside the deeds of darkness and put on the armor of light.

ROMANS 13:11–12

Beware of the voice of the enemy lulling you into a state of spiritual slumber. Be aware of where you are in your life with God. Some people think they have made headway in the way of prayer, but have allowed themselves to fall asleep, and have stopped progressing along the path. Wake from your spiritual slumber. Step away from the darkness, including dark ways of living, and step into the fullness of the light of Christ. Dress yourself in the armor of light. Your life will be a wreck unless you begin living by God's grace and guidance, doing everything you can to live out your calling as a follower of Christ.

REFLECTION QUESTION: What are some ways you need to wake up from spiritual slumber?

JANUARY 13

Brothers and sisters, I do not consider myself yet to have taken hold of it. But one thing I do: Forgetting what is behind and straining toward what is ahead, I press on toward the goal to win the prize for which God has called me heavenward in Christ Jesus.

PHILIPPIANS 3:13–14

Press on then in Christ's way of life. You are being called heavenward. Look ahead at the path that lies before you, and forget what lies behind you, as St. Paul instructs us in his letter to the Philippians. Pay little attention to what you have already gained, but instead yearn for what still lies ahead of you in your journey of faith. This is the best way to learn humility. Long for God with all your heart if you desire to grow in love and maturity. May this sacred desire be forged within your will, by God's almighty hand and by your consent. God is a great lover. Let nothing take greater place in your life than God's love. You are loved by God, and God desires to be first in your heart.

REFLECTION QUESTION: Do you focus most of your attention on the past, the present, or the future?

JANUARY 14

Jesus replied: "'Love the Lord your God with all your heart and with all your soul and with all your mind.' This is the first and greatest commandment."

MATTHEW 22:37–38

Look to God with all your heart. Keep guard over the windows and doors of your soul, allowing in no flies or pests. If you are willing to do this, cry out for Jesus's help through prayer, and very soon, he will help you. So press on then, and see how willing the Lord is to protect you. God is fully ready, waiting only for you to call out for help. What shall we do then? How shall we press on? Learn to call out to God with all your heart, with all your soul, and with all your mind. Call together other fellow travelers and journey together, moving forward with God in this way of love.

REFLECTION QUESTION: Who are you walking with in your journey of faith?

JANUARY 15

I lift up my eyes to you,
to you who sit enthroned in heaven.
As the eyes of slaves look to the hand of their master,
as the eyes of a female slave look to the hand of her mistress,
so our eyes look to the LORD our God,
till he shows us his mercy.

PSALM 123:1–2

L ift up your heart to God with a quiet stirring of love. Look to God for who God is, not just for what God can give you. Keep your attention on Jesus rather than on yourself, so that Jesus becomes the sole desire of your mind and heart. Seek to let go of all earthly attachments, so that both the thoughts of your mind and the desires of your heart are not encumbered by earthly things, either great or small. Let them be, and take no heed of them. Love is the work that most pleases God.

REFLECTION QUESTION: What earthly attachment is most difficult for you to release to God?

JANUARY 16

Come to me, all you who are weary and burdened, and I will give you rest.
Take my yoke upon you and learn from me, for I am gentle and humble in
heart, and you will find rest for your souls. For my yoke is easy and my
burden is light.

MATTHEW 11:28–30

A ll who come to Christ discover how much they are loved by God. Keep loving God and learn from Christ how to live a life that is gentle and humble. You will find great joy in this inner work of loving God. God's angels will come to your aid with all their might. Bad spirits will try to oppose you whenever you do this work of resting your life in Christ. They will try to prevent you from fully turning your heart to God. People that you meet will be wonderfully helped by this work unfolding within you, even though you may not know how. People going through fiery trials will be eased of their pain by virtue of this work. No other work is as able to cleanse your soul and make you more like Christ. Yet, this work is the lightest of all work, for Christ's burden is light and being yoked to Christ is easy. When your soul is helped by God's grace, you discover within a spirit of delight and willingness to continue resting your life in God's love. Otherwise, it is hard work and too much to bear.

REFLECTION QUESTION: Where do you find rest for your soul?

JANUARY 17

After six days Jesus took with him Peter, James and John the brother of James, and led them up a high mountain by themselves. There he was transfigured before them. His face shone like the sun, and his clothes became as white as the light. . . . While he was still speaking, a bright cloud covered them, and a voice from the cloud said, "This is my Son, whom I love; with him I am well pleased. Listen to him!"

MATTHEW 17:1–2, 5

B e persistent in turning your heart fully to God until you know God's delight within your soul. At first, you will find yourself in a kind of darkness, as in a Cloud of Unknowing.[3] You will not understand much, at first, except that you feel deep within you a deep desire for the Lord. You will learn to pray naked, allowing God's Cloud of Unknowing to cover you, though you will not understand what is happening.[4] For a time, you may not see Jesus clearly by light of understanding in your mind, or feel him in the sweetness of love in your affection. Do not be anxious or afraid. Rest your soul in the love of God, as though sitting on top of a mountain enshrouded in clouds.

REFLECTION QUESTION: How often do you pray when undressed?

JANUARY 18

For while we are in this tent, we groan and are burdened, because we do not wish to be unclothed but to be clothed instead with our heavenly dwelling, so that what is mortal may be swallowed up by life.

2 CORINTHIANS 5:4

L earn to pray naked, only clothed by God's glory, as in a cloud, as long as you may. All the more, cry with love for God's presence to cover you. For if ever you want to feel God moving in your life or see Jesus while you are still clothed with this mortal life, it is necessary that you enter into the cloud of God's presence. Persevere in this way of prayer as you are learning to do, trusting in Christ's mercy, and you can be sure to come again and again into God's glorious presence. What is merely mortal and transitory is being swallowed up by eternal life.

REFLECTION QUESTION: How might morning dressing time become a special time of prayer?

Set your minds on things above, not on earthly things. For you died, and your life is now hidden with Christ in God. When Christ, who is your life, appears, then you also will appear with him in glory.

COLOSSIANS 3:2–4

Lest you wander from the way of Jesus by following other paths, it is wise to tell you a little more of what this way of life is like. This kind of spiritual life is not measured by time as some people think. If you were to measure this approach to prayer by the clock, then consider the shortest moment anyone may imagine, shorter than a blink of the eye—never longer, nor shorter than the shortest measurement of time, according to the greatest of philosophers or scientists. The moment in which you enter into this way of life is so short that for the smallness of it, it is indivisible and incomprehensible. Enter into God's presence in the present moment.

REFLECTION QUESTION: When do you most easily hide your life in Christ each day?

JANUARY 20

As soon as Jesus was baptized, he went up out of the water. At that moment heaven was opened, and he saw the Spirit of God descending like a dove and alighting on him.

MATTHEW 3:16

This moment, the present moment, is the only time that is given to you. On the final day, God will ask you how you spent the gift of time given to you. And it is a reasonable thing to give an account of your time, for it is neither longer nor shorter, but in the infinitesimal present moment of time in which your soul is stirred and your will moved. At a particular moment, heaven opened, and the Spirit of God descended upon Jesus at his baptism. At a particular moment in your day today, heaven opens and God descends upon you. For just as there are many fractions of a second in one hour, so there are many tiny acts of the will and movements of desire in one soul, each of which are the present moment to encounter God.

REFLECTION QUESTION: How often do you encounter God's presence in your daily life?

JANUARY 21

But he said to me, "My grace is sufficient for you, for my power is made perfect in weakness." Therefore I will boast all the more gladly about my weaknesses, so that Christ's power may rest on me.

2 CORINTHIANS 12:9

Y ou have been reformed by God's grace to the first state of the human soul, as it was before humans fell away from God's glory. By the help of God's grace, be alert to that stirring of your soul at the present moment. None of these moments will then escape, but every smallest beat of time will beckon your soul toward what is most to be desired and what is highest to be willed, to be fully in God's presence. May Christ's power and love rest on you.

REFLECTION QUESTION: When have you experienced God's grace empowering your life?

JANUARY 22

Do not conform to the pattern of this world, but be transformed by the renewing of your mind. Then you will be able to test and approve what God's will is—his good, pleasing and perfect will.

ROMANS 12:2

J esus is the true measure of your soul. You are made in God's image, according to Christ's likeness. God alone is fully sufficient to fulfill the deepest desires of your will and soul. Your soul, by virtue of God's transforming grace, is being renewed to comprehend Christ by love. Ordinarily, God is incomprehensible to all created, intelligent powers, including angels and humans. God is not known by knowing, but by loving. Let your life be transformed and let your mind be renewed by entering into God's good, pleasing, and perfect presence.

REFLECTION QUESTION: In what ways has your life been transformed by God in the past year?

JANUARY 23

"For my thoughts are not your thoughts,
neither are your ways my ways," declares the LORD.
"As the heavens are higher than the earth, so are my ways higher than
your ways and my thoughts than your thoughts."

ISAIAH 55:8–9

All intelligent creatures, both angelic and human, have the power of knowledge and the power of love. By the power of knowledge alone, God is incomprehensible. By the power of love, every created being may come to know God uniquely, each in their own way. We know Jesus to the fullest only by the way of love. This is the endless and marvelous miracle of love.

REFLECTION QUESTION: How did you first come to love God?

JANUARY 24

Dear friends, let us love one another, for love comes from God.
Everyone who loves has been born of God and knows God. Whoever
does not love does not know God, because God is love.

1 JOHN 4:7–8

The marvel of love is that your soul, by virtue of God's love actively working within you, should be able to comprehend Christ and experience his incomparable love, which fills all souls and all angels and all Creation and all time. God's love has no beginning and no end, for God is love and God's love shall never cease. Whoever has the grace to see God's love shall truly see, and shall know the feeling of endless bliss. What is contrary to this is nothing but ongoing pain and sorrow, for all who refuse God's love.

REFLECTION QUESTION: Who first helped you experience the love of God?

JANUARY 25

How priceless is your unfailing love, O God!
People take refuge in the shadow of your wings.
They feast on the abundance of your house;
you give them drink from your river of delights.
For with you is the fountain of life;
in your light we see light.

PSALM 36:7–9

Therefore, whoever is transformed by God's grace, and continues to attune their soul and the stirrings of their will to the love of the Lord, shall never in this life be without some taste of the endless sweetness of Christ's presence. The presence of our Lord in this life is but an appetizer of the full feast to come in the bliss of heaven. Do not be surprised that God stirs you to this sacred work. For this is the holy work, as you shall hear, in which all people would have continued if humans had never sinned and fallen short of God's glory.

REFLECTION QUESTION: When have you feasted upon the abundance of Christ's presence?

JANUARY 26

For he has rescued us from the dominion of darkness and brought us
into the kingdom of the Son he loves, in whom we have redemption, the
forgiveness of sins.

COLOSSIANS 1:13–14

Being in the presence of our Lord is the very purpose for which you were made, the goal toward which every aspect of your life is aimed, and the design to which you will be restored again. Whenever this sacred work fails, when anyone refuses Jesus's love, a person falls deeper and deeper into trouble and further from the Lord. By attuning your soul to the way of Jesus, and by continually attending to Christ's invitation moment by moment, you will ever rise higher and higher out of the depths of darkness, nearer and nearer to God's presence.

REFLECTION QUESTION: Who do you know right now who needs Christ's loving presence?

28

JANUARY 27

What is mankind that you make so much of them,
that you give them so much attention,
that you examine them every morning
and test them every moment?

JOB 7:17–18

For this reason, take good heed of time and how you use it, for few things are more precious than the time God has given us at each moment. In a single moment of time, heaven may be won or lost. As a token that time is precious, consider God's gift of time to you. God never gives two times together, but one moment of time after another. From the beginning until this present moment, God will not reverse the order or course in the purposes of Creation. You were not made for time, but God made time for you. As ruler of Creation, in giving the gift of time to you God will not rush ahead of the stirring in your soul that occurs within time. So, when you are held accountable for your use of time, you will not be able to say in that final day, *You gave me more than I could handle, for I could only deal with life moment by moment.* Moment by moment is where you will discover God present with you.

REFLECTION QUESTION: How could you spend more time with God each day, moment by moment?

JANUARY 28

But you, Sovereign LORD,
help me for your name's sake;
out of the goodness of your love, deliver me.

PSALM 109:21

With some apprehension, you may be saying at this moment, *What shall I do?* Or, *How shall I best live to be able to make an account of the gift of time given to me?* Up to now in your life, it may be true that you've seldom given serious thought to God's gift of the present moment. How delightful that you are reading this book, which shows you are yearning for a new way of life. If you are willing to change, then be assured by the wisdom of God's Word that this change will not come by simple course of nature or by ordinary grace. You cannot change the past or the future. Moreover, regarding the future, and in view of your frailty and slowness of spirit, you will be unable to attend to even one in a hundred moments. So you are quite right in concluding, *Help me now for the love of Jesus!*

REFLECTION QUESTION: In what ways do you need God to help you right now?

JANUARY 29

Jesus knew that the hour had come for him to leave this world and go to the Father. Having loved his own who were in the world, he loved them to the end.

JOHN 13:1

Your help will come in the love of Jesus. Love is such a power that it shares all things. Love Jesus and he will share everything he has with you. In full divinity, Jesus is the creator of time. In full humanity, Jesus is the keeper of time. By his divinity and humanity together, Jesus will always be the best judge of your life, and rightfully hold you accountable for your use of time. Knit your life to Christ, by love and by faith. By interweaving your life with Jesus, you will begin to see as Jesus sees, and his love for you will be woven into your love for God and God's love for you. Jesus loves you as his own and Jesus loves you to the end of time.

REFLECTION QUESTION: How have you experienced the love of Jesus?

JANUARY 30

Mary treasured up all these things and pondered them in her heart.

LUKE 2:19

Mary, the mother of Jesus, lived by God's grace in the present moment, treasuring up all she experienced moment by moment. All the angels of heaven who never lose track of time live by God's grace in the present moment. All the saints in heaven and on earth have lived by God's grace in the present moment. By God's grace, may you take heed of time and learn to live in the present more fully in the virtue of love. Find comfort in this, consider this way of life, and pick out something of profit for your life. A word of caution: no one may truly claim fellowship with God, or with God's angels and saints, except that they become attentive to the present moment, with the help of God's grace. When you do your part, as little as that is, you will benefit everyone around you daily, and others in your life will also begin to learn their part as well in God's sacred drama unfolding day by day. Keep treasuring up in your heart the grace of God, moment by moment.

REFLECTION QUESTION: What do you treasure most in your heart?

JANUARY 31

They saw what seemed to be tongues of fire that separated and came to rest on each of them. All of them were filled with the Holy Spirit.

ACTS 2:3–4

Pay attention to the marvelous manner of this work in your soul. Once truly conceived, and suddenly stirring within you, this loving desire for God springs suddenly into flames like the spark from a match. It is marvelous to number the sparklike stirrings that may in one hour be kindled in a soul that is yielded up to this sacred fire-craft. Yet, in one stirring among all these, you may suddenly and perfectly forget all created things. Just as quickly after such a spark ignites, because of the corruption within you, you fall down again to some thought or to some ordinary daily deed, done or yet to be done. So what! Just as quickly, another spark rises within the soul suddenly as before. God breathes upon your life, fanning into flames a sacred fire.

REFLECTION QUESTION: If your soul is like a wood stove, how is your fire burning?

February

One Little Word

FEBRUARY 1

Jesus answered, "I am the way and the truth and the life. No one comes to the Father except through me."

JOHN 14:6

May you perceive the true nature of living in the way of Jesus. Understand how different this way is from your imagination, or any kind of speculative thinking. These less fruitful ways of living are most often brought into your life, not by devotion, nor by the humble and unseen stirring of love, but by pride, meddling thoughts, and illusions. It is fitting that such pride and vain thinking be cast down and crushed underfoot. If this new way of life with God is truly to be conceived within you in purity of spirit, then many current ways of thinking need to be cast away. Walking in the way of Jesus is walking in the way of truth and walking in the way of life.

REFLECTION QUESTION: How are you walking in Jesus's way, truth, and life?

FEBRUARY 2

Enter through the narrow gate. For wide is the gate and broad is the road that leads to destruction, and many enter through it. But small is the gate and narrow the road that leads to life, and only a few find it.

MATTHEW 7:13–14

Some who get to know of this way of life, either by reading or hearing about it, will suppose that the entrance into this way is through logic and brainpower. Intellectuals seek with their minds how to encounter God through the mental labor of reasoning, working hard with their minds against their better natures, fooling themselves with a pseudo-spirituality, which is neither physical nor spiritual. Such persons, whoever they may be, are too easily deceived. Enter with Jesus through the narrow gate. Enter by God's grace through faith in your heart. Enter into newness of life.

REFLECTION QUESTION: When did you enter the narrow gate that leads to life?

My message and my preaching were not with wise and persuasive
words, but with a demonstration of the Spirit's power, so that your faith
might not rest on human wisdom, but on God's power. We do, however,
speak a message of wisdom among the mature, but not the wisdom of
this age or of the rulers of this age, who are coming to nothing. No, we
declare God's wisdom, a mystery that has been hidden and that God
destined for our glory before time began.

1 CORINTHIANS 2:4–7

By God's goodness, as you open your heart to the mystery of God's merciful and miraculous love, you soon will leave behind foolish ways of living, and seek out wise counsel. Otherwise, you may fall into deliriums or other great troubles and deceits of the soul, by which you may be led astray and lost, with lasting consequences in this life and the next. Therefore, by the love of Jesus, be discerning in this endeavor, and beware of stressing your mind and soul. It is impossible to come to God by reason or brainpower alone. You are better off to learn to let go of such ideas.

REFLECTION QUESTION: What place does reason have in your faith life?

FEBRUARY 4

"What no eye has seen,
what no ear has heard,
and what no human mind has conceived"—
the things God has prepared for those who love him
—these are the things God has revealed to us by his Spirit.

1 CORINTHIANS 2:9–10

God's presence can be like a kind of darkness or a cloud. But do not think of God merely as a cloud in the sky, or the darkness within your house at midnight when the lights are out. For such darkness and clouds are easily imagined in your mind, suspended above your head on the brightest summer day. These physical elements surround you on the darkest night of winter, with the light of your imagination shining into that darkness. No, this is not the type of darkness or cloud being described here, so give up such ideas. When speaking of darkness or of clouds in these pages, imagine the lack of knowing God personally. Whatever you do not understand, and everything you once learned but have forgotten, is now dark to you, for you do not see these with the eyes of your spirit. For this reason, do not think of a cloud of the sky, but a Cloud of Unknowing that is between you and God.

REFLECTION QUESTION: Has there been a time in your life when you did not know God personally?

FEBRUARY 5

You have searched me, LORD,
and you know me.
You know when I sit and when I rise;
you perceive my thoughts from afar.
You discern my going out and my lying down;
you are familiar with all my ways.

PSALM 139:1–3

Come into the Cloud of Unknowing to live with God. Just as this Cloud of Unknowing is above you, between you and God, even so, God invites you to put a Cloud of Forgetting beneath you, between you and everything in Creation. You may think you are far from God because the Cloud of Unknowing stands between you and God; but surely, you are further from God when you have no Cloud of Forgetting between you and all Creation. When considering all Creation, do not just think of creatures, but think of everything God made as well as the conditions of every creature. God's Creation includes all things God has made, whether physical or spiritual, in the heavens, or on earth. Let all things in the created order be hidden beneath you in the Cloud of Forgetting.

REFLECTION QUESTION: When have you come to God in a way beyond words?

FEBRUARY 6

Whatever were gains to me I now consider loss for the sake of Christ. What is more, I consider everything a loss because of the surpassing worth of knowing Christ Jesus my Lord, for whose sake I have lost all things.

PHILIPPIANS 3:7–8

There is some gain to be found from meditating upon certain conditions and activities in Creation. There is much greater gain to be found in the sacred work of contemplation. Your memory or study of Creation in any of its patterns is a way of spiritual enlightenment, for the eye of your soul is opened and fixed upon God's works, as is the eye of a shooter upon a target. We are wise to meditate upon God's works, for in the details of Creation, we discover the heart and mind of the Creator. But when we focus upon Creation alone, that focal point may act as a barrier between us and God. We come closer to God when we do not allow anything but God's presence and love to fill our mind.

REFLECTION QUESTION: What have you been willing to lose for the sake of knowing Christ?

FEBRUARY 7

Do you show contempt for the riches of his kindness, forbearance and patience, not realizing that God's kindness is intended to lead you to repentance?

ROMANS 2:4

Ponder God's kindness and worth. It will profit you little to think only of historic saints, beauty in Creation, or the glories of created heavenly angels. It is better to meditate upon the joys of heaven, and as you ponder them, allow them to nourish your soul and draw your heart closer to God. For although it is good to love and praise God for what God does, it is far better to meditate upon God for who God is. Of course we are wise to meditate on God's kindness expressed in Creation and in history. But it is even better to learn to love and praise God for God's sake.

REFLECTION QUESTION: How has God's kindness influenced your life?

*No, we declare God's wisdom, a mystery that has been hidden and that
God destined for our glory before time began.*

1 CORINTHIANS 2:7

Now you may be asking, *How shall I meditate on God?* This is a mystery, for God is the greatest mystery of all. With your question, you bring that same darkness, and that same Cloud of Unknowing is present, beckoning to you to enter. Through grace, you may have a headful of knowledge about all other creatures and their ways, and you may even have a brain filled with knowledge of God's ways of working; yet, perhaps you still do not know God personally. Therefore, it is better to rely less upon head knowledge and learn to rely more on the love of Jesus, which no one can truly comprehend. Why? Because God may be loved but not fully understood. By love you may touch Christ and hold on to God, but never by your intellect.

REFLECTION QUESTION: How do you meditate on God?

FEBRUARY 9

*He made my mouth like a sharpened sword,
in the shadow of his hand he hid me;
he made me into a polished arrow
and concealed me in his quiver.
He said to me, "You are my servant,
Israel, in whom I will display my splendor."*

ISAIAH 49:2–3

Therefore, though it is good at times to think of God's kindness and worthiness, and though you can find some enlightenment in such contemplations, nevertheless, it is better to let go of these lesser ways and cover them with a Cloud of Forgetting. Step with courage up into the cloud of God's presence, with a sacred and delight-filled stirring of love, and seek to pierce that bright darkness above you. God wants to hide your life within the shadow of his mighty hand. God desires to display splendor to you. Keep aiming upward into that thick Cloud of Unknowing with the sharp dart of love, longing for Jesus and not settling for anything less.

REFLECTION QUESTION: What obstacles do you most often face when seeking to draw near to God?

FEBRUARY 10

Do you not know that your bodies are temples of the Holy Spirit, who is in you, whom you have received from God? You are not your own; you were bought at a price. Therefore honor God with your bodies.

1 CORINTHIANS 6:19–20

If any thoughts rise and press continually between you and the unknown, asking you, "What are you seeking and what do you most desire?" say to these thoughts, *God I desire, God I seek, nothing but God.* Then, if these inner voices ask you, "Who is this God you desire?," say it is the God who made you, bought you at great price, and graciously has called you higher. Say to your thoughts, *You have no expertise to know God, so be still.* Quickly quiet such thoughts with an inner stirring of love for Jesus, though these thoughts may seem to you holy and helpful for seeking God.

REFLECTION QUESTION: What do you most desire in life?

FEBRUARY 11

Finally, brothers and sisters, whatever is true, whatever is noble, whatever is right, whatever is pure, whatever is lovely, whatever is admirable— if anything is excellent or praiseworthy—think about such things.

PHILIPPIANS 4:8

It may be that spiritual thoughts will bring to mind various beautiful and wonderful insights into God's kindness, saying that God is wholly sweet, loving, gracious, and merciful. If you listen to them, they want nothing more than to continually distract your mind more and more. Eventually, they will bring you to think not only of the passion of Christ, his wonderful kindness, but also of your old wretched way of life. Then your mind will wander back to consider some previous way you used to live, until at last your mind is scattered, you know not where. The cause of this scattered or distracted mind is that you listened and answered the inner thoughts and voices in your head that want nothing more than to take you on such a wild ride, away from God's presence, here and now.

REFLECTION QUESTION: What do you like to think about when your mind wanders?

FEBRUARY 12

*And the peace of God, which transcends all understanding, will guard
your hearts and your minds in Christ Jesus.*

PHILIPPIANS 4:7

O f course, some of your inner thoughts are both good and holy. For what man or woman would think to enter a life of prayer and contemplation without many such sweet meditations upon your own mortality, or upon Christ's passion, kindness, and goodness. Surely you will err or fail in your purposes without such thoughts. Yet, when you have experienced such meditations for a long time, it is fitting to let them go, putting them under the Cloud of Forgetting, if you truly want to pierce the Cloud of Unknowing between you and God.

REFLECTION QUESTION: How do you refocus your mind when it wanders?

FEBRUARY 13

*One thing I ask from the Lord,
this only do I seek:
that I may dwell in the house of the Lord
all the days of my life,
to gaze on the beauty of the Lord
and to seek him in his temple.*

PSALM 27:4

E very human soul is seeking for something. Seek to dwell with God. Whenever you intend to begin this endeavor, and feel God's grace calling you, then lift up your heart to Jesus with a quiet stirring of love. Focus all your soul upon the one who made you, bought you, and has graciously called you into this way of life, welcoming no other thoughts but thoughts of God. If at all possible, suffice to come to Christ with a naked intent, directly, without any other cause than simply being with God, seeking God where God dwells.

REFLECTION QUESTION: What are you seeking?

FEBRUARY 14

Love is patient, love is kind. It does not envy, it does not boast, it is not proud. It does not dishonor others, it is not self-seeking, it is not easily angered, it keeps no record of wrongs. Love does not delight in evil but rejoices with the truth. It always protects, always trusts, always hopes, always perseveres. Love never fails.

1 CORINTHIANS 13:4–8

If you want to enfold your soul in God's loving presence, take one little word or phrase to hold on to in your mind and soul. Choose a short word or phrase, such as *love*, or the ancient prayer *Lord, have mercy.*[5] Choose a short word or phrase rather than a longer one, for the simpler the word or phrase, the more it will harmonize with the work of the Spirit of God within you. Choose a little word or prayer phrase that lifts your soul, and write this upon your heart, so this word or phrase will never leave you regardless of the circumstances.

REFLECTION QUESTION: What single word or phrase draws you closer to God?

FEBRUARY 15

The tax collector stood at a distance. He would not even look up to heaven, but beat his breast and said, "God, have mercy on me, a sinner."

LUKE 18:13

By this one little word, God will protect you like a shield and spear, whether you are walking in peace or in conflict. With this little holy word, you may penetrate higher into the cloud above, moving you into Christ's beautiful presence. With this same word, you may strike down all types of lesser thoughts under the Cloud of Forgetting below you. God covers us with mercy and makes our lives right again when we bow our hearts and lives before the Lord and ask for mercy.

REFLECTION QUESTION: What are some of your most frequently used short prayers?

FEBRUARY 16

*When you pray, go into your room, close the door and pray to your
Father, who is unseen. Then your Father, who sees what is done in
secret, will reward you.*

MATTHEW 6:6

If any thoughts press upon your mind, asking you many questions, answer not with many words but rather with this one little word you have chosen. If such thoughts continue to press you to explain this one word, or to provide the background of this word, tell them they have heard it, and there is nothing more to say. If you will hold true to this one little word, to this short prayer as a way to come to God, be assured that such distracting thoughts will eventually go away. Why? Because you have refused to allow them to feed upon the sweet meditations of God touched upon previously.

REFLECTION QUESTION: Where do you most often go to pray?

FEBRUARY 17

*May these words of my mouth and this meditation of my heart
be pleasing in your sight,
LORD, my Rock and my Redeemer.*

PSALM 19:14

You may be wondering about the many thoughts that press upon your mind regarding this way of prayer, whether they are good or bad. If they are bad, then why have they been so helpful to you in your devotional life? Sometimes, you have received some comfort from these many voices that have caused you to think about God. Sometimes these thoughts have brought you to tears as you meditated upon Christ's passion on the cross. Sometimes you have wept for your own wretched spiritual condition, or for other reasons, each of which have seemed completely holy and done you much good. Therefore, such thoughts should not be considered bad, but good; for with their sweet stories they do you much good. Why then, you are wondering, should you be asked to put such thoughts away, far under the Cloud of Forgetting? Bring all such questions to God, offering them as your prayer to God.

REFLECTION QUESTION: What questions or thoughts do you have that you can bring to God as prayers right now?

FEBRUARY 18

Your word is a lamp for my feet,
a light on my path.
PSALM 119:105

Ask God any good question and God will answer in the best way possible. First, when you ask God about these thoughts pressing swiftly upon your mind as you are praying, offering to help you in your prayer life, these thoughts, which you see sharply and clearly, come from your natural intelligence, printed upon your rational mind within your soul. If you are wondering whether these thoughts are good or bad, understand that they are good in nature, like a sunbeam, shining light into your soul. But such divine light can be used either for good or for bad purposes. You use this light for good purpose when you allow these thoughts to open your soul, by God's grace, to better see your own inner darkness, as well as to see Christ's passion and kindness, and to shine light upon all God's wonderful works in Creation, both natural and spiritual. No wonder that such thoughts increase your devotion to God.

REFLECTION QUESTION: What sources of light or inspiration have increased your devotion to God?

FEBRUARY 19

If you harbor bitter envy and selfish ambition in your hearts, do not boast
about it or deny the truth. Such "wisdom" does not come down from
heaven but is earthly, unspiritual, demonic. For where you have envy and
selfish ambition, there you find disorder and every evil practice.
JAMES 3:14–16

You can also use this inner light for evil when you allow these thoughts to swell your soul with pride, intellectual arrogance, or empty head knowledge. This divine light may press into your life to form you into a humble student and wise spiritual director who helps others grow in love with God. Or this same light may puff up your soul to become an arrogant scholar filled with vanity and falsehood. For some, whoever they may be, whether in a religious or secular profession, this natural intelligence is put to corrupt use when it is swollen with pride, worldly pursuits, and empty conceit by coveting worldly power, riches, vain pleasures, or the flattery of others.

REFLECTION QUESTION: What are some negative sources or corrupt influences that have troubled your mind and soul?

FEBRUARY 20

The Spirit himself testifies with our spirit that we are God's children. Now if we are children, then we are heirs—heirs of God and co-heirs with Christ, if indeed we share in his sufferings in order that we may also share in his glory.

ROMANS 8:16–17

If your inner thoughts and meditations are good in nature, you may be wondering why you are encouraged to put them under the Cloud of Forgetting, when you have used them for so much good and they have increased your devotion to God. Understand that there are two ways of living in God's big family as children of God. The first way is the active life, and the second is the contemplative life. The active way is more common and the contemplative way is more uncommon. Both ways have two levels, a higher and a lower. In both cases, these ways overlap. So even though they are distinct, neither may be experienced without some part of the other. In the active life, we share in Christ's sufferings, and in the sufferings of others. In the contemplative life, as heirs of God and co-heirs with Christ, we share in Christ's glory.

REFLECTION QUESTION: Are you more drawn to the active way of life or the contemplative way of life?

FEBRUARY 21

What does "he ascended" mean except that he also descended to the lower, earthly regions? He who descended is the very one who ascended higher than all the heavens, in order to fill the whole universe.

EPHESIANS 4:9–10

How do the active life and the contemplative life interrelate? As written above, there is a lower and higher expression of both of these ways of spiritual living. For example, take a look at the higher level of the active life. That level overlaps with the lower level of the contemplative life. You cannot be fully active without also being partly contemplative, nor fully contemplative without being partly active. The condition of the lower expression of the active life is such that it both begins and ends in this life. The uncommon or higher expression of the contemplative life is different. For the contemplative life begins in this life but continues on into eternity.

REFLECTION QUESTION: Where would you like your spiritual life to be?

FEBRUARY 22

As Jesus and his disciples were on their way, he came to a village where a woman named Martha opened her home to him. She had a sister called Mary, who sat at the Lord's feet listening to what he said.
LUKE 10:38–39

Consider the part that Mary chose, which was to sit at Jesus's feet and listen to his words. That part shall never be taken away from her. The active life, the part that Martha chose, is often troubled and upset about many things; but the contemplative person sits in peace with the one thing that will never be taken away, Christ's presence. The lower level of the active life engages in good and honest acts of service, mercy, and charity. The higher level of the active life and the lower level of the contemplative life engage in the good act of spiritual meditation, such as pondering the condition of the human soul with sorrow and contrition, meditating on Christ's passion and on the suffering of the servants of God with sympathy and compassion. Contemplatives reflect on all God's wonderful gifts such as God's kindness, as well as on God's work in Creation, in both the physical and spiritual realms, with thanksgiving and praise. The higher level of contemplation enters completely into the Cloud of Unknowing, with love stirring the soul, blindly coming into God's presence.

REFLECTION QUESTION: How does your life express each level of the active spiritual life?

FEBRUARY 23

Martha was distracted by all the preparations that had to be made. She came to him and asked, "Lord, don't you care that my sister has left me to do the work by myself? Tell her to help me!"

LUKE 10:40

In the lower level of the active life, much of the time you are living below your life's capacity, with most of your focus on external or material matters. In the higher level of the active life, as well as in the lower level of the contemplative life, you are living your life to greater capability with more of your focus on internal, spiritual matters. But in the higher level of the contemplative life, you begin living beyond your natural capacity, transcending the limits of your natural self by coming into God's presence. When you come to Christ, your purpose is to attain by God's grace what is impossible to gain by natural means. In other words, be knit personally to Jesus, your spirit interwoven with God's Spirit, in the unity of your love with God's love and the harmony of your will with God's will.

REFLECTION QUESTION: How does your life participate in the contemplative life?

FEBRUARY 24

"Martha, Martha," the Lord answered, "you are worried and upset about many things, but few things are needed—or indeed only one. Mary has chosen what is better, and it will not be taken away from her."

LUKE 10:41–42

As you try to understand this, you'll find it is impossible to come to Mary-like actions unless you break away, at least for a time, from Martha-like activity. In the same way, you will not come to Mary-like contemplation unless you break away, at least for a time, from Martha-like thinking. It is unhelpful for you, when you are meditating upon God, to allow yourself to be distracted by lower thoughts, including what you have done, and what you should be doing, no matter how worthy those lower activities are at the time. In the same way, when you are caught up in God's presence in the Cloud of Unknowing, with an earnest stirring of love for God, seek God alone.

Do not let any thought distract you from God, even thoughts of God's wonderful gifts of kindness, or God's work in Creation, either physical or spiritual. Such thoughts may rise up to distract you or press between you and God, even when these thoughts are holy, profound, or comforting.

REFLECTION QUESTION: How hard is it for you to break away from Martha-like activity to engage in Mary-like contemplation?

FEBRUARY 25

Do not be anxious about anything, but in every situation, by prayer and petition, with thanksgiving, present your requests to God.

PHILIPPIANS 4:6

Whenever distractions arise, put these things and all anxious thoughts beneath you, covering them with a thick Cloud of Forgetting. Even when they seem important or full of promise and purposeful help, let them go. By love alone, not intellect, can you reach out to Jesus in this life. As long as your soul lives within your mortal body, the clarity of your understanding of the spiritual life, and especially your understanding of God, is muddled with some manner of fantasy. Your intellect is too limited to truly know God, and unless your soul is filled with the Mary-like wonder of sitting in Jesus's presence, your mind alone may lead you astray.

REFLECTION QUESTION: When you are praying, how do you deal with anxious thoughts or distractions when they arise within you?

FEBRUARY 26

Since we are surrounded by such a great cloud of witnesses, let us throw off everything that hinders and the sin that so easily entangles. And let us run with perseverance the race marked out for us, fixing our eyes on Jesus, the pioneer and perfecter of faith. For the joy set before him he endured the cross, scorning its shame, and sat down at the right hand of the throne of God.

HEBREWS 12:1–2

When you set yourself to the work of prayer, you will find that your mind is suddenly stirred up with many thoughts pressing upon you. You are wise to push these distractions away. If you do not overcome them, they will overcome you. It is better to fill your mind with God, dwelling in the mystery of Christ's love, than to find your mind preoccupied with something far less than God. For a time, distractions beneath you may come between you and the Lord. Therefore, refuse to allow anything to distract you from being with Jesus, including clear visions, holy thoughts, or enjoyable experiences. You will discover that it is more profitable for the health of your soul, more worthy in itself, and more pleasing to God and to all the saints and angels of heaven to fix your eyes on Jesus through a blind stirring of love.

REFLECTION QUESTION: What do you do to keep focused on God when you get distracted by many thoughts while you are praying?

FEBRUARY 27

While he was speaking, a cloud appeared and covered them, and they
were afraid as they entered the cloud. A voice came from the cloud,
saying, "This is my Son, whom I have chosen; listen to him." When the
voice had spoken, they found that Jesus was alone. The disciples kept this
to themselves and did not tell anyone at that time what they had seen.
LUKE 9:34–38

You will find that your love for Jesus is also what is most helpful to all your friends, whether they are believers in God or not, spiritually alive or spiritually dead. So keep pressing into the Cloud of Unknowing, knowing it is better to have a blind encounter with Jesus, and experience God's life deep within your soul, than to have the eyes of your heart opened in contemplation with a vision of all the angels and saints of heaven, or hear all the joyful songs of those who dwell in heavenly bliss.

REFLECTION QUESTION: What do you most enjoy about spending time alone with God?

FEBRUARY 28

Come near to God and he will come near to you.
JAMES 4:8

D o not wonder at this now. There will come a time when you will understand more clearly these truths that now, by grace, you blindly grope for and experience only in limited ways currently in your life. You can be sure that you'll never have a truly clear vision of God in this life, but a true experience of Jesus you may have through the grace God gives to you. So, then, lift up your love into the cloud of Christ's presence. Let him draw your love up into that cloud, and strive by the help of God's grace to let go of lower things.

REFLECTION QUESTION: What helps you come near to God?

FEBRUARY 29

Since, then, you have been raised with Christ, set your hearts on things above, where Christ is, seated at the right hand of God.
COLOSSIANS 3:1

T houghts of anything less than Christ's life will press upon your will and into your mind, drawing you farther from God, making you less able to experience the fruit of his love for you. Do you think that the intentional removal of such thoughts or distractions will hinder you in your purpose of knowing Jesus more fully? If even the remembrance of higher things, such as a holy person or some spiritual truth, can distract you, consider all the more how the remembrance of lower things, such as people's sins or the thought of some worldly thing, will hinder you and slow you down from coming closer to God. Don't worry if such good and pure meditations about God press upon your will or into your mind.

REFLECTION QUESTION: Where do you set your heart?

March

Learning to Walk

MARCH 1

In peace I will lie down and sleep,
for you alone, LORD,
make me dwell in safety.

PSALM 4:8

Please do not misunderstand this way of faith. Though sometimes good and holy thoughts will come into your mind that seem to increase your devotion to Jesus, for a time, in the life of prayer such thoughts may be more of a hindrance than a benefit. Why is this so? Although you may encounter angels and saints along the way, all who truly seek God will not be satisfied until they find their rest and satisfaction in God alone.

REFLECTION QUESTION: What has increased your devotion to Jesus?

MARCH 2

No temptation has overtaken you except what is common to mankind.
And God is faithful; he will not let you be tempted beyond what you can
bear. But when you are tempted, he will also provide a way out so that
you can endure it.

1 CORINTHIANS 10:13

Everyone gets distracted at times by bodily or worldly temptations. Suddenly, some lesser thought or image flashes in your mind, pressing against your will to be noticed, when you were not looking for it. The pain of human sin presses against your power to resist, and though you have been washed clean and totally forgiven in your baptism, nevertheless, if such a sudden temptation is not struck down quickly, your heart will be put to the test. If the temptation comes from a source of pleasure, you'll be tempted to enjoy the feeling of it. If the temptation comes from a source of pain, you'll be tempted to avoid the pain, or waste time in some manner of grumbling, or become angry against it.

REFLECTION QUESTION: What temptations do you face most often?

MARCH 3

As you received Christ Jesus as Lord, continue to live your lives in him, rooted and built up in him, strengthened in the faith as you were taught, and overflowing with thankfulness.
COLOSSIANS 2:6–7

When temptations fasten onto a person, they are more deadly in one who is spiritually dead. For when temptation fastens onto those who are spiritually alive in Christ, because you already have forsaken the lower ways of the world, and fully committed your heart to a devout life among God's people, whether that temptation is private or public, it will not truly rule over your heart and mind. You have put your heart and mind under the care of Jesus. It doesn't matter if you are a monk or a stonemason. When temptation fastens on your heart, including temptations of pleasure or pain, you still have choices to make to overcome the danger. Remember that from the beginning of your life of faith, you have grounded and rooted your life with Christ, by the witness and wise counsel of those spiritual parents who brought you into new birth.

REFLECTION QUESTION: Where is your life rooted and grounded?

MARCH 4

What benefit did you reap at that time from the things you are now ashamed of? Those things result in death! But now that you have been set free from sin and have become slaves of God, the benefit you reap leads to holiness, and the result is eternal life. For the wages of sin is death, but the gift of God is eternal life in Christ Jesus our Lord.
ROMANS 6:21–23

If you allow any temptation that fastens onto your life to take root and flourish, then it will dig itself deeper, down into your heart and will. This especially occurs when you give temptations your full consent. Then they can become deadly. Here is a list of seven of these deadly sins: anger, envy, sloth, pride, greed, gluttony, and lust. All these deadly temptations are conceived and develop within your thoughts, your will, your physical appetites, or in your basic human desires. It is much better for you to give your full consent to the gift of God and newness of life in Christ Jesus.

REFLECTION QUESTION: Which of these seven sins do you struggle with most?

MARCH 5

"In your anger do not sin": Do not let the sun go down while you are still angry.
EPHESIANS 4:26

When something or someone has offended you, there rises in you an angry passion and an appetite of revenge. Unbridled, this passion may become deadly. God is slow to become angry. Scripture call us to "take note of this: Everyone should be quick to listen, slow to speak and slow to become angry, because human anger does not produce the righteousness that God desires."[6] When allowed to burn out of control, anger can cause big troubles, both in your life and in the lives of others around you. As St. Paul writes, "Get rid of all bitterness, rage and anger, brawling and slander, along with every form of malice" (Ephesians 4:31). It is better to deal with your anger as it arises, offering your angry heart to God at the time you become angry.

REFLECTION QUESTION: What do you tend to do when you get angry?

MARCH 6

Let us not become conceited, provoking and envying each other.
GALATIANS 5:26

Envy is another deadly force within the human soul destroying God's gift of love. Whenever you begin to disdain or loathe someone with spiteful and condemning thoughts, envy is born within you, hindering your spiritual life of love. Envy destroys your life and "rots the bones." As the ancient wise man declared long ago, "I saw that all toil and all achievement spring from one person's envy of another. This too is meaningless, a chasing after the wind." There may have been a time in your life in the past when you gave in to such empty pursuits, or were "enslaved by all kinds of passions and pleasures," a time when you "lived in malice and envy, being hated and hating one another." Hopefully, such a time is past, and you see how destructive this way of living was to your life and to others. "Therefore, rid yourselves of all malice and all deceit, hypocrisy, envy, and slander of every kind."[7]

REFLECTION QUESTION: How has envy troubled your life?

MARCH 7

Everything exposed by the light becomes visible—and everything that is illuminated becomes a light. This is why it is said:
"Wake up, sleeper,
rise from the dead,
and Christ will shine on you."
Be very careful, then, how you live—not as unwise but as wise.

EPHESIANS 5:13–15

Sometimes, when you are overcome with weariness and lack of energy or motivation for any good activity, whether physical or spiritual, you likely have given way to sloth. Sloth is a spiritual torpor, a sleepiness of the soul that lulls you into a lethargic, spiritually dull state of being. When you no longer care about caring for yourself or caring for anyone else, sloth has entered your heart and lulled you to sleep. Perhaps it is time to wake up your sleepy soul, to rise from the deadness of sloth, and let the light of Jesus illuminate your life, making visible how you are to live, as one spiritually awake, full of Christ's compassion and purpose.

REFLECTION QUESTION: When has sloth been a problem in your life?

MARCH 8

He gives us more grace. That is why Scripture says:
"God opposes the proud
but shows favor to the humble."

JAMES 4:6

If your life is filled with unhealthy pride, you will probably not know it, or if you do know it, you will not care. Pride is a soul destroyer. Let it be known that there is a certain kind of pride that is healthy; an inner, joyful confidence in who God made you to be, a child of God who is deeply loved. Mostly though, pride is a disease that distorts your vision, causing you to see your life falsely, as much more than you are or much less than you are. Both arrogance and false humility are destructive forms of pride. Think of what pleases you most. If you find greatest pleasure or satisfaction in your own personality, in your own intelligence, in your unique abilities, degrees, reputation, or even in your appearance, then you have given way to unhealthy pride. Think of where you rest your mind. Consider where you attach your heart. Examine where you focus your will. If it is mostly upon yourself, if you have allowed pride to take center place in your soul, if you feed mainly upon your own selfish desires, and want nothing more than to live with yourself at the center of your life, you are slowly killing yourself with pride. The ancient sage declares, "Pride goes before destruction, a haughty spirit before a fall." We all have choices to make daily. Choose to shed the clothes of arrogance, vainglory, and pride. "All of you, clothe yourselves with humility toward one another, because, 'God opposes the proud but shows favor to the humble.'"[8]

REFLECTION QUESTION: What woman has shown you the way of joyful confidence?

MARCH 9

Then he said to them, "Watch out! Be on your guard against all kinds of greed; life does not consist in an abundance of possessions."
LUKE 12:15

Another deadly trouble of the soul is greed. Every human has genuine needs. We are all needy people. Learn to distinguish between what is needed and what is wanted. Many things we may want are not things we really need. Those who have allowed worldly goods, wealth, vocation, possessions, or need for power take center place in their life have given way to the deadly temptation of greed. Learn to be content with a simple way of life, and find satisfaction in being close to God. As the Scriptures teach us, "Keep your lives free from the love of money and be content with what you have, because God has said, 'Never will I leave you; never will I forsake you.'"[9]

REFLECTION QUESTION: What excess belongings in your life do you need to give away?

Listen, my son, and be wise,
and set your heart on the right path:
Do not join those who drink too much wine
or gorge themselves on meat,
for drunkards and gluttons become poor,
and drowsiness clothes them in rags.

PROVERBS 23:19–21

Some give in to the deadly temptation of gluttony by centering their soul on food and drink, or any manner of physical delight that a person may taste or experience. Every human needs food and drink. Such people put their physical appetites at the center, and make their stomach into a god that must be satisfied. Your body was made by God to be a temple in which God's Spirit is pleased to live. Use your body for sacred purposes. Listen to what is wise, and set your heart on the path that leads heavenward. Remember what Jesus taught, and "do not worry about your life, what you will eat or drink; or about your body, what you will wear. Is not life more than food, and the body more than clothes?" Jesus himself was often misunderstood regarding food and drink, because he loved to be with people in their homes, sharing meals together with people. "The Son of Man came eating and drinking, and they say, 'Here is a glutton and a drunkard, a friend of tax collectors and sinners.' But wisdom is proved right by her deeds." Listen to what is wise and prove wisdom right by the way you live. "So whether you eat or drink or whatever you do, do it all for the glory of God."[10]

REFLECTION QUESTION: In what ways have food or drink been a trouble for you?

*For everything in the world—the lust of the flesh, the lust of the
eyes, and the pride of life—comes not from the Father but from the
world. The world and its desires pass away, but whoever does the will of
God lives forever.*

1 JOHN 2:16–17

There are also people who center their lives on physical beauty and physical desires. They enter the pleasure garden to indulge their senses with any manner of sexual passion, sweet-talking, or flattering others in order to seduce them with the deadly way of life known as lust. The inner appetite of lust is never quite satisfied, but always demands just a little more. If untrained in God's ways of love, the body will continue yearning for more and more physical pleasure. The eyes will keep looking for more physical beauty. The soul will keep seeking more recognition and affirmation. These lusts do not come from God. What comes from God is inner power of the Holy Spirit to walk in the way of love. "So I say, walk by the Spirit, and you will not gratify the desires of the flesh."[11]

REFLECTION QUESTION: How has lust influenced you?

*It is from within, out of a person's heart, that evil thoughts come—sexual
immorality, theft, murder, adultery, greed, malice, deceit, lewdness, envy,
slander, arrogance and folly. All these evils come from inside and defile a person.*

MARK 7:21–23

As you or anyone else hears these warnings, do not presume that you are guilty or burdened with any such sins, but weigh each thought and stirring within your heart as it comes to you. Be diligent in pulling weeds from your heart and mind when you first see them spring up as newly sprouted temptations. For unless you give weight to this danger within your own heart and deal with these first seductive thoughts, though they initially may not cause you to stumble, whoever you may be, you will not avoid plunging into a life of sorrow. In face of such deadly threats, it is impossible to completely avoid willful faults. As the psalmist prays, "Who can discern their own errors? Forgive my hidden faults. Keep your servant also from willful sins; may they not rule over me" (Psalm 19:12–13). All who are true followers of Jesus's way of perfection will seek to avoid recklessness in willful sin, knowing this approach to life leads down a deadly path of destruction. Rather, offer your life as a daily living sacrifice to God.

REFLECTION QUESTION: What help have you found in dealing with willful sins?

MARCH 13

He gives strength to the weary
and increases the power of the weak.
Even youths grow tired and weary,
and young men stumble and fall;
but those who hope in the LORD
will renew their strength.
They will soar on wings like eagles;
they will run and not grow weary,
they will walk and not be faint.

ISAIAH 40:29–31

If you want to stand and walk rather than stumble and fall in the spiritual way, never cease in your intent to pray to God for help. Keep pressing upward with a sharp dart of love into this Cloud of Unknowing that is between you and God, longing for Christ's love. Be unwilling to center your life on anything less than God's loving presence. God will give you strength, even when you are weary. God will empower you, even when you feel weak. Such a labor of love is the only thing that will ultimately loosen the soil of your hardened heart and uproot weeds that have sprung up within you. Put your hope in God, and God will renew you and strengthen you in your journey of faith.

REFLECTION QUESTION: How often do you ask God for help as you pray?

Train yourself to be godly. For physical training is of some value, but godliness has value for all things, holding promise for both the present life and the life to come.

1 TIMOTHY 4:7–8

Practice this labor of love by spiritual disciplines that train the body, mind, and will. For example, practice fasting, watchful meditation in the night, and rising early for predawn prayer. As you learn such spiritual disciplines, beware of excessive practices that do harm to your body, mind, or will. Some who seek after God have gone astray by extreme forms of ascetic practices. As you begin new ways of spiritual living, old offenses and faults will continue to stir and rise up from deep within your soul. Avoid these distractions and learn to practice spiritual disciplines with moderation. Let God's grace and forgiveness continue to fall like rain upon the dry soil of your soul.

REFLECTION QUESTION: What spiritual disciplines have brought you closer to God?

MARCH 15

Blessed are you who are poor,
for yours is the kingdom of God.
Blessed are you who hunger now,
for you will be satisfied.
Blessed are you who weep now,
for you will laugh.

LUKE 6:20–21

Cry out to God now for sorrow because of your spiritual poverty. Hunger now for God, and you will then find true contentment. Weep now as you meditate on Christ's passion upon the cross, and rejoice then over the great joys of heaven. What may be the result of such meditations? They will bring you much good, much help, much spiritual profit, and much grace. But compare all these actions to the blind stirring of love deep within your soul. Spiritual disciplines are minor and ineffective without the best part; the inward stirring of love for God is the best part that Mary experienced, even without all these other actions. Without love, spiritual disciplines offer little or no profit to the soul. Love breaks up the hard ground of the soul, uprooting the roots of sin and planting new spiritual seeds of virtue. When these seeds of good character germinate, they spring up and grow into maturity, with the warm sunshine of Jesus's love bringing light and beauty to your soul, without the intermingling of crooked or impure seeds or weeds.

REFLECTION QUESTION: What causes you to weep?

MARCH 16

If you have any encouragement from being united with Christ, if any comfort from his love, if any common sharing in the Spirit, if any tenderness and compassion, then make my joy complete by being like-minded, having the same love, being one in spirit and of one mind. Do nothing out of selfish ambition or vain conceit. Rather, in humility value others above yourselves.

PHILIPPIANS 2:1–3

Good character is nothing less than God's purpose and design for your life well measured with loving affection in your soul, simply directed to God. For God is the beginning of all virtue and good character. If you are motivated to any one virtue but allow that virtue to become intermixed with other lesser purposes, although this single good character may be uppermost in your life, it can be diminished by the presence of those lesser purposes. But if you allow one or two of Jesus's excellent virtues, such as humility or charity, to take center stage in your heart, you need nothing more, for in these you have found the best part.

REFLECTION QUESTION: Where do you see humility and love at work in your life?

MARCH 17

Who is wise and understanding among you? Let them show it by their good life, by deeds done in the humility that comes from wisdom.

JAMES 3:13

Look at the virtue of humility. This virtue cannot be perfected as long as other lesser things are mingling with God at the center of your soul. Humility will continue to be perfected in you when you allow Jesus to work in you by his Spirit. But first, learn more about humility, seeking a clear picture of this virtue. Then it will be easier to understand how humility takes root and grows in your soul. Humility arises from knowing God. Humility is nothing else but a true knowledge and experience of yourself as you are before God. For surely, whoever sees and intimately knows their true self is truly humble.

REFLECTION QUESTION: What is your definition of true humility?

MARCH 18

In the same way, you who are younger, submit yourselves to your elders. All of you, clothe yourselves with humility toward one another, because, "God opposes the proud but shows favor to the humble."

1 PETER 5:5

Two sources produce humility in a human soul. The first source is an awareness of the wretchedness and frailty of your spiritual nature, which influences every human in some part as long as you are alive, no matter how far you've matured in your spiritual life. The second source of humility is when you begin to encounter God's abounding love and beauty. Before God's presence, all Creation quakes, all preachers are silenced, and even saints and angels are blinded. We are easily overpowered by such an encounter with God's love and beauty. Without God's help, we are unable to stand in God's presence surrounded by the Cloud of Unknowing.

REFLECTION QUESTION: How have encounters with God helped you become more truly yourself?

*As God's chosen people, holy and dearly loved, clothe yourselves with
compassion, kindness, humility, gentleness and patience. Bear with
each other and forgive one another if any of you has a grievance against
someone. Forgive as the Lord forgave you. And over all these virtues put
on love, which binds them all together in perfect unity.*

COLOSSIANS 3:12–14

The second source of humility is also the highest way of perfection, for though it begins in this life, it shall last without end. The first source of humility—the awareness of the wretchedness and frailty of your spiritual nature—is imperfect, for it fades away at the end of this life like darkness fading to dawn. It also falls short of multiplying your desire for God's abundant grace as long as we live in our mortal body. As often and as long as Jesus chooses to work in this way, we will sometimes suddenly and perfectly lose ourselves in prayer before the loving presence of God, overlooking our thoughts and feelings, forgetting whether we've been holy or wretched. Instead, we remember that God has chosen us and that we are holy and dearly loved.

REFLECTION QUESTION: How has the virtue of humility grown in your life?

MARCH 20

*Humble yourselves, therefore, under God's mighty hand, that he may
lift you up in due time.*

1 PETER 5:6

Sometimes in prayer, we may forget everything else in life, and find ourselves lifted up before the loving presence of God. We experience being deeply loved by God. Whether this happens often or seldom, the experience usually lasts but a short while. In this brief time, you are made perfectly humble, for you experience no other thought or feeling but only God's love and beauty. Whenever your mind and heart is communing with lesser thoughts or feelings, although you make Christ your highest goal, you'll still discover a lesser kind of humility. Nevertheless, please welcome this saying, for even imperfect humility is good and should be sought after eagerly.

REFLECTION QUESTION: How have you been humbled, either intentionally or unintentionally?

MARCH 21

All of you, be like-minded, be sympathetic, love one another, be compassionate and humble.

1 PETER 3:8

Although it may be called imperfect humility, through this humility we gain at least an imperfect knowledge and experience of who we are. Having even a little true self-knowledge will motivate you more toward the virtue of perfect humility. In the company of a few others, grow in humility through mutual prayer, bearing one another's burdens, offering sympathy and compassion to people in their suffering. Even if all the saints and angels of heaven, or if all the holy men and women alive within God's family on earth did nothing else but pray to God that you come into perfect humility, you still need knowledge and experience of yourself before God. It is impossible to come to the perfect virtue of humility without struggling with your own shortcomings, and occasionally losing what you've imperfectly gained. Such self-knowledge comes more easily when people you love and trust help you to see who you are becoming in Christ, and help you become who you already are in God.

REFLECTION QUESTION: How have you come to know yourself better this year?

MARCH 22

You were taught, with regard to your former way of life, to put off your old self, which is being corrupted by its deceitful desires; to be made new in the attitude of your minds; and to put on the new self, created to be like God in true righteousness and holiness.

EPHESIANS 4:22–24

Therefore, strive with all your energy to gain a truer knowledge and experience of who you are in God's eyes. The more you discover your true self, the more you will also gain true understanding and deeper experience of God. As long as you are still in this mortal flesh, you will never know Jesus fully until you are united, body and soul, in eternal bliss. But as much as possible, come to know and experience Jesus as he allows himself to be known, by living as Jesus lived, fully in humility within your soul while in your mortal body. Do not think, because of these two kinds of humility, one perfect and another imperfect, that you should skip past the challenges of imperfect humility, and set out with all your heart to become perfectly humble.

REFLECTION QUESTION: Who has helped you discover your true self?

MARCH 23

When the perishable has been clothed with the imperishable, and the mortal with immortality, then the saying that is written will come true: "Death has been swallowed up in victory."
1 CORINTHIANS 15:54

Try not only to understand but also to practice contemplative spiritual disciplines. They are of greater worth than all other forms of exercise you undertake by God's grace, whether physical or spiritual. By a secret love, press with purity of heart upward toward the Cloud of Unknowing that lies between you and God. Clothe yourself with what is imperishable and you will discover the true and perfect virtue of humility without needing any special vision of anything less than the presence of God.

REFLECTION QUESTION: What is your current understanding of the contemplative life?

MARCH 24

When you pray, do not be like the hypocrites, for they love to pray standing in the synagogues and on the street corners to be seen by others. Truly I tell you, they have received their reward in full. But when you pray, go into your room, close the door and pray to your Father, who is unseen.
MATTHEW 6:5–6

Get to know perfect humility and treasure humility in your heart so that you will grow in love. The more you treasure humility in your heart, the more humble and down to earth you will become. The less you know of the two kinds of humility, the more prideful you will become. There are those who know nothing of perfect humility and have little knowledge of imperfect humility, who with that little knowledge, erroneously think they have become truly humble. They deceive themselves and clothe themselves in garments of self-righteousness that are pretending to be sacred. So strive for humility, for those whose lives are truly humble guard themselves against such hypocrisy in the present and avoid future transgressions as well.

REFLECTION QUESTION: Who helps keep you honest and down to earth?

MARCH 25

I have no greater joy than to hear that my children are walking in the truth.

3 JOHN 4

A child learns to crawl before she learns to walk. In the same way, you learn humility first by knowing your own limitations before learning of God's majesty. Those who think the only way into a life of humility is through knowledge of human wretchedness lack true wisdom. You can be confident that perfect humility is available to all and by God's grace may be truly experienced in this life by anyone who pursues this virtue. Begin by getting on your knees and humbling yourself, as you first learn to crawl before you learn to walk in the truth.

REFLECTION QUESTION: How often do you pray on your knees?

MARCH 26

It would have been better for them not to have known the way of righteousness, than to have known it and then to turn their backs on the sacred command that was passed on to them. Of them the proverbs are true: "A dog returns to its vomit," and, "A sow that is washed returns to her wallowing in the mud."

2 PETER 2:21–22

S ome have confused ideas about humility, that it only involves self-abasement by recalling our wretched condition and past transgressions. Humility is more than crawling around in the mud of human failure. Some only know humility by the experience or memory of destructive living, whether in the present or the past. Once you've discovered the life-giving way of humility, you discover it has little to with vain self-abasement, and everything to do with walking freely in God's joyful way of righteousness.

MARCH 27

This righteousness is given through faith in Jesus Christ to all who believe. There is no difference between Jew and Gentile, for all have sinned and fall short of the glory of God, and all are justified freely by his grace through the redemption that came by Christ Jesus.

ROMANS 3:22–24

There are some who have lived mostly in innocence, never having willfully pursued deadly faults, but only falling short of God's glory through their weakness and ignorance. Such people are often drawn to the contemplative life. Such a person, through wise counsel and enlivened conscience, will grow in the virtue of humility, making life changes for the good through contrition and confession, according to the plans and designs provided by God's grace.

REFLECTION QUESTION: In what ways have you fallen short of God's glory?

MARCH 28

Then he said, "Jesus, remember me when you come into your kingdom." Jesus answered him, "Truly I tell you, today you will be with me in paradise."

LUKE 23:42–43

When anyone, whether unclean or innocent, experiences God's grace to enter the contemplative life, they will soon discover another approach, the higher way of humility. Into this higher way, they rise up, stand on two feet, and begin to learn to walk. The perfect way of humility is so far above the imperfect path of humility that a few comparisons may be helpful. Think of Mary the mother of Jesus, and how different her life was from the life of the thief on the cross. Better yet, think of Jesus's perfect life on earth in contrast to the life of any other human who has ever lived. Or consider the life of an angel in heaven who never knows any weakness, in contrast to the life of a frail human on earth.

REFLECTION QUESTION: What story in Jesus's life do you enjoy thinking about?

MARCH 29

During the days of Jesus's life on earth, he offered up prayers and petitions with fervent cries and tears to the one who could save him from death, and he was heard because of his reverent submission. Son though he was, he learned obedience from what he suffered and, once made perfect, he became the source of eternal salvation for all who obey him.

HEBREWS 5:7–9

Some may think there is no perfect way of humility, but only the imperfect way of humility that comes by knowing our own human weakness and wretchedness. If that is true, then how did Jesus learn humility while living a fully human life yet without sin? Into this perfect way of humility you are called, both in the Gospels, through the example of the life of Jesus, and today as God continues to invite you into a life continually perfected by the grace of our Lord Jesus Christ as he is for all eternity, perfect by nature.

REFLECTION QUESTION: What example in Jesus's life encourages you to grow closer to God?

MARCH 30

Humble yourselves before the Lord, and he will lift you up.

JAMES 4:10

By virtue of learning to walk in the higher way of perfect humility, a person who once groveled in the mire may discover their life truly called into a life of loving God. By this way, you will come into a life of maturity quicker than by any other way. God loves to lift us up into the higher way of love. Walking in this higher way is also the swiftest way to experience Christ's love deeply through the forgiveness of your sins.

REFLECTION QUESTION: When have you known an inner stirring of your soul to love God?

MARCH 31

"For my thoughts are not your thoughts,
neither are your ways my ways,"
declares the LORD.
"As the heavens are higher than the earth,
so are my ways higher than your ways
and my thoughts than your thoughts."

ISAIAH 55:8–9

There is no presumption in daring to seek this higher way of perfection, even if you've lived the most wretched life. In the time you still have to amend your ways, when you feel that inner stirring of your soul to the contemplative life of love, by the guidance of a wise mentor, with your own conscience humbly hungering for Christ's love, quietly press toward the Cloud of Unknowing that rests between you and God. God's thoughts will always be higher than our thoughts. God's ways are always higher than our ways. Keep thinking God's thoughts. Keep seeking God's ways. God will keep lifting you up.

REFLECTION QUESTION: What time of day do you find best to think about God?

April

One Thing of Worth

APRIL 1

When one of the Pharisees invited Jesus to have dinner with him, he went to the Pharisee's house and reclined at the table. A woman in that town who lived a sinful life learned that Jesus was eating at the Pharisee's house, so she came there with an alabaster jar of perfume.

LUKE 7:36–37

In Luke's Gospel, a woman went to the house of a religious leader named Simon.[12] Jesus was already reclining at table with Simon when this woman arrived. She was living a sinful life at the time, and when she heard Jesus was dining at Simon's house, she pressed on, inviting herself over to be with Jesus, bringing with her an alabaster jar of expensive perfume. Though uninvited, she entered into the dining room where Jesus was reclining. She immediately knelt down and began weeping at Jesus's feet. Wetting his feet with her tears and wiping them with her hair, she poured out the expensive perfume upon his feet. The aroma of the perfume filled the room.

REFLECTION QUESTION: What extravagant act of devotion have you offered to God?

APRIL 2

As she stood behind him at his feet weeping, she began to wet his feet with her tears. Then she wiped them with her hair, kissed them and poured perfume on them.
When the Pharisee who had invited him saw this, he said to himself, "If this man were a prophet, he would know who is touching him and what kind of woman she is—that she is a sinner."

LUKE 7:38–39

Remember how Jesus loved while having dinner at a Pharisee's home when this sinful woman came to Jesus. She wept at Jesus's feet, pouring expensive perfume onto his feet and wiping them with her hair. The religious leader Simon was shocked by her behavior, and was also shocked that Jesus allowed her to act this way. Simon's heart harshly judged Jesus and also condemned the woman. To Simon, the fact that Jesus allowed this woman to touch him and offer him such devotion revealed that Jesus was not a prophet, not sent by God to guide the faithful closer to God. Simon was a religious leader; in his eyes, Jesus must either be ignorant, foolish, or something worse. Simon was also deeply embarrassed that the woman, who was living a sinful life, would step foot into his home and disturb his dinner, and bring impurity upon his household. His heart was not moved with compassion, but with religious judgment.

REFLECTION QUESTION: What most motivates your heart?

APRIL 3

Jesus answered him, "Simon, I have something to tell you."
"Tell me, teacher," he said.
"Two people owed money to a certain moneylender. One owed him five hundred denarii, and the other fifty. Neither of them had the money to pay him back, so he forgave the debts of both. Now which of them will love him more?"
Simon replied, "I suppose the one who had the bigger debt forgiven."
"You have judged correctly," Jesus said.

LUKE 7:40–43

Jesus told Simon about a moneylender and two debtors, one who owed a little, the other who owed a huge amount. The first owed the equivalent of two months' wages. The other owed ten times as much, nearly two years' worth of salary. Both debtors were forgiven their debts. Jesus asked Simon which debtor loved the moneylender more. Simon replied, "I suppose the one who had the bigger debt forgiven." In this reply, you can hear Simon's heart hesitating to hear the meaning of the story, and also the way the story was being lived out right before his eyes in his own life and in the life of this sinful woman. Jesus assured Simon that he answered correctly. All the eyes at that dinner table were upon Jesus, wondering what he would do next.

REFLECTION QUESTION: Where do you focus the attention of your heart?

APRIL 4

Then he turned toward the woman and said to Simon, "Do you see this
woman? I came into your house. You did not give me any water for my
feet, but she wet my feet with her tears and wiped them with her hair.
You did not give me a kiss, but this woman, from the time I entered, has
not stopped kissing my feet. You did not put oil on my head, but she has
poured perfume on my feet.

LUKE 7:44–46

The ordinary practice of hospitality in Jesus's time when guests arrived for dinner was for the host to provide a basin of water to allow the guests to wash their feet. After this washing, the guests would be welcomed with a friendly kiss. Guests also would be offered a small jar of olive oil to ceremonially receive a touch of oil on their head as an additional welcome blessing. None of these ordinary practices of hospitality were offered to Jesus by this religious leader. Jesus was not welcomed warmly by Simon, but treated inhospitably. As Jesus entered Simon's home for dinner, he was ignored, and the customary ceremonies of welcome were neglected. On the contrary, when a sinful woman entered without an invitation, she offered Jesus extravagant hospitality. She was weeping and kneeling at Jesus's feet, expressing her broken heart before Jesus. This woman's tears wet Jesus's feet, and she dried his wet feet with her hair. Then she kissed Jesus's feet over and over as an expression of her great love. Finally, she brought out a jar of her own perfume, and poured out the perfume upon Jesus's feet, filling the room with the fragrance of her devotion.

REFLECTION QUESTION: How have you offered your devotion to Jesus?

APRIL 5

Therefore, I tell you, her many sins have been forgiven—as her great
love has shown. But whoever has been forgiven little loves little.

LUKE 7:47

Without the grace of Jesus at work within her, this woman would no more have been able to turn away from a life of habitual sin than she would have been able to buy the forgiveness of her sins. Therefore, she pressed forward with true love and inner desire into the Cloud of Unknowing. She learned to love blindly what she could never have seen clearly in this life by simple light of reason, nor experience by the sweetness of mere human affection. She was so caught up in this way of love that she had very little awareness of her past life of sin. She became so deeply attuned to Jesus's love that she also had little awareness of her surroundings in Simon's house. This true story from the Gospel reveals the way of true love, encouraging us to experience God's love beyond anything seen or unseen in this mortal life.

REFLECTION QUESTION: What does this story tell you about the way of true love?

APRIL 6

Then Jesus said to her, "Your sins are forgiven." The other guests began to say among themselves, "Who is this who even forgives sins?"

LUKE 7:48–49

When Jesus said to the woman, "Your sins are forgiven," it was not because she remembered her sinful life that she was forgiven. Nor was she forgiven because she humbled herself by looking at her wretchedness only. Look what wonders may come to all who quietly press on in the way of great love. This woman certainly knew sorrow, weeping for her sins, humbled by the memory of her life of wretchedness. We are wise to do the same. Recall our own shortcomings, and allow our heart to be humbled by the memories and sorrows for all our sins. Yet, learn from this woman who loved Jesus greatly. Every day she carried the burden of deep sorrow for her sins, hiding this load deep within her heart in a way she could never forget. It was not the memory of her sins that most moved her. The story makes clear that her greatest sorrow, her heart's true desire, her deepest pain within her soul, was her longing to be loved. She languished almost to death for lack of love. Once she was truly loved, she longed for even greater measure of this love, for it is the condition of a true lover that the more you experience, the more you long for. She knew with sorrow that she was not worthy of this love, and that her sins had separated her from God whom she sought to love. But she also knew that this sorrow was due more to a languishing sickness of the soul from her lack of love. So what should she do? Should she plunge herself from the height of her desire for love down into the dark depths of sin? Should she debase her soul by searching among the stinking garbage heap of her sins, looking at each past misdeed one by one, examining and weeping over each? No, surely not. Jesus gave her true knowledge of grace within her soul, so she never needed to wallow in her sins again.

REFLECTION QUESTION: When did you first know that you were truly and deeply loved by God?

APRIL 7

Jesus said to the woman, "Your faith has saved you; go in peace."
LUKE 7:50

Those who come to God by faith, longing to be loved, will be saved and find true inner peace. Those who discover the contemplative way of love discover inner peace and freedom from the meddlesome aspects of the active life. Contemplatives learn inner contentment without the need to defend their way of life even in face of active people who speak out against them. In Luke we also find the story when Jesus came to the house of Martha and Mary her sister. All the time that Martha was busy preparing food to serve to Jesus and his followers, Mary, her sister, sat at Jesus's feet. As she sat, she listened to Jesus's teaching, paying little attention to anything else, including her sister's actions in the kitchen, though Martha's labors were good and valuable. Like Mary, take time daily to sit and listen to Jesus.

REFLECTION QUESTION: Where do you sit and listen to Jesus?

APRIL 8

The decrees of the LORD are firm,
and all of them are righteous.
They are more precious than gold,
than much pure gold;
they are sweeter than honey,
than honey from the honeycomb.
PSALM 19:9–10

Martha was involved in the first part of the active life, actively serving others. The second part of the active life, overlapping with the first part of the contemplative life, is to focus on Jesus and the sweetness of his voice and words. Jesus's words are sweeter than honey, and more precious than finest gold. Listening to the voice of Jesus is better and holier than the first part of the active life, for it leads a person into the contemplative way. Mary looked beyond Jesus's humanness, beholding with all the love of her heart the sovereign wisdom of God hidden in Jesus's presence and words.

REFLECTION QUESTION: What is the sweetest taste to your soul at this time?

APRIL 9

We also have the prophetic message as something completely reliable, and you will do well to pay attention to it, as to a light shining in a dark place, until the day dawns and the morning star rises in your hearts.
2 PETER 1:19

From her seat at Jesus's feet she would not move, nor did she pay any attention to what was being done around her. Instead, she sat attentively before Jesus. With a sweetness of secret desire and love, she pressed toward that high Cloud of Unknowing between herself and her God. There was never a purer creature in this life on earth, nor ever shall there be, as those ravished in contemplation and love of God. Into this high and wonderful Cloud of Unknowing between humans and God Mary pressed with a secret love. This love is the one thing needed in this life, the best and highest part of contemplation, that one thing that will never be taken away from Mary, nor from anyone who finds this one thing.

REFLECTION QUESTION: What are you paying attention to most at this time?

APRIL 10

You too, be patient and stand firm, because the Lord's coming is near.
Don't grumble against one another, brothers and sisters, or you will be
judged. The Judge is standing at the door!

JAMES 5:8–9

Mary's sister, Martha, complained to Jesus, demanding that Jesus tell her sister to get up and help with the preparations so that Martha would not be doing all the work by herself. While this complaining was going on, Mary continued to sit quietly, answering with not a single word. Nor did Mary grumble against her sister for any complaint she made. When you begin to grumble in your spirit or complain against a family member or friend, consider Mary, who sat quietly at the feet of Jesus and did not say a word, but simply listened to the Lord. This is not so amazing, really, for Mary had another kind of work to do that Martha had not yet discovered.

REFLECTION QUESTION: What do you do when you begin to feel irritated?

APRIL 11

This is what the Sovereign LORD, the Holy One of Israel, says:
"In repentance and rest is your salvation,
in quietness and trust is your strength,
but you would have none of it."

ISAIAH 30:15

Therefore, Mary had no need to listen to her or answer her complaint with defensiveness or rebuttal. Pay attention to all these works and words and actions shown between these two sisters. They are set as an example of the active and contemplative ways of life that have been heard and lived among people of faith throughout the ages. In Martha, we recognize activists, who have been guided by her way of life, a necessary and vital aspect of life. In Mary, we recognize contemplatives, who conform their way of life after hers, having chosen the one thing needed in this life, the one thing that is not only better, but that also will never be taken away.

REFLECTION QUESTION: How do you find rest for your soul after you've grown weary?

APRIL 12

Do not let any unwholesome talk come out of your mouths, but only
what is helpful for building others up according to their needs, that it
may benefit those who listen.

EPHESIANS 4:29

Just as Martha complained long ago about Mary, to this day activists complain about contemplatives, often ignorant of their way of life. For there are people, whether men or women, secular or sacred, involved in worldly affairs or not, people who are stirred by grace and wise counsel to forsake outward business and set themselves to live the contemplative way according to their ability, attitude, and acumen. Just as quickly as a person enters into this contemplative way, their family and friends, along with many others who know nothing of such inner soul stirrings nor of the contemplative manner of life, may rise against them with complaints, saying to them they are wasting their life on empty pursuits.

REFLECTION QUESTION: What has been stirred in your soul recently?

APRIL 13

Come, let us go up to the mountain of the LORD,
to the temple of the God of Jacob.
He will teach us his ways,
so that we may walk in his paths.

ISAIAH 2:3

There are many who have tried to walk in this way of contemplation, attempting to forsake the way of the world. Where they could have become Christ's faithful followers and contemplatives, because they refused to be governed by any true spiritual counsel, they have fallen into ways of darkness, focusing their lives upon corruption. Some have become two-faced, pretending to be full of spiritual light when they are really full of ignorance. Some have departed from God's presence, falling into reckless and destructive ways as they slander what is good and holy. It is best not to speak anything more of such troubling matters. Nevertheless, whenever needed, God will grant you favor to better understand the conditions and causes of such failings to better equip you to walk in the way of love.

REFLECTION QUESTION: Who taught you to walk in the way of the Lord?

APRIL 14

*Seek first his kingdom and his righteousness, and all these things will be
given to you as well.*
MATTHEW 6:33

Some may think less of Martha because she complained to Jesus about her sister Mary. But Martha was a deeply spiritual woman, highly to be admired among the wise ones of the Bible. She came to Jesus first when her brother had died. Yes, she complained about her sister as some do today about the contemplative way of life. But it is better not to say anything negative about Martha or about any of Christ's servants who are seeking to do the will of God. For if you think about her complaint, you will quickly recall the situation in which she made this criticism. She did not know what was going on in Mary's heart, and she was seeking to serve her guests with excellence. Later, it was Martha who went out first to meet Jesus when her brother Lazarus had died. Seek first to be near to the Lord.

REFLECTION QUESTION: What are you seeking first in life?

APRIL 15

*As for God, his way is perfect:
The LORD's word is flawless;
he shields all who take refuge in him.*
PSALM 18:30

Up to this point, Martha had yet to hear about the way of perfection. Also, when she did speak, she spoke politely and briefly, giving her good reason to be excused from the criticism of others. In the same way, active men and women today need to be given lots of grace when they criticize the contemplative life, even if they do so harshly. It is far better to make allowances for such people who are still living in ignorance. For what reason? Martha understood very little of what was going on in Mary's heart when she brought her complaint to the Lord.

REFLECTION QUESTION: What questions do you have about the contemplative life?

Do not store up for yourselves treasures on earth, where moths and vermin destroy, and where thieves break in and steal. But store up for yourselves treasures in heaven, where moths and vermin do not destroy, and where thieves do not break in and steal. For where your treasure is, there your heart will be also.

MATTHEW 6:19–21

Similarly, there are many active people today who understand very little of what goes on in the soul of contemplative people who turn away from the busyness of this world and draw near to God, seeking to become God's treasured people, allowing their lives to be filled with the treasure of God's holiness, goodness, and love. If they truly knew of this inner life of contemplation, they would not say what they say. Therefore, it is better to give them grace, for they currently know no better way than the way they are living at the time. Also, consider your own numerous faults from the past, whether in word or deed, because of your blindness. Just as surely you desire to receive God's grace to pardon your faults, so, with love and compassion, it is better to overlook the ignorant words and deeds of others and simply press on in the calling of life to which you are called by God. As Jesus taught, "So in everything, do to others what you would have them do to you."[13]

REFLECTION QUESTION: Where is your heart's treasure?

APRIL 17

I will show you the most excellent way.

1 CORINTHIANS 12:31

When you set out upon the pathway of love, it becomes easier and easier to overlook the faults of active, busy people who fail to understand your contemplative ways. The more you are caught up in Christ's love the less attention you will give to what others say against you. Learn from Mary, who was not distracted when her sister Martha spoke against her. Follow her example and God will continue to do for you what Jesus did for her. What did Jesus do for Mary? Recall when Martha asked him to act as judge between these two sisters. Martha asked Jesus to order her sister to leave her contemplation and come help serve in the kitchen. Nothing secret is hidden from God's eyes, and so Jesus saw Mary's spirit ardently caught up in love.

REFLECTION QUESTION: When did you, in your daily living, first set out upon the pathway of love?

APRIL 18

The Advocate, the Holy Spirit, whom the Father will send in my name, will teach you all things and will remind you of everything I have said to you. Peace I leave with you; my peace I give you. I do not give to you as the world gives. Do not let your hearts be troubled and do not be afraid.
JOHN 14:26–27

Affectionately, Jesus answered Martha on behalf of Mary, because Mary would not be distracted from her love. How did Jesus speak to Martha? Not as a judge, but rather as an advocate coming to the defense of the one being loved. Two times Jesus called Martha by name, a gentle and loving way to get her attention and to help her more fully listen to what he was to say. "Martha, Martha, you are worried and upset about many things," Jesus told her. Those who walk in the active way of life are often preoccupied and worried about many things. You busy yourself first with the things you need. Then you get busy with many charitable actions arising from your concern for others.

REFLECTION QUESTION: How has God encouraged you?

APRIL 19

For Christ's love compels us, because we are convinced that one died for all, and therefore all died.
2 CORINTHIANS 5:14

As with Martha, understand that such charitable actions are good and healthy for your soul. Nonetheless, do not think that such actions are the highest work of the soul or better than other kinds of work of the soul. As Jesus told Martha, "only one thing is necessary."[14] What is that one thing? Assuredly, the one thing most important is God's love. May God be fully loved and praised above all other activities that you may do, whether physical or spiritual. Some will try to love Jesus in little portions while at the same time attempting to love this life fully by getting busy with many important daily activities, whether physical or spiritual. They end up being divided in their soul and frustrated within. It is better to die to every lesser love and pursue the one love that is truly necessary for life.

REFLECTION QUESTION: What compels you?

APRIL 20

No one can serve two masters. Either you will hate the one and love the other, or you will be devoted to the one and despise the other. You cannot serve both God and money.

MATTHEW 6:24

Have you ever wondered if it's possible to love God and at the same time serve God through physical and spiritual activities? Imperfectly, yes. But to grow in perfect love, learn from Mary, who chose the best part that would never be taken away from her. Why is this so? This best part, the inner awakening of perfect love for God, begins on earth but will continue without an end in the perfect joy of heaven. Loving is the one thing necessary—loving God and being loved by God.

REFLECTION QUESTION: What distracts you most from loving God more fully?

APRIL 21

This is my prayer: that your love may abound more and more in knowledge and depth of insight, so that you may be able to discern what is best and may be pure and blameless for the day of Christ, filled with the fruit of righteousness that comes through Jesus Christ—to the glory and praise of God.

PHILIPPIANS 1:9–11

You may be wondering about the meaning of "Mary has chosen the best part."[15] When someone talks about "what is best" that means likely there also is "what is good," and "what is better." The best is third and highest in the order of these. What are these three good things of which Mary chose the best? God's people, through the centuries, have celebrated two ways of living, the active way and the contemplative way. These two ways of spiritual life are seen in the lives of Martha and Mary, the two sisters in the Gospel story. Martha is the active person and Mary the contemplative. Within these ways of living are discovered the way to God, and from them we may discern what is the best way.

REFLECTION QUESTION: Who taught you to discern what is best?

APRIL 22

Stand at the crossroads and look;
ask for the ancient paths,
ask where the good way is, and walk in it,
and you will find rest for your souls.
But you said, "We will not walk in it."
JEREMIAH 6:16

Within these two ways of living are also discovered three parts: what is good, better, and best, as described earlier in this writing. The first part of these three is revealed in physical actions of mercy and love and may be known as the first degree of the active life. The second part of these two lives is witnessed in spiritual meditation upon our own wretchedness, upon Christ's passion, and upon the joys of heaven. The first part of the active life is good. The first step into the spiritual life is a step away from what is not good, into the good way, into the ancient way of faith.

REFLECTION QUESTION: When did you take your first steps into the ancient and good way?

APRIL 23

For now we see only a reflection as in a mirror; then we shall
see face to face. Now I know in part; then I shall know fully, even as I
am fully known.
1 CORINTHIANS 13:12

The second part—the better one—is even better for us, for it is the second degree of the active life, and is also the first degree of the contemplative life. The higher ways of the active life and the lower ways of the contemplative life overlap and may be understood as a spiritual sisterhood, like the kinship of Martha and Mary. An active person may journey into the contemplative life and discover new ways of experiencing God's presence. A contemplative person may engage in the active life according to the greatness of the need.

REFLECTION QUESTION: When have you enjoyed being in God's presence?

APRIL 24

All the nations you have made
will come and worship before you, Lord;
they will bring glory to your name.
For you are great and do marvelous deeds;
you alone are God.
Teach me your way, LORD,
that I may rely on your faithfulness;
give me an undivided heart,
that I may fear your name.

PSALM 86:9–11

The third part—what is best for us—is discovered within the mysterious Cloud of Unknowing when we are drawn into God's love by a secret inner longing for God alone. The first part is good, the second is better, but this third part is best of all. This is the best part that Mary chose. Jesus did not say Mary had chosen the best life but rather the best part, for there are but two ways of living and both ways are good. Within these two ways of living, Mary made a choice for what is best. As Jesus promised, this best part shall never be taken away from any who chose it. For what is good and what is better are both valuable and honorable, yet they both end with the mortal life you are now living.

REFLECTION QUESTION: How might you live more often with an undivided heart?

APRIL 25

But grow in the grace and knowledge of our Lord and Savior Jesus
Christ. To him be glory both now and forever! Amen.

2 PETER 3:18

In the life to come, there will be no more need for acts of mercy to help those who are hungry, thirsty, dying, sick, homeless, in prison, or in need of burial. For in the life to come there is no longer any hunger, thirst, sickness, homelessness, prison, or death. Also, in the life to come, there is no longer any reason to weep for your own wretchedness, nor even to weep for Christ's passion. But the third part, that part which Mary chose, may you also choose, and thus by God's grace, discover what is best. To be more direct, all who chose this best part are chosen by grace. So grow in this grace with increasing desire, for this highest way of life shall never be taken away from you, but shall last into eternity.

REFLECTION QUESTION: What most encourages grace to grow within your life?

APRIL 26

God again set a certain day, calling it "Today." This he did when a long
time later he spoke through David, as in the passage already quoted:
"Today, if you hear his voice,
do not harden your hearts."

HEBREWS 4:7

So hear God's voice as he calls out to you in the active way of life. Just as Jesus spoke to Martha on behalf of Mary, so God calls to you. Be actively involved in what is good and what is better, in the first part and in the second, now in one and now in the other. If you are able, seek to engage in both the active and contemplative ways of life, uniting them together into your daily way of life. But beware of complaining or of interfering with contemplatives, for you do not know what is in their hearts. Learn from them how to rest and play and pray. With Mary, they have chosen the third and best part.

REFLECTION QUESTION: How do you hear God's voice?

APRIL 27

His mouth is sweetness itself;
he is altogether lovely.
This is my beloved, this is my friend,
daughters of Jerusalem.

SONG OF SONGS 5:16

How sweet was the love between Mary and her beloved. Jesus has great love for you when you turn away from your distracted life and come to sit at his feet. Try to understand the love you share with God, not as some shallow romance, but as the real love story witnessed in the Gospel of Luke. Mary found the highest and purest kind of love in Jesus. His mouth was "sweetness itself" to her. Jesus found in Mary, to his great delight, a heart so deeply rooted in love for God that nothing would satisfy her nor hold her heart except the love of God.

REFLECTION QUESTION: What is your love story?

APRIL 28

Do not be afraid, for I know that you are looking for Jesus, who was crucified. He is not here; he has risen, just as he said. Come and see the place where he lay. Then go quickly and tell his disciples: "He has risen from the dead and is going ahead of you into Galilee. There you will see him." Now I have told you.

MATTHEW 28:5–7

Place before your heart the story of three women who loved Jesus with wondrous love: Mary, the sister of Martha; Mary Magdalene; and the woman who anointed Jesus at Simon's home.[16] Like Martha's sister, Mary, Mary Magdalene also sought Jesus with great love. She came to the tomb with a broken heart that would not be comforted even by angels. For as she was weeping, an angel spoke affectionately to her. Even as this angel spoke to her such words of comfort, Mary could not stop weeping out of her great love for Jesus. She who came seeking for the King of angels wouldn't be comforted by mere angels.

REFLECTION QUESTION: Who has sought to comfort you in your spiritual journey?

In accordance with your great love, forgive the sin of these people, just as you have pardoned them from the time they left Egypt until now.

NUMBERS 14:19

Anyone who truly looks into the Gospel stories will find many examples of perfect love written to inspire such wondrous love. In the same way, this writing you now are reading is intended to inspire this same love. If you desire one such example of the love Jesus has for you and for all who come to him with such wondrous love, consider the story already told above. Remember the troubled woman who turned away from her life of sin when she was called into the grace of the contemplative life of love. Discover Jesus's heart in the love story between a sinful woman and Jesus in the home of Simon, the religious leader. Jesus confronted those who spoke against her, and he came to her defense because of her great love. He also challenged the religious teacher Simon in his own house before his own guests for his negative attitude toward this woman. Jesus asked Simon which person had greater love, the one who was forgiven little or the one who was forgiven much. Of course, her love was a surpassing love, for she knew she had been forgiven with an even more wondrous love. This is the love that God has for all who turn away from their own brokenness and are called by grace into a life of love.

REFLECTION QUESTION: How has God's love been seen in your life through forgiveness?

APRIL 30

The people of Israel are oppressed,
and the people of Judah as well.
All their captors hold them fast,
refusing to let them go.
Yet their Redeemer is strong;
the Lord Almighty is his name.
He will vigorously defend their cause
so that he may bring rest to their land.

JEREMIAH 50:33–34

With all your heart, truly begin to conform your way of loving and your way of living by God's grace and wisdom. Seek to live according to the pattern of love and life found in these women whose Gospel stories are shared above. Be confident that God will answer today in the same way Jesus loved those women long ago. Jesus defended those women from people who maligned them. Daily and secretly in your heart, God will spiritually defend you from those who misunderstand you, or who speak against you. God will bring you rest.

REFLECTION QUESTION: How has God brought you spiritual rest?

May

Everyday Grace

He has reconciled you by Christ's physical body through death to present you holy in his sight, without blemish and free from accusation—if you continue in your faith, established and firm, and do not move from the hope held out in the gospel.
COLOSSIANS 1:22–23

While you labor in this new way of life, there will always be some who speak or think negatively against you just as they did to some women in the Bible. You may even have inner thoughts or doubts calling you into question, telling you that your new way of life is useless. Give little attention to such negative words or thoughts, nor allow them to distract you from your secret spiritual labor of love. God will answer these accusers in God's own time and way, turning such negative thoughts and words away and convicting the souls of those doing the maligning. As you press on in the labor of love, undistracted by such accusers and accusations, Jesus will support you, stirring others to provide, in body and in spirit, everything you need in this life.

REFLECTION QUESTION: What do you do when you hear negative thoughts?

MAY 2

*You have delivered me from death
and my feet from stumbling,
that I may walk before God
in the light of life.*
PSALM 56:13

Some are confused and in error when they think Christ only calls people into the contemplative life after all their physical needs have been secured. They show their ignorance. Jesus will bless you with life's necessities, or will strengthen you and give you patience in your spirit to endure hardships. Either way, it makes no difference to a true contemplative. If you wonder at this, you may have allowed uncertainty to creep into your heart. Turn away from the distractions of this world and turn fully to God. There will always be those who prefer fanciful or spiritual-sounding arguments to walking with God in the light of life.

There will always be people who prefer to stumble in the dark. We are better off to put our trust in God. Be confident when you turn from the world to God.

REFLECTION QUESTION: Are you stumbling in the dark or walking in the light?

MAY 3

I have come that they may have life, and have it to the full.
JOHN 10:10

When you set out to enter the contemplative way, as Mary did, seek to humble your life before the wonder and worth of Jesus's perfect love. Live by love rather than living buried beneath your own pile of imperfections. It is much better to gaze on God's beauty and worth than glare at your shortcomings. Those who truly humble themselves before the Lord will not be in want, either in body or spirit. Why is this true? Because you have found the source of every abundance, Jesus Christ. Whoever finds Jesus, as the Good Book reminds us, finds life to the fullest.

REFLECTION QUESTION: What kind of life do you want with God?

MAY 4

We ought always to thank God for you, brothers and sisters, and rightly so, because your faith is growing more and more, and the love all of you have for one another is increasing.
2 THESSALONIANS 1:3

How do virtues grow in the soul? Take a look at the virtue of love. Because of God's great love at work in our soul, we are able to love others and love God more and more. Love, faith, and humility grow in your soul when you set aside or abandon the things of this world. Press on with even the smallest measure of blind love, penetrating into the mysterious Cloud of Unknowing. As you enter into God's love, the virtue of humility is genuinely perfected within your soul. The virtue of love grows in the same way.

REFLECTION QUESTION: How has the virtue of love increased in your life?

MAY 5

The LORD is compassionate and gracious,
slow to anger, abounding in love.

PSALM 103:8

As Bernard of Clairvaux affirmed long ago, there are four degrees of love.[17] First, we learn to love ourselves for our own sake. Second, we learn to love God for our own sake. Third, we gradually learn to love God for God's sake. Fourth, we learn to love ourselves for God's sake. True love is loving God above all else, for God's sake alone. True love is loving others for God's sake. True love is also loving yourself for God's sake. In this virtue of love, God is loved for God's sake alone, above all other creatures and things on earth. This is well and good. The heart of love is being loved by God and learning to love ourselves for God's sake. This love is discovered in the naked movement of your soul toward God.

REFLECTION QUESTION: What is your understanding of love?

MAY 6

Let us love one another, for love comes from God. Everyone who loves
has been born of God and knows God. Whoever does not love does not
know God, because God is love.

1 JOHN 4:7–8

The virtue of love grows when you apprentice yourself to Jesus. Do not ask for pleasure. Do not ask for pain. Ask only for God's love. Whether you are in pain or in pleasure really doesn't matter. What matters, and what is God's greatest desire for you, is that you learn to love as Jesus loves. In the virtue of love, God is perfectly loved for God's sake alone. In the virtue of love, learn to love yourself for God's sake alone. Nothing on earth comes above your love for God. As you grow in love, you will learn to love Christ more and more, even turning away from what is most beautiful and sacred on earth in order to commune more fully with God.

REFLECTION QUESTION: Who taught you to love?

MAY 7

I was hungry and you gave me something to eat, I was thirsty and you gave me something to drink, I was a stranger and you invited me in.

MATTHEW 25:35

True charity involves loving others for God's sake. Pick the low-hanging fruit on the tree of charity by looking upon all people with one love for God's sake. Whether family or stranger, friend or enemy, charity looks upon all people as God's beloved. Think of all people as members of God's family, and no one a stranger. Think of all people as friend and no one as enemy. See the face of Jesus in the face of all. For Jesus will tell you on the final day, "I was a stranger and you invited me in."[18] Even those who cause you pain or hardship, love calls you to love them as God loves them.[19] True love reaches out to such people with an inner stirring of the soul to will them as much good as possible, as you would for your closest friend.

REFLECTION QUESTION: Who have you welcomed into your life recently?

MAY 8

If you really keep the royal law found in Scripture, "Love your neighbor as yourself," you are doing right. But if you show favoritism, you sin and are convicted by the law as lawbreakers.

JAMES 2:8–9

When you look at others, try to discover how to see all people through God's eyes, whether they are friend or enemy, family or stranger. Do not show favoritism. This way of viewing all people without bias or prejudice will continue to grow and will be perfected as you draw nearer to Jesus and place all things under God's love. The more you grow in this way of seeing others, the more your life will deepen in virtue and charity, so that you will more gladly share life and prayers together with others, especially with your fellow faith pilgrims.

REFLECTION QUESTION: In what ways are you showing favoritism rather than loving as God loves?

MAY 9

You have heard that it was said, "Love your neighbor and hate your enemy." But I tell you, love your enemies and pray for those who persecute you, that you may be children of your Father in heaven.
MATTHEW 5:43–45

Be willing to step down from the heights of loving contemplation to personally show love to others. As charity invites you, share God's love with your enemies as though they are your friends, with strangers as though they are part of your family. Love those who do not love you, with the same love or an even greater love than you have for your friends. At first, this will seem difficult, even impossible. But as you yield your life to God, God's love will continue to well up within you like a healthy spring of water, overflowing into the lives of others, even into the lives of those who do not love you in return.

REFLECTION QUESTION: Who are the people that are hardest for you to love?

MAY 10

The LORD your God is God of gods and Lord of lords, the great God, mighty and awesome, who shows no partiality and accepts no bribes. He defends the cause of the fatherless and the widow, and loves the foreigner residing among you, giving them food and clothing.
DEUTERONOMY 10:17–18

When you are caught up in God's love, you learn to see others for who they are, not merely as friend or enemy, family or foreigner. Of course, when a few specific people come to mind as your heart reaches out to them, it is right to express personal affection for these people, as charity calls. Jesus gave special affection to Mary and Martha of Bethany, as well as to Peter and John and a few others during his time on earth. In general, it is better to show no partiality, but to love God above all others. In this way, you will learn to love all others simply and naturally for God's sake, as you love yourself.

REFLECTION QUESTION: When in your life have you offered kindness to a foreigner?

MAY 11

*If, by the trespass of the one man, death reigned through that one man,
how much more will those who receive God's abundant provision of
grace and of the gift of righteousness reign in life through the one man,
Jesus Christ!*

ROMANS 5:17

Just as all people are separated from God's love through Adam's fall
from grace, so will all people who seek grace through Jesus Christ be
reunited with God through Christ's passion, that is, through his death
and resurrection. In a similar way, the more you grow in your love for
God and the more your spirit is united with God's Spirit, the more your
life will reveal Jesus's way of life. The more you receive God's abundant
gift of grace and the more God's gift of new life reigns in your life through
Christ, the more you will view all people through Christ's eyes, giving no
partiality to anyone, but loving all with God's eternal love.

REFLECTION QUESTION: What hindrances in your life make it hard for
you to love?

MAY 12

*God has put the body together, giving greater honor to the parts that
lacked it, so that there should be no division in the body, but that its
parts should have equal concern for each other. If one part suffers, every
part suffers with it; if one part is honored, every part rejoices with it.
Now you are the body of Christ, and each one of you is a part of it.*

1 CORINTHIANS 12:24–27

If one of the limbs on your body hurts, your other limbs also feel the
pain. If one of your limbs is healthy, the rest of your body enjoys greater
health as well. This is how it is in Christ's body, among Christ's people,
the church. Christ is head of the body, the church. When you are enlivened
by God's love, you become a member of Christ's body. If you desire to follow Jesus and grow in God's love, then train yourself in the holy work of
laying down your life for your brothers and sisters. Just as Jesus laid down
his life by offering his body on the cross, so we are called to lay down our
life by giving greater honor to members of Christ's body who lack honor.

REFLECTION QUESTION: What are some of your prejudices?

MAY 13

You see, at just the right time, when we were still powerless, Christ died for the ungodly. Very rarely will anyone die for a righteous person, though for a good person someone might possibly dare to die. But God demonstrates his own love for us in this: While we were still sinners, Christ died for us.

ROMANS 5:6–8

Jesus did not die only for his close friends and family, but for all people in all times, without any favoritism or partiality shown to one person over another. While we had our backs turned away from God, Christ died for us. Everyone who turns away from sin and asks for God's mercy will be forgiven through the grace of God given at the cross. Discover grace at the cross, and you will grow in the virtues of humility and love, along with all other virtues. With the smallest impression of Christ's love, all the virtues are planted in the soul and begin to grow. Then, we will begin to experience God's love within us and be more and more willing to lay down our lives for others.

REFLECTION QUESTION: Is your life turned away from God or turned toward God?

MAY 14

Anyone who enters God's rest also rests from their works, just as God did from his. Let us, therefore, make every effort to enter that rest.

HEBREWS 4:10–11

Make every effort now, while you are able, to press upward into the majestic Cloud of Unknowing. Once within this cloud, you will find rest for your soul. In the beginning, it takes real effort on your part, an intense labor of your soul. Every day, receive God's grace, and your spiritual strength will grow and grow. Over time, through weeks and years of practicing being in God's presence, you will begin to experience God's grace more and more in the everyday places of your soul. Think of this as everyday grace, because Jesus loves to meet you and work with you every day, refreshing your soul.

REFLECTION QUESTION: How do you practice being in God's presence?

MAY 15

Jesus said, "Peace be with you! As the Father has sent me, I am sending you." And with that he breathed on them and said, "Receive the Holy Spirit. If you forgive anyone's sins, their sins are forgiven; if you do not forgive them, they are not forgiven."

JOHN 20:21–23

Some of you who are reading this may be wondering what kind of effort or labor is involved. Before we look at what is your work, clearly understand how Jesus is working his everyday grace within you. The sacred flame of love that is sparked within your will is not your own doing, but is a gift from Christ's hand. His hand and breath are always ready to kindle this flame within every human soul ready and willing to receive such a gift. Jesus loves to move within our soul, breathing the breath of God into our life, preparing us to join with God in this great work of love, as he has been doing since long before we were aware of God's presence.

REFLECTION QUESTION: How is Jesus working everyday grace within you?

MAY 16

In all my prayers for all of you, I always pray with joy because of your partnership in the gospel from the first day until now, being confident of this, that he who began a good work in you will carry it on to completion until the day of Christ Jesus.

PHILIPPIANS 1:4–6

What is God's great work of love in you, and how may you join God in this labor? Seek to cast down all lesser thoughts, distractions, and worldly worries, burying them under the Cloud of Forgetting, as was written earlier this year. Make this your effort and God's grace will assist you daily. The quickening of love within your soul is God's work alone. Keep doing your little work of love and God promises never to fail to do his great work of love within you. Keep at your work and know that Jesus is paying attention.

REFLECTION QUESTION: What little work of love will you do today?

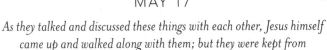

MAY 17

*As they talked and discussed these things with each other, Jesus himself
came up and walked along with them; but they were kept from
recognizing him.*
LUKE 24:15–16

Be aware of Jesus's presence with you, standing and abiding with you. Press on with spiritual discipline now, and in due time you will come to know God's refreshing presence that brings rest to your soul. At first, when you are not as spiritually fit for this work, the labor will seem difficult and even painful. The spiritual life is like walking in the mountains. At first, when you are not acclimatized to the altitude or not in shape, even though you walk in a beautiful place surrounded by glory, the labor of simply walking will seem difficult and even painful. You will wonder if you can continue and why you are doing what you are doing. After a while though, as you build up your spiritual strength, this same effort will become easier and easier, bringing deep refreshment for your soul.

REFLECTION QUESTION: Where are you growing in strength in your spiritual journey at this time?

MAY 18

*No discipline seems pleasant at the time, but painful. Later on,
however, it produces a harvest of righteousness and peace for those who
have been trained by it.*
HEBREWS 12:11

Very few people enjoy physical training at first. In the beginning, training the body is painful. Runners preparing for a race train by running. Athletes get better at their sport by physical training that increases over time. Weavers learn to weave by weaving. All this training costs energy and at first feels painful. Training for a spiritual journey may also feel painful at first. But the further you are trained in Jesus's way of love, the less you will seem to be working, and the more God will be working everyday grace within you, often without your awareness. This may occur during short periods of time, or remain with you over longer periods of time. Jesus desires to bring you greater joy in your journey of faith, as you draw nearer and nearer to God.

MAY 19

For my eyes have seen your salvation,
which you have prepared in the sight of all nations:
a light for revelation to the Gentiles,
and the glory of your people Israel.
LUKE 2:30–32

As you draw near to Jesus and become enveloped in the Cloud of Unknowing, he will at times shine light into this Cloud of Unknowing to reveal to you some of the mysteries of his love, of which humans have little understanding and few words to adequately describe. Then you will once again experience the spark of God's love igniting your innermost affections, more than you imagine possible or could possibly describe in words. This is Jesus's work within the human soul, a kind of work that goes far beyond your ability to understand or speak about with your limited human speech even if you made great effort to do so.

REFLECTION QUESTION: When has God's light helped you understand the mysteries of God's love?

MAY 20

The disciples were even more amazed, and said to each other,
"Who then can be saved?"
Jesus looked at them and said, "With man this is impossible, but not
with God; all things are possible with God."
MARK 10:26–27

One of the most important acts in the contemplative journey of love is the work of letting go of lesser thoughts, distractions, and worries when you experience God's everyday grace stirring within your soul. Speak of this work as often as you please. It is easier to understand than to undertake. Without God's grace at work in the everyday places of your soul, both kinds of work are impossible for you. But with God's everyday grace at work within your soul, nothing is impossible.

REFLECTION QUESTION: What do you do now that once seemed impossible?

MAY 21

You have shown me the way of life,
and you will fill me with the joy of your presence.
ACTS 2:28 NLT

Some may ask who is invited into this beautiful way of life. Above all, I want you to know that this way of life is not your work or effort but is a gift of grace given to all who are willing to receive. You still may have many questions about how a person is invited to enter into this way of life. If you want to know who is invited, be assured that anyone who turns away from the lesser things of this world to set their heart and mind on things above has already received this gift of grace. Some of you are actively involved in doing good in this life, seeking to make a difference in the lives of others. This is a beautiful expression of Christ's love at work in this world. As you offer his love to others, continue to receive God's love for you into your soul.

REFLECTION QUESTION: Who has been most helpful to you along your spiritual journey?

MAY 22

There is a great difference between Adam's sin and God's gracious gift.
For the sin of this one man, Adam, brought death to many. But even
greater is God's wonderful grace and his gift of forgiveness to many
through this other man, Jesus Christ.
ROMANS 5:15, NLT

This call into the contemplative way of living always comes as a gift of grace. Jesus gives the gift of his grace to any and all who open their hearts to receive it. God invites all kinds of people into a life of grace including thieves, bullies, crooks, heavyweights, hoodlums, scoundrels, the hard-hearted, reprobates, skeptics, evildoers, hypocrites, drug addicts, black sheep, pagans, hustlers, tyrants, rebels, tycoons, self-centered, freethinkers, outlaws, infidels, scapegoats, agnostics, and even true believers. Whoever you are, Jesus invites you to receive God's gift of grace and to allow God's wonderful grace to begin to work a new way of life and love within your soul.

REFLECTION QUESTION: How has God's grace changed your life?

MAY 23

Those who have had a bath need only to wash their feet; their whole body is clean. And you are clean, though not every one of you.
JOHN 13:10

Most people put on clean clothes after bath time, not before. In the same way, you are wise to clothe yourself with Jesus's new clothes after you've allowed your soul to be cleansed of inner impurities. Follow the instructions Jesus gave long ago to his earliest followers. As Jesus washed his people's feet, he taught us God's way of washing us clean. God also spoke a warning long ago through Paul regarding preparing your heart for intimate time with God in worship: "Everyone ought to examine themselves before they eat of the bread and drink from the cup."[20] Learn to examine your heart as you enter into times of prayer.

REFLECTION QUESTION: What needs to be washed clean in your life?

MAY 24

Brothers and sisters, since we have confidence to enter the Most Holy Place by the blood of Jesus, by a new and living way opened for us through the curtain, that is, his body, and since we have a great priest over the house of God, let us draw near to God with a sincere heart and with the full assurance that faith brings, having our hearts sprinkled to cleanse us from a guilty conscience and having our bodies washed with pure water.
HEBREWS 10:19–22

Soul examination involves spiritual bathing as found in the book of Hebrews. When we take time and effort to examine our inner life, confessing any corruption or sin we discover there, God washes our hearts. The Holy Spirit removes all our guilt. Christ cleanses our conscience from all sin. Newly washed by God, we are free to draw near to God with sincere hearts through the new and living way Christ opened for us. Consider the clear counsel of James, who wrote, "Therefore confess your sins to each other and pray for each other so that you may be healed. The prayer of a righteous person is powerful and effective" (James 5:16).

REFLECTION QUESTION: Who do you meet with to pray together?

MAY 25

If we confess our sins, he is faithful and just and will forgive us our sins and purify us from all unrighteousness.
1 JOHN 1:9

The roots of the soul are too often planted in corrupted soil. When this is the case, you bring impurities up from your roots, into your innermost being, even when you've confessed your sins to each other and prayed together. Therefore, whoever will continue to grow in God's love is wise to root your life in good soil, allowing Jesus to cleanse your soul of all impurity. After being washed clean, you will be ready to continue growing in this new way of love with all eagerness and humility. Too long, you've been prevented from entering this way of love. But understand that you've been called into this way even from childhood, back when your life was less caught up in impure ways.

REFLECTION QUESTION: What childhood memory do you have when your life was more innocent?

MAY 26

Still others, like seed sown among thorns, hear the word; but the worries of this life, the deceitfulness of wealth and the desires for other things come in and choke the word, making it unfruitful.
MARK 4:18–19

As long as you are living within your mortal flesh, your soul will often experience barriers between you and God, and you will sense a mysterious Cloud of Unknowing hiding God from your awareness. One example of these barriers is the ongoing frustration you experience when you are distracted by lesser thoughts, anxieties, and cares that insert themselves into the middle of your times of prayer and devotion. Such thoughts and worries are like weeds that choke off the life of God growing in your soul. In wisdom, God created you to live as a good garden, producing much fruit. It is better to weed your garden and let nothing come between you and God.

REFLECTION QUESTION: What weeds of worry are growing in your garden right now?

MAY 27

Although they claimed to be wise, they became fools and exchanged the glory of the immortal God for images made to look like a mortal human being and birds and animals and reptiles.

ROMANS 1:22–23

When first humans willfully chose to disobey God's Word by putting Creation above the Creator, and by subjecting their souls to creaturely desires above God's desires, they separated themselves from God's love and ways. The long shadows of this separation continue to trouble humans today. People today still elevate created things above the Creator, exchanging the glory of God for mere images or idols. This can even take place within a soul that desires to seek Christ above all else. For those same ancient, willful, and lesser desires proudly assert themselves into our soul even as we are seeking Jesus, and thus become obstacles in the way of coming closer to God.

REFLECTION QUESTION: When have you put something created above the Creator?

MAY 28

Not only so, but we also glory in our sufferings, because we know that suffering produces perseverance; perseverance, character; and character, hope. And hope does not put us to shame, because God's love has been poured out into our hearts through the Holy Spirit, who has been given to us.

ROMANS 5:3–5

When you deeply yearn for the purity of heart that was lost when sin entered in, and when you begin striving for that inner state of wholeness free from trials and troubles, you begin to discover what perseverance is all about, the willingness to press on no matter how much pain you feel. Both saints and sinners striving to become godly learn to endure hardships on their way to holiness. Those who learn to endure hardships and persevere through times of suffering discover the wonder of living by hope. Of course, people accustomed to a life of sin are also often accustomed to greater hardships that naturally come from living separated from God. Nonetheless, some who have known terrible troubles from living in corruption and sin have more quickly ascended into the heights of holiness than those who have meandered in religious mediocrity. Press on then with perseverance, in the face of suffering and adversity, allowing God's love to be poured into your hearts through the Holy Spirit, present with you right now.

REFLECTION QUESTION: How have your life challenges strengthened you and given you hope?

MAY 29

The servant came back and reported this to his master. Then the owner of the house became angry and ordered his servant, "Go out quickly into the streets and alleys of the town and bring in the poor, the crippled, the blind and the lame."

"Sir," the servant said, "what you ordered has been done, but there is still room."

Then the master told his servant, "Go out to the roads and country lanes and compel them to come in, so that my house will be full."

LUKE 14:21–23

The abundance of God through Christ invites us into a life of unexpected surprises and wonders. God loves to unfold miracles in lives of people who were overlooked by this world. Most onlookers did not notice what was going on in the lives of their neighbor, or family member, or friend. Some marvel at the amazing beauty and power of God's grace in this life, but more often, these wonders are hidden. On the final day, as the morning mist clears, all people will see God's glory and all the gifts they've been given by God. On that final dawning day, there will be some who were overlooked or disdained in this mortal life, some who were belittled and rejected as sinners, and some who were reviled as the lowliest of society. On that final day, many supposed sinners will surprise many supposed saints when they are seen sitting together with Jesus and all God's people in the full glory of the eternal feast that awaits all who have entered into life with God.

REFLECTION QUESTION: When have you been surprised by the goodness and grace of God?

MAY 30

Because of God's tender mercy,
the morning light from heaven is about to break upon us,
to give light to those who sit in darkness and in the shadow of death,
and to guide us to the path of peace.
LUKE 1:78–79 NLT

There will also be some on that final day who were in positions of spiritual authority on earth, who seemed full of honor and religious dignity, highly esteemed as sacred leaders or evangelists or workers of miracles or preachers or leaders of spiritual movements. Yet, as the morning mist clears, and all is seen in the eternal light of Christ's dawning glory, some who knew religious power and glory in this mortal life will be seen as something else, living in shadows of hypocrisy, deception, and infamy. But God is full of tender mercy, and is moved with compassion toward all his children, even upon those who have been deceived and in the dark. The light of Christ's presence shines upon every person walking in darkness, revealing who we truly are as in the light of morning dawn, guiding us along the path home.

REFLECTION QUESTION: How has Christ's presence been like a light in your life?

MAY 31

*Christ died and returned to life so that he might be the Lord of both
the dead and the living. You, then, why do you judge your brother or
sister? Or why do you treat them with contempt?
For we will all stand before God's judgment seat.*

ROMANS 14:9–10

Let it be clearly known that no human is the final judge of another in this life, either for good or for evil. Beware of those who arrogantly think they know the eternal state of another person's soul. You are not the judge over someone's soul. Leave that to Christ Jesus and to God's mercy. It is better to stop passing judgment on others. That is God's business not ours. Nevertheless, know for certain that everything you do in this life in word or deed, whether good or evil, will finally be brought into the light of Christ's eternal dawn.

REFLECTION QUESTION: How often do you pass judgment on someone else?

June

Grace and Goodwill

JUNE 1

Be strong in the grace that is in Christ Jesus. And the things you have heard me say in the presence of many witnesses entrust to reliable people who will also be qualified to teach others.

2 TIMOTHY 2:1–2

Who may rightly judge the life of another? Whenever you point a finger at another person, you are wise to remember that you have several fingers pointing back at you. Whenever you start a fire, you are wise to remember the power of fire to both warm and burn, to create and destroy. There are many to whom God gives the power to kindle spiritual fire in others, people who are granted spiritual authority for the care of the soul of another, including spiritual mentors, formal and informal. In previous centuries, such people were sometimes called curates, for they labored in the cure of souls, seeking to heal the soul of many ills. Formal mentors may include priests, pastors, chaplains, monastics, and spiritual directors. Informal spiritual mentors may be called upon to discern the condition of the soul of another and to hold someone accountable.[21]

REFLECTION QUESTION: Who is mentoring you now?

JUNE 2

The tongue is a small part of the body, but it makes great boasts. Consider what a great forest is set on fire by a small spark. The tongue also is a fire, a world of evil among the parts of the body.

JAMES 3:5–6

Mentoring is best done confidentially and quietly, with the inspiration of the Holy Spirit in mature love. Let every person who enters this sacred work beware. Do not presume or pretend to be the ultimate judge of another person's faults. Rather, let your own soul be ignited by God's Spirit for this warming work within the soul of another, lest you scorch another with your hasty judgment.[22] So, beware of blaming or condemning others. If you are to judge anyone, judge your own life in God's radiant light, with the guidance of a wise spiritual mentor.

JUNE 3

Not that I have already obtained all this, or have already arrived at my goal, but I press on to take hold of that for which Christ Jesus took hold of me.
PHILIPPIANS 3:12

Once you've set out along this new journey, with the encouragement and support of a sacred community and a soul mentor, keep turning away from what lies behind, and keep pressing on toward what is ahead. Once Christ has taken hold of you, keep taking hold of Christ, and press on in the journey together with Jesus as your Guide. If any past memories of your old way of life crawl up behind you and threaten to disrupt your spiritual journey, or if any new temptations or sparks of sin fly up in your soul along the way, crush these sparks under foot with a spirited step of love, treading them down as you journey forward. After these distracting thoughts and temptations have been extinguished, cover them with the Cloud of Forgetting, as if they were never part of your life. As often as such sparks of temptations or old shameful regrets rise up, keep crushing them under foot. Make this a regular, daily habit.

REFLECTION QUESTION: Where are you in your spiritual journey with Christ?

JUNE 4

I went past the field of a sluggard,
past the vineyard of someone who has no sense;
thorns had come up everywhere,
the ground was covered with weeds,
and the stone wall was in ruins.
I applied my heart to what I observed
and learned a lesson from what I saw.
PROVERBS 24:30–32

It is better to pull weeds in a garden when they first appear. If this work of weeding your garden becomes tedious, call in support from others who may assist you in living with greater freedom from regrets and distracting temptations to sin. Others may know spiritual practices or disciplines that you've never learned, wise practices that can assist you in your journey with the Lord. But the best way forward is to simply come to Christ Jesus. Let him tend to your soul, pulling weeds from your inner life, and rebuild your life. Learn from him how to live and grow fruitful by staying near him, your gardener, as you keep pressing on in the way of love.

REFLECTION QUESTION: What weeds are growing in your life?

JUNE 5

I lift up my eyes to the mountains—
where does my help come from?
My help comes from the Lord,
the Maker of heaven and earth.
PSALM 121:1–2

E ven wise saints get distracted from their prayers. What has helped you deal with distractions in the past? How do you currently face distracting thoughts or desires? Here's a spiritual practice you may find helpful: Whenever thoughts or desires sneak in between you and God, do everything in your power to look past these distractions, as if you are looking over the shoulders of someone standing next to you, focusing instead upon a mountain view of great beauty far off in the distance. Seek what is higher and more glorious, focusing your attention on what is beyond you, as if looking upon a glorious sunset of colors captured in a great cloud suspended above a mountain range in the distance.

REFLECTION QUESTION: What often distracts you when you pray?

JUNE 6

Love and faithfulness meet together;
righteousness and peace kiss each other.
Faithfulness springs forth from the earth,
and righteousness looks down from heaven.
PSALM 85:10–11

A s you focus your gaze on this luminous Cloud of Unknowing, within a short time you will be less distracted by those immediate thoughts or desires pressing on you. This approach to distractions is nothing else but your yearning for God's presence, to feel and see God's presence, and to personally know the love of God. Knowing Christ's love is also to know God's peace, and thus find rest for your distracted soul. As you are faithful to focus your eyes upon Jesus, God's love will meet you. As you are true to the right way God wants you to live, God's peace will meet you. Love and peace will come to you. Keep looking heavenward.

REFLECTION QUESTION: In what ways are love and peace missing from your life?

JUNE 7

We do not have a high priest who is unable to empathize with our weaknesses, but we have one who has been tempted in every way, just as we are—yet he did not sin. Let us then approach God's throne of grace with confidence, so that we may receive mercy and find grace to help us in our time of need.

HEBREWS 4:15–16

There is another way of dealing with distractions you may want to learn as well. Imagine your distractions are like an attacking bear.[23] Sometimes, you are truly defenseless before such attacks. Sometimes the best approach is to humble yourself, falling to the ground, lying prostrate and still upon the earth, as if cowering and playing dead before an angry bear. Sometimes, it is folly to strive against overpowering distractions. A better approach is to yield your soul to Jesus, knowing that you are overcome in your battle against these distractions. Cry out to God for mercy and protection against your enemies. You may feel as if you've been defeated or overcome by these distracting thoughts and desires, as if cowering at the feet of an enemy. But know with full confidence that when you lie still, humbling your heart and calling out to Christ for protection, Jesus will come to your aid in times of need.

REFLECTION QUESTION: How has the Lord helped you in a time of need?

JUNE 8

*The Lord God formed a man from the dust of the ground and breathed
into his nostrils the breath of life, and the man became a living being.*

GENESIS 2:7

God will defend you. You will become like water that flows down through the cracks and escapes notice. As you humble yourself in the Lord's presence, you admit you are powerless over these attacking thoughts and desires, you realize your life has become unmanageable, and you see your need for Christ's saving grace. The closer you bow to the earth, the more you know your own frailty and God's love. Without God's breath of life in your nostrils, you are dust. This is the way of humility, to bow down to the dust. Jesus loves to come down to all who truly humble themselves, to lift you up, breathe into your soul the breath of life, and mightily defend you in the presence of your enemies. With great love God will come to you, to rescue you from your tormentors, as a father rescuing his child from an attack. The Lord will gather you in his arms and wipe away the tears from your eyes. Christ cherishes your life.

REFLECTION QUESTION: How has God rescued your life?

JUNE 9

*I consider that our present sufferings are not worth comparing with
the glory that will be revealed in us. For the creation waits in eager
expectation for the children of God to be revealed.*

ROMANS 8:18–19

Do not be burdened with spiritual practices. God's glory and grace will help you grow as you practice what you are learning. May you be equipped not only to walk in the way of love but also to teach others the way of love. Learn the joy of helping others enter into this lifelong journey of faith, empowered by God's glory and grace. Step forward then along your spiritual journey, with the prayers of others to energize you along the way. Be willing to face suffering and pain with humility of heart, knowing there is no quick or easy way to grow in the art of spiritual living. Know also that any present sufferings we face in this life cannot compare to the glory that awaits us in our life with God.

REFLECTION QUESTION: Who are you helping enter into their journey of faith?

JUNE 10

The crucible for silver and the furnace for gold,
but the LORD tests the heart.

PROVERBS 17:3

For a time, you may go through a fiery trial of purification. If so, God is allowing you to be purified as silver in a crucible, or as gold refined in a furnace. Over time, the pain will subside, as your soul is strengthened and conditioned, and you will be better able to practice the spiritual life without so many troubles. Jesus will give you gifts along the way, gifts of grace to help wash you clean, and also take away the pain of sin. Consider the ill choices you've made and bad habits you've formed that separate you from God's presence and God's love. No matter how much you grow in this life, you will always know something of the pain and long shadows cast by original disobedience in the Garden of Eden. This pain, though constantly present in your soul, will not trouble you much, at least not in comparison with the ongoing troubles you bring on yourself by your own wanderings, distractions, and temptations. Be prepared to face many troubles and hurts ahead. Though the Lord allows these tests to come, God never leaves us or forsakes us in times of trial.

REFLECTION QUESTION: How has your life been tested or purified by trials?

JUNE 11

The word of God is alive and active. Sharper than any double-edged
sword, it penetrates even to dividing soul and spirit, joints and marrow;
it judges the thoughts and attitudes of the heart.

HEBREWS 4:12

Some times of trial arise from that ancient scar on the human soul, springing up anew in every generation with new movements of corruptions, separation from God's love, and many forms of brokenness. Take up the double-edged sword of discernment, alive and active and sharper than any human-made sword, able to penetrate deep within the soul, to divisions of soul and spirit, able to discern the deepest thoughts and intentions of the heart. With this sharp blade, like a skillful surgeon, cut away what is fruitless and lifeless, anything that is not part of

Christ's life for you. Learn and understand that your life will always have uncertainty, unrest, and troubles.

REFLECTION QUESTION: How has God's Word helped you discern what to cut away from your life?

JUNE 12

Out of his fullness we have all received grace in place of grace already given.
JOHN 1:16

There is no turning back, but only pressing forward, even when you are overcome with a fear of failing. May God give you grace to overcome the pain of failures, as mentioned earlier, as well as grace upon grace from Christ's fullness to strengthen you along the way. May God's grace be present in your life even through fierce storms of temptations, weariness of loss, and darkness from shadows of the past. Though ever present along the way, these troubles shall have little power to afflict you as long as you journey together with Jesus, filled with God's grace.

REFLECTION QUESTION: How have you received God's grace upon grace?

JUNE 13

In him we have redemption through his blood, the forgiveness of sins, in accordance with the riches of God's grace that he lavished on us. With all wisdom and understanding, he made known to us the mystery of his will according to his good pleasure, which he purposed in Christ.
EPHESIANS 1:7–9

If you ask what is the best way to enter into this new way of life, Jesus will come to you personally with the riches of God's grace and goodwill to guide you. Find people who are humble of heart, who know how little they know, yet know the mystery of God's will in Christ. Together with such spiritual guides, call upon almighty God for help in learning to walk in this way of love. This work is primarily Christ's beautiful grace lavished upon you and now working in your soul, as God makes known to you the mystery of his goodwill according to his good pleasure.

REFLECTION QUESTION: In what ways have you experienced the mystery of God's good pleasure?

JUNE 14

Therefore, my dear friends, as you have always obeyed—not only in my presence, but now much more in my absence—continue to work out your salvation with fear and trembling, for it is God who works in you to will and to act in order to fulfill his good purpose.

PHILIPPIANS 2:12–13

Not even saints or angels come into this new way of life by their own merits, but only by God's grace. Understand that God gives good gifts according to God's good pleasure, to habitual sinners as well as to saints, to those who have offended against God's laws, and to those who have never grieved God greatly. God is known as all-merciful and almighty, able to give mercy according to God's choice, working in whatever way God chooses. God gives us grace when and where God chooses. God works with whomever God chooses to work, working with goodwill to fulfill God's wonderful purpose in our lives.

REFLECTION QUESTION: What are a few of the good gifts God has given to you?

JUNE 15

He gives us more grace. That is why Scripture says:
"God opposes the proud
but shows favor to the humble."
Submit yourselves, then, to God.

JAMES 4:6–7

God loves to gives grace and work God's goodwill in any soul that is able to receive these gifts. God delights to give these gifts to any and all hearts open to receive. There is no person, whether impure or innocent, without the grace of God at work already. God gives freely to all who are able to receive such a gift. For God's gifts are not given because a person is innocent, nor are they withheld because a person is impure. Pay attention, for God loves to shower gifts upon even those who some may think unworthy. Keep yielding your life to God, and God will continue to give you favor.

REFLECTION QUESTION: How has God's grace changed your life?

JUNE 16

When they go with their flocks and herds
to seek the LORD,
they will not find him;
he has withdrawn himself from them.

HOSEA 5:6

Note that God's gifts are sometimes withheld and sometimes withdrawn. For, some who have received Christ's gift of grace have also had those gifts later withdrawn due to their folly. Beware how you look upon another person's soul. The closer you come to living according to God's truth, the easier it is to wander into error. If you are confused about these matters now, it may be better for you to lay these matters aside until they become clearer along the way. Christ will come and guide you, lest you stumble over these matters and injure yourself.

REFLECTION QUESTION: When have you sensed that God withdrew from your life?

JUNE 17

Pride goes before destruction,
a haughty spirit before a fall.
PROVERBS 16:18

Keep on your toes, alert to the dangers of pride. Pride shuns God and corrupts God's good gifts, turning them into entitlements or means to dominate. Pride weakens corrupt hearts to stumble further into corruption. Humility, by contrast, openly receives God and God's good gifts with gratitude. A humble person understands that God gives freely without anyone earning this favor. Humility empowers us to continue in God's sacred work, a work that is impossible without such an open and willing heart. You will be more and more able to continue in this work the more your soul is united to God's good pleasure working within you without wandering away from Jesus.

REFLECTION QUESTION: In what ways do you struggle with pride?

JUNE 18

Do not be afraid, little flock, for your Father has been pleased to give
you the kingdom.

LUKE 12:32

As you discover an inner desire to do the sacred work of contemplation, you will also discover the ability for this work rising inside of you. Without Christ's will at work within you, it is as though you are dead, without any longing or desire for God. Apart from God's good pleasure working in your soul, as much as you try, even with all your will and desire put to the effort, it will come to nothing. Do not fear. God takes great pleasure in giving amazing gifts to us, including the gift of God's kingdom! Your will and desire for this contemplative life are not based on knowledge, but upon what is unknowable by reason alone. The contemplative life is a gift of God's grace and goodwill for you.

REFLECTION QUESTION: What spiritual gifts has God given you?

JUNE 19

I became a servant of this gospel by the gift of God's grace given
me through the working of his power.

EPHESIANS 3:7

Allow God's grace to work in you, guiding your life wherever God's goodwill leads. Let God's grace be the leading actor in your life and you in a supporting role. Pay attention to the working of grace in your life, but do not try to be the lead actor. Do not go meddling with God's grace working in you, as if you could improve on Christ's plans for your life. The more you meddle the more you'll be in a muddle. Be like wood from a tree or stone from the earth. Offer your life for God's service. As a carpenter or a mason, Jesus will continue crafting the material of your life into something beautiful.

REFLECTION QUESTION: What evidence to you see of God's grace working in you?

JUNE 20

Jesus replied, "Anyone who loves me will obey my teaching. My Father will love them, and we will come to them and make our home with them."

JOHN 14:23

Be like a home, and God's grace will be the homemaker dwelling in you. Act as though you are blind at home. Let go of your need to know everything. Sometimes, knowledge can be more of a hindrance than a help in the contemplative life. It is sufficient for you to experience God's grace stirring in you with the new life that you've never previously known or understood. May this stirring of delight for Jesus be sufficient, greater than any pleasures on earth, as you stand before the Lord without shame, clothed only in God's delight.

REFLECTION QUESTION: How at home are you with God?

JUNE 21

Even though I walk
through the darkest valley,
I will fear no evil,
for you are with me;
your rod and your staff,
they comfort me.

PSALM 23:4

Be confident that Jesus is stirring your will and your desire with God's will and with heavenly desire, without need for any lesser methods or human intervention. Fear no evil or dark shadows, for the Lord, your shepherd, is with you; his rod and my staff are here to comfort you. Sometimes, God's unseen staff will ward off unknown evil and protect your life, though you are unaware of what's happening. At times, God's unseen rod will strike, convicting your heart of wandering from God's path, guiding you back onto the right path. Occasionally, you may find your soul troubled by some spiritual force, whether of the darkness or of the light. Do not fear these interruptions, but find rest for your soul in God alone.

REFLECTION QUESTION: What phrase from Psalm 23 do you love the most, and why?

JUNE 22

Here I am! I stand at the door and knock.
If anyone hears my voice and opens the door, I will come in and eat
with that person, and they with me.

REVELATION 3:20

As long as God's grace dwells in you, no other force can truly harm you. Throughout the ages, people have tried many methods of drawing close to God. During your life, as well, you may have attempted many approaches to try and get closer to Christ. No matter what method or practice, everything depends upon the gift of God's grace at work in your innermost being. Every good practice hangs on God's grace and goodwill, like a door hanging on hinges. Christ is knocking, desiring to enter. Regardless of what method you may use, God's grace and goodwill are given freely without any merit or payment. Listen to Christ's voice and open the door into this new way of life.

REFLECTION QUESTION: What methods have you found helpful for getting closer to Christ?

JUNE 23

Keep this Book of the Law always on your lips; meditate on it day and
night, so that you may be careful to do everything written in it. Then
you will be prosperous and successful.

JOSHUA 1:8

There are a few basic spiritual practices that are to become a regular part of your daily life to help you grow closer to God, including reading, meditating, and praying. These three practices have been described in detail in many previous books by wise saints, so I will not go into great detail here to explain them.[24] These three belong together, as three strands of one rope: reading Scripture, meditating on Scripture, praying Scripture. Whether you are a beginner or a well-seasoned veteran of the spiritual life, you are wise to learn to hold onto these three as a mountain climber relies upon a well-crafted three-strand rope.

REFLECTION QUESTION: What spiritual practices do you hold on to?

JUNE 24

He said to them, "This is what I told you while I was still with you: Everything must be fulfilled that is written about me in the Law of Moses, the Prophets and the Psalms." Then he opened their minds so they could understand the Scriptures.

LUKE 24:44–45

To learn to think clearly, one must first read the Bible, or listen to others read Scripture aloud. Reading and hearing others read are both valuable ways of developing our mind and heart. We learn by reading books, especially God's good book, the Bible. But like young children, we may also learn by hearing others read aloud. A pastor or priest also helps others grow by spending time weekly reading, studying, and then preaching Scripture. In other words, people grow not only by their own reading, but by attending worship services where they hear God's Word. We learn to pray by first reading and studying. At every stage of our journey, our prayers grow from this.

REFLECTION QUESTION: When has a sermon or a reading from the Bible helped you grow?

JUNE 25

Do not merely listen to the word, and so deceive yourselves. Do what it says. Anyone who listens to the word but does not do what it says is like someone who looks at his face in a mirror and, after looking at himself, goes away and immediately forgets what he looks like.

JAMES 1:22–24

Let us look together at two pictures to better understand the truth: first a mirror and second a pool of water. God's Word is like a mirror. In your spiritual life, the eye of your soul is your reason. Your conscience is like the spiritual reflection you see in the mirror. When you look at your face in a mirror, you check for any blemishes or dirt. Without a mirror you cannot see these blemishes or dirt, but must rely upon the eyes of another person. In the same way, in the spiritual life, without reading or hearing God's Word, it is impossible for you to understand the true condition of your soul, for you are blinded by habits of sin and darkness, unable to see any corruption, blemish, or dirt upon your soul.

REFLECTION QUESTION: How has the Bible been like a mirror for you?

JUNE 26

*"Go," he told him, "wash in the Pool of Siloam" (this word means
"Sent"). So the man went and washed, and came home seeing.*

JOHN 9:7

The second picture of a pool of water follows from the first, the image of the mirror. When you look in a mirror, whether a physical one or the spiritual mirror of God's Word, you begin to discover blemishes and dirt on your face or on your soul. At that moment and not before, you hurry to a pool or a basin of water to wash away the dirt. The pool of water for our soul is discovered among God's people, the church. The water is the cleansing and healing work of God's Spirit upon your soul through mutually confessing your souls to one another, and receiving Christ's forgiveness, assurance of pardon, and healing grace.

REFLECTION QUESTION: Where do you go to wash your soul?

JUNE 27

*Come near to God and he will come near to you. Wash your hands, you
sinners, and purify your hearts, you double-minded.*

JAMES 4:8

With any kind of blemish or filth, a person may come to God's deep well of mercy, and with the waters of God's grace, with prayerful confession of sin, we are washed clean and made new. So, as you can see, the three ancient spiritual practices of reading, study, and prayer are intimately related. Whether you are young or old, educated or uneducated, immature or mature, there is no clear thinking without reading or hearing. The more you read and study Scripture, the more you will commune with God in prayer, and the more your spiritual life will grow. The more you grow, the more you see your need for daily time before the mirror of God's Word, and daily time at the pool of God's grace to be washed clean and made new.

REFLECTION QUESTION: How has your life been washed clean and made new?

JUNE 28

*When Daniel learned that the decree had been published, he went home
to his upstairs room where the windows opened toward Jerusalem.
Three times a day he got down on his knees and prayed, giving thanks to
his God, just as he had done before.*

DANIEL 6:10

Like a person who lives in a chalet nestled in an alpine meadow, some contemplatives view the glory of the lofty sacred mountains without exerting much effort. With a quick glance out the chalet window, their meditation may be either of the valleys plunging down into their own human frailty, or of mountains soaring above in God's eternal goodness. They do not require the long climbing labor of reading and study to arrive at these visions. Rather, they are given sudden epiphanies and unexpected intuition as a gift from God not based upon any human achievement. A person may either look downward into the valley of their own sorrows, or upward into the heights of sacred goodness. As long as you are stirred by God's grace and guided by wisdom, both visions have something valuable to teach the human soul.

REFLECTION QUESTION: From what window in your home do you most enjoy the view?

JUNE 29

Abide in Me, and I in you.
JOHN 15:4A NASB

In the same way, consider choosing a single sacred word or phrase such as *joy, grace,* or perhaps *abide in me.* Choose a single word or a short phrase and think about that word or phrase, focusing your mind on that one word. Most people begin to analyze that word, pondering the meaning, the spelling, and other qualities of it. Even better, increase your devotion for Jesus through that single word by entering into the reality behind it like opening a window and seeing mountains. In your heart, walk in the valley or climb the mountain with the word. In your soul, experience joy and grace. With your innermost being, come face-to-face with Jesus and abide with him. You cannot meet Jesus face-to-face through reason alone or by mere intellectual effort. But, you can know Jesus and God's grace at work within your soul through the little window of a single sacred word or a short phrase.

REFLECTION QUESTION: What one word or short phrase will you choose as a way to pray?

JUNE 30

In him was life, and that life was the light of all mankind. The light shines in the darkness, and the darkness has not overcome it.
JOHN 1:4–5

Like a shuttered window, that single word may be opened, if opened whole and not broken into many shards by intellectual analysis. Human frailty and sin blind the soul like a shuttered window, allowing very little of Christ's light to shine within. Those who know of the beauty beyond the shuttered window take every effort to unlatch the shutters, swing them back, open the window, and lean out and catch the vision of the heights of mountain glory beyond the alpine meadows. While this intense inner work of meditation proceeds, as you are striving inwardly to clear away the obstacles to visions of God's glory, outwardly you may remain calm and quiet in your body, without even much change upon your face. Such meditations may continue as you are sitting, traveling, lying down in your bed, standing in the kitchen, or kneeling at prayer. Wherever you are, others will see you at peace and full of serenity as your soul finds rest in Christ's life and glory.

REFLECTION QUESTION: How has Christ's light shone into your heart and life this year?

July

Help, Thanks, Wow![25]

JULY 1

They asked each other, "Were not our hearts burning within us while he talked with us on the road and opened the Scriptures to us?"

LUKE 24:32

Just as sparks from a fire fly up into the starlit heavens, so your meditations and prayers also suddenly fly up into heaven without even trying when you are well kindled in the grace of this spiritual life. Consider also prayers of the heart offered to God in secret, not merely the prayer times offered when you join together with others in worship. All who pray know that there is no single best way to pray. Many helpful forms or patterns of prayer have been handed down from the saints of old, and all have power to draw the soul into Christ's presence. Therefore, pray as you are able according to the way you've been taught. Offer your prayers from the heart, that your prayers may ever rise suddenly up into the starlit skies of God's presence without any special effort or planning, but spontaneously like sparks ascending from a bonfire.

REFLECTION QUESTION: In what ways is your prayer life like a bonfire?

JULY 2

When you pray, do not keep on babbling like pagans, for they think they will be heard because of their many words. Do not be like them, for your Father knows what you need before you ask him.

MATTHEW 6:7–8

As you pray, let your words be few—the fewer, the better. As mentioned above, learn to pray using a single sacred word or phrase, even a one-syllable word such as *help, thanks,* or *wow.*[26] One syllable may be better than two. Of course you may use more syllables and more words, according to the leading of the Spirit upon your heart at the time. A spiritual person will learn over time to be in tune with the highest and best movements of God's Spirit, no matter the number of words or time elapsed.

REFLECTION QUESTION: Do you tend to pray with many words, or few?

JULY 3

*Be pleased to save me, L*ORD*;*
*come quickly, L*ORD*, to help me.*
PSALM 40:13

To better understand this simple way of prayer, look at an example from human experience. When a person faces a life-threatening emergency, such as a house fire or a heart attack, or some other danger, suddenly they cry out for help. This cry for help is bold, desperate, and full of spirit, driven by need for help and haste. As a result, not many words or syllables are used. Often, such a person uses but a single word, such as *Help!* Why? When life is threatened by such a danger, there is no time to waste on lengthy descriptions of need. There is only time to cry out loudly with intensity of spirit but a single word, such as *Fire!* or *Help!* This one word, as short as it may be, pierces quickly through all other voices, stirring the ears of hearers to respond quickly and come to the rescue.

REFLECTION QUESTION: When have you cried out to God for help?

JULY 4

In his temple all cry, "Glory!"
PSALM 29:9

As the ancient people of Israel prayed, learn to pray using a little word or a short phrase. Sometimes simply pray, *Glory!* Cry out to God, declaring God's glory as your adoration. Rather than speak or think about this word or phrase, offer this simple word or phrase secretly from the depths of your spirit. God loves those who pray the Psalms daily, for the Psalms are the prayer book of the Bible. Yet, there is a potential danger of thinking that you become more spiritual through recitations of lengthy psalms, mumbled without thought or meaning. In the spiritual realm, all is in unity, whether height, depth, width, or length. When short, simple prayer comes from the secret depths of your spirit, such a prayer pierces quickly into the height, depth, width, and length of heaven. God loves to hear your cry for help, and will cover you with glory in the Cloud of Unknowing.

REFLECTION QUESTION: What are some short, simple prayers you pray?

JULY 5

I pray that you, being rooted and established in love, may have power,
together with all the Lord's holy people, to grasp how wide and long
and high and deep is the love of Christ, and to know this love
that surpasses knowledge—that you may be filled
to the measure of all the fullness of God.

EPHESIANS 3:17–19

D o you wonder why a short little prayer of just one small syllable pierces into the heights of heaven more easily than lengthy prayers? When you pray with your whole being, from the height and depth of your soul, from the width and length of your spirit, such a prayer is always heard. From the height comes all your energy; from the depth comes wisdom; from the length comes enduring affection; and from the width comes compassion. Root and establish your prayers in the love of God, a love that far surpasses our understanding or comprehension. Prayer is not mainly about thinking but about loving. May you know inwardly this love that surpasses knowledge. Pray simple, short prayers, and your life will be filled with all the measure of God's fullness of love.

REFLECTION QUESTION: When have you been overwhelmed with the love of God?

JULY 6

Christ himself gave the apostles, the prophets, the evangelists, the
pastors and teachers, to equip his people for works of service, so that the
body of Christ may be built up until we all reach unity in the faith and
in the knowledge of the Son of God and become mature, attaining to the
whole measure of the fullness of Christ.

EPHESIANS 4:11–13

G rasp the length of the fullness of Christ by taking hold of God's steadfast love that endures forever. Grasp the width of the fullness of Christ by experiencing Christ's compassion for all people. Grasp the height of the fullness of Christ by climbing up into the strongholds of God's fortress. Grasp the depth of the fullness of Christ by plunging down into the ocean of Christ, the wisdom of God. Our Lord continues to give gifts to us to equip us for a life of caring and serving others, uniting our lives together in the body of Christ. God desires that we will grow and mature, attaining more and more of the fullness of Christ.

REFLECTION QUESTION: How is your life growing spiritually?

JULY 7

Our citizenship is in heaven. . . . The Lord Jesus Christ, who, by the power that enables him to bring everything under his control, will transform our lowly bodies so that they will be like his glorious body.

PHILIPPIANS 3:20–21

Allow your soul to be transformed by God's grace into the image and likeness of God your creator, and know that you are truly heard when you pray simply from the heart. Even those who have turned away from God, who think of God as an adversary, may by God's grace cry out with a short prayer for help and be heard. When prayer comes from the height, depth, length, and breadth of a person's soul, no matter how dark or hideous the state of that soul, God hears our cry and comes quickly to help.

REFLECTION QUESTION: What is the state of your soul right now?

JULY 8

Since we have now been justified by his blood, how much more shall we be saved from God's wrath through him! For if, while we were God's enemies, we were reconciled to him through the death of his Son, how much more, having been reconciled, shall we be saved through his life!

ROMANS 5:9–10

Imagine you live next door to someone who despises you. In the middle of the night, you hear your neighbor cry out one little word, *Fire!* Without thinking much about it, out of compassion in your heart you are awakened with this heartfelt cry for help. Even though it is the middle of a winter night and cold, and even though the person has been mean and rude to you, still you offer your help to your neighbor, doing what you can do to help put out his fire or rescue him from the flames. If a mere mortal will help such a neighbor at such a time, to have mercy and pity on his enemy who has been so unkind, how much more mercy and pity shall Jesus have for all who cry out for help. He will come quickly to the rescue.

REFLECTION QUESTION: How has God helped you in a time of distress?

JULY 9

To those who have been called, who are loved in God the Father and kept for Jesus Christ: Mercy, peace and love be yours in abundance.

JUDE 1–2

God responds to prayer, coming to be present when a cry comes from the height, depth, length, and breadth of a human soul. You will receive an abundance of mercy, mercy without comparison from the height, depth, length, and breadth of heaven when you call with your whole heart to God. Whenever you are merciful to another it is the result of God's grace transforming your soul, helping you learn to love your enemy who is your neighbor, whereas mercy is God's heart and inner nature, flowing out of the height, depth, length, and breadth of God's innermost being.

REFLECTION QUESTION: Where have you experienced God's mercy touching your life?

JULY 10

One day Jesus was praying in a certain place. When he finished, one of his disciples said to him, "Lord, teach us to pray. . . ."

LUKE 11:1

Learn to pray from the height, depth, length, and breadth of your spirit, not with many words but with a short, sacred word from the heart. Heartfelt prayers are best expressed in fewer words, even through a single word. What word should this be? As mentioned above, short, prayerful words such as *help, thanks,* or *wow* are best, as they express the fullness of the human heart in simplicity and intent. To better know what kind of words to use as you pray, seek to better understand the true nature of prayer.

REFLECTION QUESTION: Who taught you to pray?

The Spirit helps us in our weakness. We do not know what we ought to pray for, but the Spirit himself intercedes for us through wordless groans. And he who searches our hearts knows the mind of the Spirit, because the Spirit intercedes for God's people in accordance with the will of God.

ROMANS 8:26–27

The heart of prayer is to direct your life fully Godward. When you turn your heart to God, asking for help, you receive God's grace and Jesus removes your corruption, washing you clean. Just as all human degradation may be summarized by the little word *sin*, whether in action or intention, so the removal of all human corruption may come from praying a little word such as *help* through action and intention. In the same way, when you've received good gifts of grace, either with a single word, in your thoughts, or especially with your ardent desire, offer up the simple word *thanks* with no more words needed. God already knows your heart. From the goodness of God's heart flow all good gifts to those who open their hands and hearts with humility and gratitude. The Lord loves to hear us cry out with surprise and wonder, like little children, by simply praying *wow!* Do not marvel at these three short words, *help*, *thanks*, and *wow*, as though they are the only words that will work. If other short words of prayer better express your heart longing for God's presence, be encouraged to use such words as well. Your heart is what matters to God, much more than your words.

REFLECTION QUESTION: What prayers from the heart do you pray to God?

Christ did not enter a sanctuary made with human hands that was only a copy of the true one; he entered heaven itself, now to appear for us in God's presence.

HEBREWS 9:24

Prayer is not primarily about words. You can spend all your life buried in books on prayer and never learn to pray or spend any time in Jesus's presence. Although study is valuable when joined with prayer, you will never enter into God's presence by mere reason or book knowledge, but only by the grace of our Lord Jesus Christ within the Cloud of Unknowing. Therefore, learn the simple, heartfelt way of prayer, stirred by Christ's presence to use a single word expressing your whole heart. Of course you may choose other single words as better prayer windows opening your whole soul, but choose them as God's Spirit inspires you to do so. Even if the Spirit inspires you to pray other words than those mentioned in these days, do not leave these simple prayer words behind, for they are wise, heartfelt words that can help bring your heart before God.

REFLECTION QUESTION: How do you pray without using words?

JULY 13

When my life was ebbing away,
I remembered you, Lord,
and my prayer rose to you,
to your holy temple.[27]

JONAH 2:7

Just because you are learning to pray with short words, this does not mean God prefers only short times of prayer with you. Learn to pray continually. Make your whole life a prayer to the Lord. Pray through the day. Pray through the night. Pray when you are feeling great. Pray when you are in the dark and in trouble. Learn to pray from the height and depth of your heart and soul, with length and breadth of time, until you see your heart's longing fully answered by God's grace. Think of that neighbor mentioned before who cried out in the middle of the winter night when his house caught on fire. He never stopped crying *Help!* and *Fire!* until someone awoke and came to his rescue.

REFLECTION QUESTION: Where in the Bible do you go to learn to pray?

JULY 14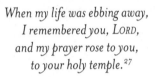

Then I acknowledged my sin to you
and did not cover up my iniquity.
I said, "I will confess
my transgressions to the Lord."

And you forgave
the guilt of my sin.
PSALM 32:5

In the same manner, when you cry out to God, do not become diverted by less important matters. For example, when you pray to confess your sins, bring your whole self to God through a single word prayer rather than trying to intellectually analyze your shortcomings in the form of a lengthy discourse. You'll discover it is a waste of time when you try to assess which sin is better or worse according to different categories of sin, such as the seven deadly sins of pride, anger, envy, greed, sloth, gluttony, and lust. You will not find it helpful to focus your attention upon certain sins as some are prone to do, as though some sins are more serious in comparison to other sins. In truth, all sins are destructive, separating you from God, stealing away your inner peace. God loves to forgive.

REFLECTION QUESTION: What sin has God forgiven in your life?

JULY 15

The tax collector stood at a distance and dared not even lift his eyes to
heaven as he prayed. Instead, he beat his chest in sorrow, saying, "O
God, be merciful to me, for I am a sinner." I tell you that this sinner,
not the Pharisee, went home justified before God.
LUKE 18:13–14 NLT

Sin is like a lump of cancer in your body. Just as all cancer is serious and life-threatening, deal with any and all sin in your life as serious and life-threatening. As soon as this lump is detected, cry out with your spirit through a single-word prayer such as *Help!* or *Thanks!* Or even a short phrase such as the prayer of the tax collector, who prayed with a heart full of sorrow, "Be merciful to me." Learn to pray using your whole soul focused through a single word or short phrase. Learn from Jesus in the Gospels how to pray, rather than merely reading a book about prayer or taking a class on prayer.

REFLECTION QUESTION: What are you learning about how to pray?

JULY 16

*Deep calls to deep
in the roar of your waterfalls;
all your waves and breakers
have swept over me.*

PSALM 42:7

Prayer is much more than a mental exercise. It is the pure cry of your spirit to the Spirit of God, without any concern that you are pronouncing things correctly or not. That is not to say you are never to pray with a flood of words. There are times when your spirit becomes too heavy with the weight of sin and sorrow, when your speech and your eyes may overflow with a torrent of tearful words in prayer bursting forth from your soul like the release of a pent-up underground spring. Deep calls out to deep. The depths of God's Spirit call out to the deep places within your spirit. Such prayer times are most welcome by God as well.

REFLECTION QUESTION: When has God called out to your spirit in the depths of your life?

JULY 17

*The whole earth is filled with awe at your wonders;
where morning dawns, where evening fades,
you call forth songs of joy.*

PSALM 65:8

Learn to pray using a short little word such as *Wow!* Fill your spirit with a prayerful sense of wonder at all God's works without the need to mentally analyze or categorize these works. Some approach prayer as some kind of scientific exercise, assessing God's works as to whether they are good, better, or best, including God's works in the physical and spiritual realms. Others think of prayer as an expression of grace-grown virtues in a person's life. They may look for evidence of God's grace expressed by such virtues such as humility, love, patience, self-control, hope, faithfulness, temperance, purity, or voluntary poverty.[28] Such approaches to prayer are not as helpful as simply turning toward God with a sense of wonder expressed through a simple word or phrase.

REFLECTION QUESTION: What fills you with wonder?

JULY 18

When Jesus spoke again to the people, he said, "I am the light of the world.
Whoever follows me will never walk in darkness, but will have the light of life."

JOHN 8:12

In God's light, we see light. All radiance of virtue comes from one source, from one fountain of light and life. Come to Christ, and you will begin to experience all these virtues together in their outward working and inward nature. Enter into life with God and all goodness and virtue is yours shining forth from the light of life. There is no need to pursue one virtue or another, but only the need to follow Jesus's life unfolding within your life by grace. Nothing in your mind and heart will bear fruit except by the grace of God, as Jesus's light of life shines within you.

REFLECTION QUESTION: How has the light of Christ changed your way of life?

JULY 19

Jesus went throughout Galilee, teaching in their
synagogues, proclaiming the good news of the kingdom, and healing
every disease and sickness among the people.

MATTHEW 4:23

As long as you live in a wretched, far-from-God state of life, you will continue to have within you the diseased lump of sin threatening your life and well-being. This lump of sin is united to your thoughts and will, enmeshed in the very fabric of your being. To be cured of this disease, learn to pray using single-word prayers such as *help, thanks,* and *wow.* Know this simple truth: the more you know Jesus, the less you'll know sin; and the more you are free of sin, the more you will be free to grow in God.

REFLECTION QUESTION: What diseases have troubled you?

JULY 20

Rejoice always, pray continually, give thanks in all circumstances; for
this is God's will for you in Christ Jesus.

1 THESSALONIANS 5:16–18

If you want to know how often to come to God in prayer, never stop praying. Make your whole life a prayer to God. In all your other life activities, such as eating, drinking, sleeping, caring for your body, reading, or talking with friends, in all these you are wise to practice moderation, so that these activities are not neglected nor do they dominate your life. But learn to pray continually as a way of life, just as much as breathing is a way of life. Just as plants grow in communion with the air all around them, the sun beaming upon them, and the soil in which they are planted, continue growing in communion with God, Father, Son, and Holy Spirit

REFLECTION QUESTION: What does "pray continually" mean to you?

JULY 21

Return to your rest, my soul,
for the Lord has been good to you.
PSALM 116:7

I am not saying that you will always be fresh and full of energy in your prayer life. Sometimes sickness and other unexpected troubles in body, mind, and soul will afflict you, hindering you. Natural daily demands will divert your attention from the heights of love. All the more, learn to pray continually, even in the face of such demands. Prayerfully and playfully allow Jesus to be involved in your life and will, with God's love your highest aim. Take good care of your body and keep physically fit to avoid, as much as possible, getting sick. Commit to your well-being in body, mind, and spirit. Avoid causing your own weakness and frailty through neglect of your physical, mental, or spiritual health. A life of continual prayer calls for rest and quietness, with health and wholeness in body and soul.

REFLECTION QUESTION: How do you rest your body and soul?

JULY 22

Dear friend, I pray that you may enjoy good health and that all may go
well with you, even as your soul is getting along well.
3 JOHN 2

Therefore, allow God's love to faithfully guide you in body and soul, while you care for your well-being and personal health. If sickness comes, be patient and humbly call on Christ's mercy to dwell within you to bring you back to health. All shall be well.[29] Your patient endurance in love and prayer through times of sickness as well as in times of various kinds of trouble pleases God so much more than any similar devotions you may offer when in times of fullness of health.

REFLECTION QUESTION: How does physical sickness influence your spiritual health?

JULY 23

As the Father has loved me, so have I loved you. Now remain in my love. If you keep my commands, you will remain in my love, just as I have kept my Father's commands and remain in his love.

JOHN 15:9–10

You may be wondering how to live a balanced life, especially regarding such ordinary habits as eating and sleeping. Seek to live a life of moderation.[30] The only life habit to pursue with complete abandonment is loving God. Do this at all times, loving Jesus continually, without holding anything back, and you will begin to discover how to live in every other area of your life with balance and moderation. The more you remain in Christ's love, the more your life will find balance. The more you abandon yourself, night and day, to the love of God in all things, the more all things will come into greater focus and greater balance.

REFLECTION QUESTION: How do you keep your life balanced?

JULY 24

Do not worry about your life, what you will eat or drink; or about your body, what you will wear. Is not life more than food, and the body more than clothes?

MATTHEW 6:25

Wake up and begin paying attention to the spiritual life of love growing within your soul. Do not worry so much about eating, drinking, sleeping, speaking, and all other physical activities. Life is so much more than all these. The less you focus your attention on these the more they will come into true focus. In truth, you will learn moderation in all these physical areas of life by paying proper attention to them, not by centering your life on these physical demands. It is better to abandon yourself more and more to God's love. Learn to weigh your well-being less by such outward measurements and more by how much you are offering your soul to the love of God.

REFLECTION QUESTION: How much do you worry about food, sleep, clothes, and other things?

JULY 25

Do not worry, saying, "What shall we eat?" or "What shall we drink?"
or "What shall we wear?" For the pagans run after all these things, and
your heavenly Father knows that you need them.
MATTHEW 6:31–32

No matter how much effort you put into your spiritual life, when you try to improve your life through your own willpower you will keep falling short of your desired goal as long as it is you doing all the work. Learn to put such vain efforts beneath you, treading them then down under you in the Cloud of Forgetting.[31] When you stop focusing so much attention on yourself and begin abandoning yourself to God's love, Jesus will empower you by lifting up your heart with a deep stirring of love. So turn your attention away from self and turn toward God. The more you desire God today, the less you will be troubled by self-centeredness. The more you lack God, the more selfishness will dominate your life. In your place of great need, then, welcome Christ's goodness to help you. The more you abandon yourself to God's love today, the more you will discover love flowing into every part of you.

REFLECTION QUESTION: What has helped you turn back to God during the day?

JULY 26

We must pay the most careful attention, therefore, to what we
have heard, so that we do not drift away. For since the message
spoken through angels was binding . . . how shall we escape if we ignore

so great a salvation? This salvation, which was first announced by the
Lord, was confirmed to us by those who heard him.
HEBREWS 2:1–3

S eek God alone, more and more, in every movement of your mind and will. Take every thought and feeling captive, offering them to God. When any thought or feeling that is not of God comes to your awareness, tread it down beneath you into the Cloud of Forgetting. Learn to pay less attention to what other people think of you and also what other people are doing. Learn also to focus less of your attention upon yourself, your deeds, including what you do for the Lord, just as you are learning to focus less of your attention on others and their deeds. Live as a lover. Lovers love their beloved as much or more than their own lives, and are willing to lay their lives down for the sake of the one whom they adore.

REFLECTION QUESTION: How do you pay attention to God's Word?

JULY 27

Do not worry about tomorrow, for tomorrow will worry about itself.
Each day has enough trouble of its own.
MATTHEW 6:34

P ut aside your own drives and desires except those that move you to desire God more. Tread down any obstacle as though under your feet, including any thoughts, worries, or desires that get in between you and Jesus. When you discover any unhealthy lump of sin in you, deeply interwoven into the tissue of your soul, see it as an obstacle hindering your life with God. Do this today. Let each day be sufficient to deal with each obstacle. Tomorrow will come when it comes. Learn today to remove all the hindrances you discover inside yourself that keep you from Christ. Ask Jesus today for help in removing these obstacles to love.

REFLECTION QUESTION: How much do you worry about what may happen in the future?

JULY 28

First take the plank out of your own eye, and then you will see clearly to
remove the speck from your brother's eye.
MATTHEW 7:5

Cast off everything that hinders your life with God, and seek to untangle your life from every sin. Deal first with the obstacles in your soul, before you try to deal with the hindrances in the lives of others. For you will never see clearly enough to help others remove the irritating grains of sand in their lives until you first remove the troublesome sand dunes from your own life. Seek God's grace to remove the dirt from your life, and you'll discover you no longer stand in judgment of others, including their actions and words, as well as no longer getting puffed up with arrogance from your own actions and words.

REFLECTION QUESTION: What irritating hindrances need to be removed from your life right now?

JULY 29

I have been crucified with Christ and I no longer live, but Christ lives in me. The life I now live in the body, I live by faith in the Son of God, who loved me and gave himself for me.

GALATIANS 2:20

Learn to live more fully in God's presence, encompassed in the Cloud of Unknowing, with nothing between you and the Lord, fully present in your mind and heart before the Lord. When Jesus comes to live in you, you no longer live in the same way as you did previously, but you die to your old way of living, and the life you now live in the body, as Paul reminds us, you live by faith in Christ. Christ comes to live with you, taking up residence in your innermost being. Your old way of thinking and feeling has also been crucified with Christ, and God's life and love are beginning to mature within you.

REFLECTION QUESTION: How is Christ's way of life beginning to mature within you?

JULY 30

Trust in the LORD and do good;
dwell in the land and enjoy safe pasture.
Take delight in the LORD,
and he will give you the desires of your heart.

PSALM 37:3–4

You may be asking how to fully die to self, in mind and heart, with your whole being before God. As with shedding worn-out clothes, you are right in thinking that the more fully you die to self, the more you shed old hindrances in your life with Christ. To answer your question about how to more fully die to self: without God's grace fully and freely given, and without your willingness to receive grace, you will not be able to sacrifice your old way of life. When you put your trust in God and seek to live Christ's way of life, God will begin to plant new desires in your heart. So, delight yourself in this new way. In your mind and heart, be clothed anew in Christ's way of life. As strange as this sounds, God's grace arises out of the ongoing pain and weakness in your soul. Take delight in God's work in those places in your life, and God's desires will continue to well up within you.

REFLECTION QUESTION: What do you delight in most often?

JULY 31

He says, "Be still, and know that I am God;
I will be exalted among the nations,
I will be exalted in the earth."

PSALM 46:10

In this place of grace in your soul where you are suffering most, be gentle and attentive to your physical needs. Do not be harsh with your body or spirit, but rather learn quietly to rest your soul by sitting in stillness with your body almost as though you are sleeping, especially in those deepest places of your soul where you are grieving and weary with sorrow. Cease struggling against these places of pain and learn to be still before God. God will be exalted in your life just as God is exalted over the nations. Know God's presence deep within your soul where you ache and suffer. Unite your life and sorrow with life and sorrow of Jesus. Jesus wants you to know him and the power of his resurrection within your body, mind, and spirit.

REFLECTION QUESTION: When do you quietly rest your life in the Lord?

August

Playful Prayer

AUGUST 1

I want to know Christ . . . to know the power of his resurrection and
participation in his sufferings, becoming like him in his death, and so,
somehow, attaining to the resurrection from the dead.

PHILIPPIANS 3:10–11

Scripture invites us to know Christ and experience his great power. We do this by participating in Christ's sufferings, and thus we become like him in life and death. By doing so, we will surely experience the resurrection from the dead. Everyone suffers, but the more we are in tune with Jesus in our innermost being, the more we will truly experience sorrow for the simple reason that we are becoming more and more in tune with Jesus's sufferings within our soul. All other sufferings we experience in this life pale in comparison to this deepest kind of suffering.

REFLECTION QUESTION: How do you face suffering?

AUGUST 2

Now I am happy, not because you were made sorry, but because your
sorrow led you to repentance. . . . Godly sorrow brings repentance that
leads to salvation and leaves no regret, but worldly sorrow brings death.
See what this godly sorrow has produced in you.

2 CORINTHIANS 7:9–11

Spiritual suffering comes not only from feeling emotions of loss and sadness, but also from experiencing sorrow in your innermost being. Anyone who has never known this spiritual sorrow will still know suffering of various kinds, but may not yet have experienced this deepest kind of sorrow. Spiritual sorrow has the capacity to wash the soul clean, not only of soul dirt, but also of the inner pain and regret that comes from separation from God. When your soul is washed clean by spiritual sorrow, you are more and more able to receive Christ's joy, as your mind and heart become less self-centered. When such spiritual sorrow runs deeply within you, your soul will fill with sacred desire for God, strengthening you to endure the pain of sorrow in your mind and heart.

REFLECTION QUESTION: How have you experienced godly sorrow that has helped you?

AUGUST 3

Blessed are those who mourn,
for they will be comforted.

MATTHEW 5:4

There will come times when you enter into true knowledge and experience of God's presence in purity of spirit, yet feel hesitant and remorseful because of your knowledge of the filthy, unclean, or sick condition of your soul. If you want to continue to mature as a follower of God, learn from the teachings Jesus gave upon the Mount of Beatitudes. The sick condition of your soul will cause you to mourn with spiritual sorrow. Jesus will bless you as you mourn for this desperate condition of your soul. Through your spiritual sorrow, which may be accompanied with weeping, lament, and struggle, you offer your life as a living sacrifice to God. Such honest and sacrificial living is pleasing to God.

REFLECTION QUESTION: When has God comforted you in a time of mourning?

AUGUST 4

All this is for your benefit, so that the grace that is reaching more and
more people may cause thanksgiving to overflow to the glory of God.

2 CORINTHIANS 4:15

When you struggle, beware of carrying such a heavy burden of sorrow that your soul is crushed under the weight. Some live under such crushing weight of sin and sorrow that they even yearn to escape this life, looking for a way out of the pressure even through thoughts of suicide. Such thoughts come from spiritual darkness and soul sickness and never from God. God wants you to thrive with well-being in your soul in this present moment, overflowing with thanksgiving for the amazing gift and worthiness of your life. God will give you your heart's desire even in the midst of your struggles, and you will find more compassion for others.

REFLECTION QUESTION: How often does your heart overflow with thanksgiving?

AUGUST 5

*This is how love is made complete among us so that we will have
confidence on the day of judgment: In this world we are like Jesus. There
is no fear in love. But perfect love drives out fear, because fear has to do
with punishment. The one who fears is not made perfect in love.*

1 JOHN 4:17–18

Spiritual sorrow and spiritual desire are two essential elements for
your spiritual journey. You were created by God to yearn for God
and to learn God's goodwill. Every person has their own unique
ability, in both body and soul, according to their unique position and
personality. Do not live in fear. Christ's perfect love chases away our fears.
Keep pressing on through experiences of spiritual sorrow and desire,
allowing your life to be transformed by the renewing of your mind and
heart, encouraged in your heart and united to Christ in perfect love, so
that you may experience more fully the riches of understanding and the
mystery of life with God.[32]

REFLECTION QUESTION: What influence has Christ's perfect love had
in your life?

AUGUST 6

*Let me live that I may praise you,
and may your laws sustain me.
I have strayed like a lost sheep.
Seek your servant,
for I have not forgotten your commands.*

PSALM 119:175–76

People who hike sometimes get lost in the wilderness. In the same
way, anyone on a spiritual journey may find themselves occasionally
losing their way. This is especially true for those who are new to
walking in the way of Jesus. People get weary, grow impatient trying to
follow maps and guidebooks, or give up altogether seeking guidance or
help. In such a frame of mind, when you are praying, it is easy to get lost,
and wander off into fantasies of your own making. People get lost trying
to follow intensive physical regimens or unhealthy spiritual illusions as
if they were the real way. These troubles do not come from God but arise
from sensual lust, emotional longings, or self-centeredness.

REFLECTION QUESTION: When you were spiritually lost, how did you find your way home?

AUGUST 7

Endure hardship as discipline; God is treating you as his children. For what children are not disciplined by their father? If you are not disciplined—and everyone undergoes discipline—then you are not legitimate, not true sons and daughters at all.

HEBREWS 12:7–8

There are many kinds of hardships in the spiritual life. When you are newly enrolled in the school of devotion, spiritual sorrow and spiritual desire may at first lift up your heart into the Cloud of Unknowing in God's presence with an unceasing yearning to feel Christ's love filling your soul. But just as swiftly, some will receive these teachings not as God has intended them but in an unhealthy way, inflicting on their body or soul severe forms of discipline as though emotional or physical suffering is the quickest road to spiritual maturity. What they lack in divine grace, they try to make up for with human willpower, straining their bodies with extreme acts of discipline. Within a short time, they burn out and grow weary, becoming weak in body and soul. These tiring pursuits lead them to contort their lives even further in search of empty physical or sensual pleasures with little regard for the actual way God made bodies and souls to be refreshed and renewed.

REFLECTION QUESTION: How has God disciplined you?

AUGUST 8

Each person is tempted when they are dragged away by their own evil desire and enticed. Then, after desire has conceived, it gives birth to sin; and sin, when it is full-grown, gives birth to death.

JAMES 1:14–15

If not misled on false paths, some people may still, through spiritual blindness, wander off into sensual passions, deceived by their own evil desires into believing that any arousal of physical appetite must be good. Their bodies, so to speak, catch fire, enflamed with intense passions sparked by their misunderstanding of how God has designed bodies and souls to work together. Some also get caught up in misguided spiritual fervor conceived by dark forces of corruption, giving birth to spiritual pride, fleshly lusts, and vain speculations. May God have mercy upon us and lead us away from such empty ways.

REFLECTION QUESTION: How do you face times when you are tempted by intense lust or fervor?

AUGUST 9

The wisdom that comes from heaven is first of all pure; then peace-loving, considerate, submissive, full of mercy and good fruit, impartial and sincere.

JAMES 3:17

There are some people who pursue spiritual life with God unwisely. They believe they have been filled with the fire of love, sparked and kindled by the grace and goodness of God's Spirit, but they've allowed themselves to be deceived, allowing their lives to be filled with passion for recognition, pride, or impurity. From these impure seeds spring noxious weeds of many kinds of trouble: hypocrisy, erroneous ways of thinking and believing, or spiritual wandering and becoming lost in the thorny wilderness of self-delusion. Just as true spiritual wisdom comes to all who enroll in God's school of devotion, even so, spiritual deception comes to all who enroll in the world's school of pretense. Spiritual forces of evil have their followers and devotees who stumble in the darkness of deception and folly, thinking they are living fully for God. Spiritual forces of good have many followers who walk with wisdom, purity, humility, mercy, impartiality, and sincerity.

REFLECTION QUESTION: How has spiritual wisdom come into your life?

AUGUST 10

Anyone who claims to be in the light but hates a brother or sister is still in the darkness. Anyone who loves their brother and sister lives in the light, and there is nothing in them to make them stumble. But anyone who hates a brother or sister is in the darkness and walks around in the darkness. They do not know where they are going, because the darkness has blinded them.

1 JOHN 2:9–11

God's people express their feelings and thoughts in a wide variety of ways that are pleasing to God, including loving others as brother and sister. But there are also those who get lost in self-deception, expressing their wayward feelings and twisted thoughts in a wide variety of states of mind and conditions of heart that are not honoring to God. We are wise not to dwell on these shadows. Rather, we are wise to press into the light of love, walking this ancient way of prayer. All who walk this ancient way are assailed at times by such deceptive feelings or thoughts. Seek to live in the light of love and walk with a few brothers or sisters in this way.

REFLECTION QUESTION: When have you been in the dark or unsure how to live?

AUGUST 11

Jesus said to him, "Today salvation has come to this house, because this man, too, is a son of Abraham. For the Son of Man came to seek and to save the lost."
LUKE 19:9–10

Sometimes, even learned men and women with degrees in theology have gotten lost by following deceptive shadows. There is little or no benefit in chasing shadow stories. But there may be some benefit, only, from a few words of warning about those who have wandered from the way and gotten lost in the darkening woods of deception. May these words encourage you to press along the way of love. Know with confidence that Jesus continues to come to seek and find the lost. Therefore, be vigilant in your spiritual journey, and look to Christ when assailed with deceptions, doubts, and darkness, and he will lead you back to the path of life.

REFLECTION QUESTION: How has Jesus saved you?

AUGUST 12

I will give you a new heart and put a new spirit in you; I will remove from you your heart of stone and give you a heart of flesh.

EZEKIEL 36:26

For the love of God, be playful as you pray. Be gentle with yourself and do not strain yourself with unnatural attempts to pray beyond your capacity. Let your prayer life be motivated by prayerful playfulness rather than arrogance. Arrogance gives birth to unhealthy appetites and addictions, but prayerful playfulness promotes down-to-earth humility and spiritual growth. Therefore, be prayerful and playful. If an arrogant person attempts to climb up the holy mountain of the Lord by sheer willpower, their heart of stone will weigh them down so much they will be unable to ascend.[33] Stones are hard and heavy and can be harmful to the human body. In the same way, a heart filled with stones can make any spiritual discipline difficult, putting an unhealthy strain upon the soul. Christ loves to remove stones from our heart. God loves to give us a new heart.

REFLECTION QUESTION: How playful is your prayer life?

AUGUST 13

As the deer pants for streams of water,
so my soul pants for you, my God.
My soul thirsts for God, for the living God.
When can I go and meet with God?

PSALM 42:1–2

Like stones in a dry riverbed without water, a heart of stone is in a dry place away from the flow of God's grace. Such dry souls sometimes injure themselves by excessive acts of devotion, and then cause these wounds to fester, thinking they are doing something spiritually heroic. Be on your guard against such empty ways of living. Instead, learn to love genuinely, and be gentle with yourself, in body and soul. Seek to live by God's goodwill with a gracious and humble spirit, rather than with a gluttonous or overhasty spirit. No matter how spiritually hungry and thirsty you are, there is no need to devour spirituality. Thirst for God. Hunger for God's way of life. Come to God to have your spiritual thirst quenched in God's gracious presence.

REFLECTION QUESTION: Is your soul thirsty for God?

AUGUST 14

You were once darkness, but now you are light in the Lord.
Live as children of light (for the fruit of the light consists in all
goodness, righteousness and truth).

EPHESIANS 5:8–9

As children of the living God, learn to be playful as you pray. First, learn to play hide-and-seek. Hide from whatever is false, ignoble, wrong, impure, repulsive, corrupt, detestable, or dishonorable. Seek whatever is true, noble, right, pure, lovely, admirable, excellent, and praiseworthy. Second, play make-believe. Pretend you are not pretending in your faith in God. Act as though you are not trying hard to impress God, but simply living a life that is pleasing to God, regardless of whether God is paying attention. Of course, God is always paying attention and is delighted when you want to please God with your thoughts and actions. God takes delight in the children of light.

REFLECTION QUESTION: How do you like to play?

AUGUST 15

You are all children of the light and children of the day. We do not
belong to the night or to the darkness. So then, let us not be like others,
who are asleep, but let us be awake and sober.

1 THESSALONIANS 5:5–6

Learn to play these two little childlike games of hide-and-seek and make-believe and you'll discover God's grace flowing into your actions and feelings, causing you to become more like Christ, both in your mind and heart. As you play hide-and-seek, and play make-believe, you'll discover more and more of God's goodness filling your life. Like a loving father or mother who loves to get down on their knees to play games with their beloved child, God will come to be with you, covering you with kisses and hugs.

REFLECTION QUESTION: What are your thoughts about being called a child of the light?

AUGUST 16

To what can I compare this generation? They are like children sitting in the marketplaces and calling out to others:
"We played the pipe for you,
and you did not dance;
we sang a dirge,
and you did not mourn."

MATTHEW 11:16–17

You may be surprised at this invitation to be childlike and playful in your prayer life. Some view this way of prayer as childish, silly, or lacking in maturity. There are specific reasons to call you to this way of prayer. Consider what was written in Scripture centuries ago. Jesus invites us to pray to our Father. Jesus welcomed little children to come to him, and he blessed the children and told us that unless we become like little children, we would not be able to enter the kingdom of heaven. Such instructions have been practiced by countless wise and prayerful people through the ages.

REFLECTION QUESTION: What is the difference between being childlike and childish in prayer?

AUGUST 17

Jesus told them, "You are going to have the light just a little while longer. Walk while you have the light, before darkness overtakes you. Whoever walks in the dark does not know where they are going. Believe in the light while you have the light, so that you may become children of light." When he had finished speaking, Jesus left and hid himself from them.

JOHN 12:35–36

Here are a few reasons to pray playfully. First, when you play hide-and-seek in a secret prayer place, you tend to pray with less thought for what you may get, and worry less about what others think of your prayer. In your hiding place of prayer, you will be less distracted, your prayers will be more quickly answered, and your heart will be more richly rewarded. Another reason to play hide-and-seek as you pray is that in secret, you are less inclined to rely on many words, excess emotions, and strange bodily contortions. In secret, you are more inclined to pray simple, pure prayers from the depths of your heart. Such playful prayer will help ignite your soul with sparks of love, kindling your heart and Christ's heart together in spiritual unity and goodwill.

REFLECTION QUESTION: When and where do you pray in secret?

AUGUST 18

God is spirit, and his worshipers must worship in the Spirit and in truth.

JOHN 4:24

Understand that God is Spirit, and all who want to pray learn to pray in the Spirit and in truth. If you desire deeper union with Jesus, discover the joy of praying genuinely and deeply in your spirit before God's Spirit, rather than thinking prayer is only about words and body posture. God knows all things, and nothing is hidden from him, either in body or soul. The deeper something is hidden in your soul, the more openly it is known to God. As the ancient songwriter prayed, "Deep calls to deep" (Psalm 42:7). Physical desires are farther from God's heart than spiritual desires. All human desire is a mixture of body and soul. When you overly stress your body or your soul in prayer, you are less able to draw close to God than when you come to God simply, genuinely and deeply, with a childlike and playful spirit.

REFLECTION QUESTION: How do you worship in the Spirit and in truth?

AUGUST 19

The Lord your God is with you,
the Mighty Warrior who saves.
He will take great delight in you;
in his love he will no longer rebuke you,
but will rejoice over you with singing.
ZEPHANIAH 3:17

God takes delight in you as you pray, playing such games as hide-and-seek or make-believe. When you hide the longings you have for God deep within your life, God finds them delightful, rejoicing over you. So hide your love for Jesus deep within your spirit, far from any carnal or worldly desires which only corrupt your love and further separate you from God. Know with confidence that the more you aim your life heavenward, the less you will be corrupted by the empty pursuit of worldly appetites, and the nearer you will draw to God.

REFLECTION QUESTION: How do you respond to God's taking great delight in you as you pray?

AUGUST 20

Every good and perfect gift is from above, coming down from the Father of the heavenly lights, who does not change like shifting shadows.

JAMES 1:17

The nearer you come to God, the more he delights to come near to you.[34] The nearer you are to Christ, the more clearly you see and know God. Seeing and knowing God is a gift of grace given to you and every good gift comes from God, who does not change. You live in a constantly changing world of shadows and light, summer and winter, night and day. The more you live with the Lord, the more you'll discover what does not change, and the more you will become more like Jesus, pure in your spiritual life, for God is Spirit.

REFLECTION QUESTION: What are some of the good gifts God has given to you?

AUGUST 21

The Lord said to Samuel, "Do not consider his appearance or his height, for I have rejected him. The Lord does not look at the things people look at. People look at the outward appearance, but the Lord looks at the heart."

1 SAMUEL 16:7

Another reason to pray secretly, as though playing hide-and-seek, is that humans too often value outward appearances more than the matters of the heart. When you place a higher value on the physical realm than on the spiritual realm, you confuse spirit and flesh, and thus end up trying to show off or look good rather than allowing the innermost stirrings of your heart be known. Prayer is much more than mere physical motions, bodily postures, or spoken words. When you show off in prayer, you end up wasting your words, like trying to explain heavenly mysteries to a drunkard. Most of what you say is made cheap by the attempt. Rather than attempting to impress someone by your spirituality with many words, it is far better to pray simple, honest, and heartfelt prayers in your prayer room where nobody is watching you but God.[35]

REFLECTION QUESTION: How do you use your body and your spirit in prayer?

AUGUST 22

Shout for joy to the Lord, all the earth.
Worship the Lord with gladness;
come before him with joyful songs.

PSALM 100:1–2

God loves hearing you pray in a variety of ways. If your heart is moved to pray with words spoken with your mouth, then pray verbal prayers. If your spirit is bursting with exuberant praise, then shout and sing for joy! If you are stirred within to express your devotion, try praying short prayers of adoration such as "Good Jesus! Fairest Jesus! Sweet Jesus!" These are only suggestions. There are many short prayers of adoration. God forbid that you think there is only one way to pray. Learn to pray simple prayers in the secret place within your heart.

REFLECTION QUESTION: What are some of the ways you are moved to pray?

John answered them all, "I baptize you with water. But one who is more powerful than I will come, the straps of whose sandals I am not worthy to untie. He will baptize you with the Holy Spirit and fire.

LUKE 3:16

Know that God created you to be whole, uniting your life as body and spirit. Christ wants you to love and serve with your body and soul together, as is fitting, and he will reward you with joy and delight in both body and soul. As a deposit of that future reward, the Holy Spirit kindles within your body or soul the flame of God's love, not just occasionally, but as often as he desires, enflaming your life with a fullness of wonder, sweetness, and delight. This holy fire does not come to you from outside your body through the windows of reason. Rather, this holy fire comes from deep within you, rising and springing up abundantly from your spiritual gladness and true heart devotion. Do not be suspicious of this wonder, sweetness, and delight. Once you've experienced God's love, you'll know this holy fire kindled within you is genuine.

REFLECTION QUESTION: When has the Holy Spirit kindled holy fire within you?

AUGUST 24

Dear friends, do not believe every spirit, but test the spirits to see whether they are from God, because many false prophets have gone out into the world.

1 JOHN 4:1

As for every delight, gladness, or sweetness, though you do not know the source, use discernment and test every spirit. For these things may be good or bad: either they are created by a good spirit if they are truly good, or they are created by bad spiritual forces intended to bring harm and trouble. Do not let yourself be tricked or deceived by erroneous ways of thinking. Stay away from excessive or abusive patterns of spiritual living. Rather, be stirred by love, by spiritual love for God dwelling in your heart. This love is kindled by God's Spirit without any other means. Therefore, you can be sure this holy fire within you is not tainted by any fantasies or falsehoods that otherwise trouble your life.

REFLECTION QUESTION: How do you test or discern what is good?

AUGUST 25

"What shall I do, Lord?" I asked.
"Get up," the Lord said, "and go into Damascus. There you will be told
all that you have been assigned to do." My companions led me by the hand
into Damascus, because the brilliance of the light had blinded me.

ACTS 22:10–11

Regarding other wonders, delights, and sweet experiences, how can you know whether they are good or bad, to be welcomed or rejected? The most important matter is to fulfill the desire and stirring of your heart toward loving God, in both your words and your way of living. There are many sounds and delights that come to you through the window of your mind. They may be good or bad, light or dark, true or false. Learn to discern by hiding yourself in God's Cloud of Unknowing, blinded by the brightness of the light of Christ's presence, prayerful in devotion to the Lord.

REFLECTION QUESTION: In recent weeks, when has your heart been stirred to love God?

AUGUST 26

Do not lie to each other, since you have taken off your old self with
its practices and have put on the new self, which is being renewed in
knowledge in the image of its Creator.
COLOSSIANS 3:9–10

In such a state of soul, as you hide yourself in God's Cloud of Unknowing, you will be able to discern what is good from what is bad, what is light from what is dark, what is true from what is false. If at first you are surprised by these experiences of wonders and delights flooding into your mind, unsure if they are reliable or not, continue to unite your heart to Jesus in prayer. Allow your life to be transformed and your mind renewed. As you are being renewed in knowledge, your life is being reshaped into the beautiful image of Christ. Give credibility to experiences of wonder and delight by testing and approving these according to God's good and pleasing will. By the Holy Spirit at work within you, through the wise counsel of a mature spiritual mentor, you will continue to grow in your ability to discern all that is full of wonder, sweetness, and delight.

REFLECTION QUESTION: Who is a wise mentor in your life?

AUGUST 27

When he arrived and saw what the grace of God had done, he was glad and encouraged them all to remain true to the Lord with all their hearts. He was a good man, full of the Holy Spirit and faith, and a great number of people were brought to the Lord.

ACTS 11:23–24

The essence of spiritual growth into full maturity is nothing more than the pursuit of God's goodwill. As Barnabas did when he arrived in Antioch, go grace-hunting, looking for evidence of the grace of God at work in people's lives. Pursue God's goodwill, by following the humble stirring of love in your heart toward God. God's goodness and grace will be your guide in this life and will bring you to endless joys in the life to come. God's goodwill is the essence of all good living, and without it no good actions may be begun or completed. Keep pursuing God's good and pleasing will, with an attitude of gladness and delight in God that influences your whole way of life.

REFLECTION QUESTION: What are your thoughts about grace-hunting?

AUGUST 28

Jesus, full of joy through the Holy Spirit, said, "I praise you, Father, Lord of heaven and earth, because you have hidden these things from the wise and learned, and revealed them to little children. Yes, Father, for this is what you were pleased to do."

LUKE 10:21

God's goodwill is at the heart of all spiritual growth. Every sweet gift and delight in this life, whether physical or spiritual, is lightweight and insignificant unless it is weighed by God's goodwill. They are lightweight in comparison to the eternal weight of glory that awaits us. You may enjoy many gifts and delights in this life without ever knowing God's goodwill or the joy of being drawn closer to

Christ through these earthly gifts. In the bliss of heaven, every wonder, all sweetness, and every delight is united with the essence of God's goodwill, unable to be separated from the presence of God.

REFLECTION QUESTION: What sweet gift or delight has God revealed to you?

AUGUST 29

Flee from all this, and pursue righteousness, godliness, faith, love, endurance and gentleness.

1 TIMOTHY 6:11

In the same way, your entire body and soul will united with the essence of God's goodwill in the endless joys of the life to come. So the essence of all spiritual growth in this life is found in pursuing God's goodwill in all things. Pursuing God's goodwill includes the pursuit of a life of righteousness, godliness, faith, love, endurance, and gentleness. Surely, all who experience this spiritual growth within their souls know there is no sweetness and no pleasure more delightful than living according to God's goodwill in all things.

REFLECTION QUESTION: What are you pursuing?

AUGUST 30

We fix our eyes not on what is seen, but on what is unseen, since what is seen is temporary, but what is unseen is eternal.

2 CORINTHIANS 4:18

May you begin to see how sweet it is to focus all your attention upon the unseen, humble stirring of love within your soul toward God's goodwill. As strange as it may sound, give less attention to every other pleasure and delight, whether physical or spiritual, whether happy or holy. If they show up in your life, then welcome them. But do not rely too much upon them, at the risk of becoming dependent upon these and not upon God. When you give too much focus of your heart to earthly delights and demands, whether sacred or profane, whether pleasures or pains, they begin to require more and more of your attention, draining you of strength.

REFLECTION QUESTION: What do you fix your eyes on?

AUGUST 31

I am not saying this because I am in need, for I have learned to be content whatever the circumstances. I know what it is to be in need, and I know what it is to have plenty. I have learned the secret of being content in any and every situation, whether well fed or hungry, whether living in plenty or in want.

PHILIPPIANS 4:11–12

Some people are motivated to love God in order to get spiritually high or have some mystical experience. If these experiences are taken away or never come, they find themselves discontent and full of grumbling. Such love is impure and immature. No matter whether your body is well fed or hungry, comforted by pleasurable spiritual feelings or distressed by sorrow and pain, may you learn the secret of being content without grumbling at life's experiences. Be just as content not to have such lofty experiences as to have them according to God's goodwill. You'll discover that some people experience such spiritual delights often, while others seldom know any kind of spiritual sweetness or comfort in this life. For love to grow in purity and maturity, learn contentment in plenty and in want by being transformed from within by the love of God.

REFLECTION QUESTION: What is the secret of being content in plenty or in want?

165

September

Transformed from Within

SEPTEMBER 1

*There are different kinds of gifts, but the same Spirit distributes them.
There are different kinds of service, but the same Lord. There are
different kinds of working, but in all of them and in everyone it is the
same God at work.*

1 CORINTHIANS 12:4–6

According to God's goodwill, he gives to every person the unique gifts that will benefit them and others they serve. Some people are so emotionally vulnerable and tenderhearted that unless they are often comforted by sweet spiritual feelings and consolations, they may not otherwise endure the wide variety of temptations and troubles they will suffer in this life, either physically or spiritually. Others are so physically frail that they lack strength to endure any kind of purifying spiritual discipline such as fasting from food, or anything else that would otherwise weaken their body. Instead, by God's goodwill at work within them through sweet spiritual feelings and tears of joy, they are purified and mature in love.

REFLECTION QUESTION: What gifts or talents has God given you?

SEPTEMBER 2

*But to each one of us grace has been given as Christ apportioned it.
This is why it says:
"When he ascended on high,
he took many captives
and gave gifts to his people."*

EPHESIANS 4:7–8

Some people are so strong in their hearts that they already practice the presence of God in their soul, offering up their lives in reverence and humble stirrings of love according to God's goodwill. Because they are already so well fed and mature, they need very little spiritual food in the manner of sweet comforts, pleasures, or spiritual delights. Which kind of person is holier than the rest, and which is dearer to God? All God's people are beloved by God, and every person receives the unique gifts and expressions of the Spirit at the right time and in the right way, according to God's grace. The gifts given to us by God are given not just for our use, but for the common good of others in the body of Christ.

REFLECTION QUESTION: How are you putting your spiritual gift to use to help others?

SEPTEMBER 3

My child, listen and be wise:
Keep your heart on the right course.

PROVERBS 23:19 NLT

Incline your heart with all humility to the unseen movement of God's love within you.[36] I am not talking about your physical heart, but the heart of your spiritual life: the center of your being. Be careful not to confuse what is spiritual with what is physical. Such confusions are often the cause of many misunderstandings, especially among the curious and those with vivid imaginations. Hide your desire for God deep within your heart and set your heart to journey with God into the Cloud of Unknowing. Too often, people try to put on a show for God or try to impress God with their religious acts or spiritual devotion. There is no need to try to show off for God. God already knows your heart.

REFLECTION QUESTION: Upon what path do you set your heart?

SEPTEMBER 4

I pray that out of his glorious riches he may strengthen you with
power through his Spirit in your inner being.

EPHESIANS 3:16

You know well that when you choose to hide your desire for God deep within, you cast that desire deeper into your spirit where God loves to dwell. Therefore, be alert in your thinking, making sure you understand spiritual instructions in a spiritual way rather than in a bodily way. Misunderstandings arise even with very small words, such as *inward* or *upward*. Get these two little words wrong and you may also be thinking in a wrong way about bigger aspects of the spiritual life. Some erroneously think *inward* means navel-gazing or selfish spiritual pursuits or focusing upon the inside of their physical body. Some erroneously think *upward* means escaping the body or mystical visions or getting on some kind of magic elevator. God invites you *inward*, into a closer life where you remain in Christ just as Christ remains in you. God calls you up with an *upward* call, to press higher and aim higher with your whole being toward life with the Lord.

REFLECTION QUESTION: How do you remain in Christ?

SEPTEMBER 5

I could not address you as people who live by the Spirit but as people who are still worldly—mere infants in Christ. I gave you milk, not solid food, for you were not yet ready for it. Indeed, you are still not ready.

1 CORINTHIANS 3:1–2

Consider a young person who has recently turned away from the empty pursuits of the world, and has enrolled in God's lifelong school of devotion. At first, out of eagerness and youthful zeal, this person weans herself away from worldly passions through the pursuit of prayer, acts of devotion, and humbly confessing her heart to a wise mentor. As a result, this woman is able to understand, with greater and greater clarity the way of the spiritual life, both when she hears people talk about this life, or when she reads about this way of life in a book. We grow slowly in the spiritual life, maturing according to God's design and goodwill.

REFLECTION QUESTION: What pursuits have helped you grow?

SEPTEMBER 6

Pray for us. We are sure that we have a clear conscience and desire to live honorably in every way. I particularly urge you to pray so that I may be restored to you soon.

HEBREWS 13:18–19

Let's imagine a woman opening a prayer book that encourages her to hide her spiritual desires within, or to climb up in the spiritual life above herself. Still young in her spiritual journey, without the maturity to see the life of the soul with clarity, whether from physical perspective or intellectual curiosity, this woman will most likely misunderstand what is meant by hiding within or climbing up and above. She has a natural tendency to pretend she is more mature than she really is, and thus falls victim to fear or pride, or perhaps pretending she's holier than her neighbor. Hiding within has nothing to do with fear. Climbing up and above has nothing to do with pride. The spiritual life is not about trying to become holier than anyone else. God is not calling us into a life of fear or hypocrisy, but of inner integrity and authentic spiritual life with Jesus.

REFLECTION QUESTION: Who is helping you grow in your prayer life?

SEPTEMBER 7

Love must be sincere. Hate what is evil; cling to what is good. Be devoted to one another in love. Honor one another above yourselves.

ROMANS 12:9–10

Free yourself from trying to pretend to be something you are not. You are being called into a life of genuine honesty, wisdom, and humility. There will be voices within that will grumble against the counsel of wise mentors, acting as though they know better how to live the spiritual life than anyone else. There will be forces within that try to elevate you above others. There will be weights upon your soul that will try to drag you down into a hypocritical, two-faced life. You will live much of the time with a divided life, with part of your soul yearning for God while another part of your soul is filled with empty and selfish pursuits. Avoid ways of life that lack sincerity, wisdom, and humility. It is better to humbly incline your whole heart to the unseen movement of God's love growing within you.

REFLECTION QUESTION: Who have you asked to mentor you or help you grow?

SEPTEMBER 8

I rise before dawn and cry for help;
I have put my hope in your word.
My eyes stay open through the watches of the night,
that I may meditate on your promises.

PSALM 119:147–48

How does a person stay spiritually healthy? Read Scripture slowly and meditate on what you've read. Learn to listen to God's Word with your heart and don't just read with your mind. Those who read, study, and listen only with their mind or their feelings evaluate everything they read from a limited point of view. The spiritual life goes deeper than intellect and emotions. When you apply only logic or emotions to the spiritual life, you end up misunderstanding and misdirecting your way of life. Beware of using only reason to understand the inward, spiritual way of life. You'll end up straining your brain trying to figure out mysteries too deep for words.

REFLECTION QUESTION: Do you meditate on God's Word when you awake in the night?

SEPTEMBER 9

Taste and see that the Lord is good.

PSALM 34:8

You may try to use your physical eyes to look at eternity, your physical ears to try to listen to the voice of God, or your physical hand to try to hold the hand of God. Some have also attempted to use their nose to smell the fragrant aroma of Christ's love, or their taste buds to savor God's goodness. Such attempts have some value for our spiritual growth, for God created the universe and your senses. In a limited and temporal way, God's goodness is evident through the use of your senses. Because God declared all that he made very good, God's goodness may be discovered in Creation through our five senses.

REFLECTION QUESTION: How do you experience God's goodness?

He has made everything beautiful in its time. He has also set eternity in the human heart; yet no one can fathom what God has done from beginning to end.

ECCLESIASTES 3:11

Though our five physical senses are given to us by God to help us experience our earthly life, when we use those same senses to comprehend the spiritual life, we will discover how limited they are to bring insight to eternal life. We will get dizzy the more we attempt to try to understand with our senses, logic, or emotions what is best known by spiritual insight and heavenly radiance. On earth, there are many ways a soul may be misguided: through delicious tastes, fragrant smells, harmonious sounds, and voluptuous sights. In the pursuit of such fleeting experiences, some believe they have discovered their soul's true resting place, but end up deceived. Many earthly ways, though good in their rightful place, when placed at the center of our life as the main attraction will lead us away from the path of spiritual growth.

REFLECTION QUESTION: Which of your senses do you rely on the most?

SEPTEMBER 11

*Those who cling to worthless idols
turn away from God's love for them.*

JONAH 2:8

Where you center your life is what you worship. Center your life on food and food becomes your god. Center your life on music and music is what you begin to worship. The same thing is true for sex, sleep, alcohol, entertainment, work, and a multitude of other potential idols. How much longer will you "love delusions and seek false gods" (Psalm 4:2)? The more we cling to what is of this earth, the more we forget about God and turn away from God's love. The more we cling to Christ, turning away from temporal pursuits and empty fantasies, the more we will grow in spiritual health, filled with God's love.

REFLECTION QUESTION: What are you clinging to?

"Why have we fasted," they say,
"and you have not seen it?
Why have we humbled ourselves,
and you have not noticed?"
Yet on the day of your fasting, you do as you please
and exploit all your workers.
Your fasting ends in quarreling and strife
and in striking each other with wicked fists.
You cannot fast as you do today
and expect your voice to be heard on high.

ISAIAH 58:3–4

Many strange practices arise from those who pursue empty fantasies and deceptions in the spiritual life. Some view the spiritual life as a masquerade or a carnival, where people wear elaborate masks and parade about as they take pleasure in many forms of self-indulgence, hoping the time of penance and fasting never comes. Everyone who seeks the Lord and his ways knows such times of fasting do come, for the spiritual discipline of fasting is an essential practice in encouraging growth in body and spirit. Learn to pray within the Cloud of Unknowing, with your soul bared to God, without any need to cover your life with falsehoods and masks before God.

REFLECTION QUESTION: How do you fast?

SEPTEMBER 13

Isaiah was right when he prophesied about you hypocrites; as it is written:
"These people honor me with their lips,
but their hearts are far from me.
They worship me in vain;
their teachings are merely human rules."
You have let go of the commands of God and are holding on to human traditions.

MARK 7:6–8

God's way of prayer is lost on those who pursue a life of hypocrisy. Some masquerade with bulging eyes, staring into the dark as if mesmerized by spiritual phantasms. The more you stare into the dark, the darker your soul will become. Some become giddy in their spirit, staggering about as though intoxicated by mystical experiences beyond their imaginings. Some pretend to be overly humble by bowing their head as though a heavy stone hung about their neck. Some go out of their way to get attention with their voices, by crying and wailing, by whining and ranting, or by a torrent of many words that have little or no connection to their inner lives. God did not create you for a life of hypocrisy but for a life of love. May your heart come near to God as you seek to live as God's true follower and friend.

REFLECTION QUESTION: How do you deal with hypocrisy?

SEPTEMBER 14

May God be gracious to us and bless us
and make his face shine on us—
so that your ways may be known on earth,
your salvation among all nations.

PSALM 67:1–2

Many crude and crass practices emerge from a life of hypocrisy. One of the strange aspects of hypocrisy is that people will pretend to have nothing to do with crazy or crass spiritual practices while in public with others, but behind closed doors, at home, they will indulge in duplicitous ways. If you try to gently challenge such a person on their double way of life, you may find yourself confronted with a burst of outrage and denial, with the hypocritical person defending themselves, claiming their whole life is lived for God in love and truth. Unless God's mercy shines the miracle of love into their lives, they will continue to live in the dark, fooling themselves by thinking they are living the spiritual life while they are playacting, deceiving themselves, and infecting others with their self-made fantasies. May God be gracious to us and help us be gracious with others.

REFLECTION QUESTION: In what ways have you been faking it?

SEPTEMBER 15

Jesus said to the crowds and to his disciples: "The teachers of the law and the Pharisees sit in Moses' seat. So you must be careful to do everything they tell you. But do not do what they do, for they do not practice what they preach. They tie up heavy, cumbersome loads and put them on other people's shoulders, but they themselves are not willing to lift a finger to move them."

MATTHEW 23:1–4

Here are a few of the people you may meet at life's masquerade. You may know one of these people personally. You may also discover you are one of them. First, you'll meet people who might be dressed in religious garb, hanging their heads down with the burden of religious traditions, who declare proudly, "We've always done it this way." These people expect others to live under the weight of many religious rules and regulations. They value external forms of crippling spirituality and ignore internal ways of liberating spirituality. Too often, they are unable to listen to the needs of others because they are burdened with customs. They bow their heads low, burdened with the weight of guilt and fear, making them unable to look up and see any other way of life. They disdain the ways of others, condemning with their mouths before they've listened with their ears. There are people who live by fear of breaking one of life's many unwritten rules. These people are unable to experience joy in life because they are too busy trying to adhere to the laws of religion.

REFLECTION QUESTION: What is keeping you from experiencing the joy of life?

Then you will call, and the LORD will answer;
you will cry for help, and he will say: Here am I.
If you do away with the yoke of oppression,
with the pointing finger and malicious talk,
and if you spend yourselves in behalf of the hungry
and satisfy the needs of the oppressed,
then your light will rise in the darkness,
and your night will become like the noonday.
ISAIAH 58:9–10

You may also have met the pointers, those who use their fingers to point out what is wrong with the world, including in your life. These people masquerade as judges. They love to judge before thinking, point before pondering, condemn before caring. Sometimes they point at their own bodies, condemning themselves for falling short of perfection, unable to receive the gift of grace because they are too busy shaming themselves or feeling guilty about everything they do not like about their lives. Most of their energy, however, is devoted to pointing at others, looking down their noses, past their outstretched fingers at all they dislike. They are blind to grace at work in the hearts of another because they are too fixated on external failures.

REFLECTION QUESTION: What hinders you from receiving the gift of God's grace?

SEPTEMBER 17

Since the promise of entering his rest still stands, let us be careful that
none of you be found to have fallen short of it.
HEBREWS 4:1

At the masquerade ball, you may also bump into busy people who never sit still, but are always on the move, on the go, heading someplace, or returning from someplace. Because their hearts are never at rest, their bodies also are always on the move. When they are standing, you'll see their bodies shifting from side to side as though they are in a hurry to get going again, telling you with their actions that they do not have time to talk to you, but need to move along. Even when sitting or lying in bed, their bodies seldom settle down, but wiggle and move and toss and turn. They also move from job to job, from house to house, from group to group, unable to commit to long-term relationships or to a life of stability because of their restless hearts.[37] Learn to enter into God's gift of rest. Settle your soul in the peace of Christ.

REFLECTION QUESTION: How easy is it for you to enter into God's rest?

SEPTEMBER 18

Lord, you alone are my portion and my cup;
you make my lot secure.
The boundary lines have fallen for me in pleasant places;
surely I have a delightful inheritance.

PSALM 16:5–6

Another group of people at the carnival are the conductors, who beat the air with their arms as though they are conducting an orchestra, or swimming across a lake. They love to talk with their hands and arms, filling the room with grand gestures, seeking the center of attention in any group. They deal with their heart's insecurities and their need for approval by asserting themselves into a group, pretending to be a symphony conductor, and orchestrating and manipulating the lives of others, even when no one has asked them to do so. We are wise to settle our lives within God's delightful inheritance, finding our soul security in God alone.

REFLECTION QUESTION: What helps you settle your soul and find security?

SEPTEMBER 19

Among you there must not be even a hint of sexual immorality, or of
any kind of impurity, or of greed, because these are improper for God's
holy people. Nor should there be obscenity, foolish talk or coarse joking,
which are out of place, but rather thanksgiving.

EPHESIANS 5:3–4

Finally, you'll find people masquerading as clowns or jugglers. They are always acting funny and laughing at their own jokes. They mask grief and insecurities by acting funny or cracking jokes, dealing with sober pains and sorrows through humor, as they giggle, juggle, and laugh their way through life. How easy it is to join in with crass or vulgar language among those who have not yet become followers of Jesus. In Christ, we are freed from such improper ways. As "fools for Christ" (1 Corinthians 4:10), we are empowered to pursue what is pleasing to God, by offering prayers of thanksgiving instead of empty words or vulgarities.

REFLECTION QUESTION: How often do you engage in crass joking or ungodly speech?

SEPTEMBER 20

They are darkened in their understanding and separated from the life of God because of the ignorance that is in them due to the hardening of their hearts. Having lost all sensitivity, they have given themselves over to sensuality so as to indulge in every kind of impurity, and they are full of greed. That, however, is not the way of life you learned when you heard about Christ and were taught in him in accordance with the truth that is in Jesus.

EPHESIANS 4:18–21

There are many inept ways of spirituality. All these can be transformed by the power of God's grace. When these crass and crude ways take command in a person's life, in such a way that you are unable to depart from them whenever you choose, they reveal the deeper problem of pride and arrogance. Then God's grace is unable to work upon the human soul. These are but some of the strange spiritual practices to avoid in this life. The more a person indulges in such masquerades, the harder it will be to find your way out of a life of hypocrisy and deceit, and the more these awkward ways of living will taint a person's inner being. This is especially true among people who are predisposed to instability in their heart and restlessness in their minds, who have not yet been willing to put off the old way of living and let themselves be loved with God's love. Today, may you be embraced by the Cloud of Unknowing and transformed by the grace of our Lord Jesus Christ.

REFLECTION QUESTION: Which old ways of life have you put behind you?

SEPTEMBER 21

Therefore, if anyone is in Christ, the new creation has come:
The old has gone, the new is here!

2 CORINTHIANS 5:17

You are being invited to be transformed from the inside out. Allow Christ's life to transform your life in body and spirit. As your life is being transformed by God's grace at work in you, others will begin to take notice of this change, and will be irresistibly drawn to you. Even the worst-tempered or ill-mannered person who begins to allow Jesus's life to live within them will discover God's grace working deep within their hearts, changing their inner motives and attitudes, causing their outlook on life and purpose for living to be beautifully transformed. All who come to know such people who have been helped by the grace of God will be encouraged and filled with delight when they discover the transformation that has taken place within a human soul.

REFLECTION QUESTION: How has Christ transformed you?

SEPTEMBER 22

But by the grace of God I am what I am, and his grace to me was not
without effect. No, I worked harder than all of them—yet not I, but the
grace of God that was with me.

1 CORINTHIANS 15:10

Yearn for this gift of new life, and begin allowing God's grace to reshape your life. Whoever lives in this way of grace discovers the joy of a well-disciplined life and all the benefits that come from such a way of living. With discernment, you will be able to observe many other ways of living, testing and approving God's goodwill at work in others. Observe and get to know the character and personality of others, including those who are very different from your way of life. By God's grace, you are who you are, and God's grace continues to work within your life, making you more and more who God intends for you to be.

REFLECTION QUESTION: What is the evidence of God's grace at work in you?

SEPTEMBER 23

The people walking in darkness
have seen a great light;
on those living in the land of deep darkness
a light has dawned.

ISAIAH 9:2

L ook for God's goodwill at work in people's lives: even people who currently live in the darkness of ignorance, rebellion, or wretchedness may be changing within for the good. God's light continues to shine into the darkness of this world. People who have been living in darkness keep discovering God's light shining into their lives unexpectedly. Seek the light of Christ already present and shining in people's lives. Shine Christ's light reflected through your life into the life of others. As others look into your life, and come to know the transformation underway, they will be drawn to God by help of the Holy Spirit working within your innermost being.

REFLECTION QUESTION: How has Christ's light shone through your life into others?

SEPTEMBER 24

If any of you lacks wisdom, you should ask God, who gives generously to
all without finding fault, and it will be given to you.

JAMES 1:5

A s you are transformed from within, your heart attitude and your words begin to reveal the heart of Jesus and God's Word, including fruitful ways of living with wisdom, passion, sincerity, and truth, without any deceit, hypocrisy, or superficial spirituality. There will always be those who pour all their energies, both in the inner and outer realms, into vain attempts to look better than they are, focusing all their attention on how to dress themselves with the clothes of religion. Whenever you discover your life in such a lack of wisdom, ask God to give you wisdom from above.

REFLECTION QUESTION: When have you asked God to give you wisdom?

Live in harmony with one another. Do not be proud, but be willing to associate with people of low position. Do not be conceited.

ROMANS 12:16

Some people work hard to appear more spiritual than they really are, putting on the outward look of saints. They learn how to speak religious-sounding words and make sacred gestures. They think in vain that if they put on a good enough show, no one will see their hearts of darkness and deceit. Such people live more for the fleeting approval of others than they do for the love of God, the saints, and all the holy angels. They get more stressed out about one misused word that makes them look bad before a fellow human than they do about a thousand self-centered thoughts or a whole pile of harmful attitudes of the heart. God knows that wherever you find a heart full of self-conceit, you also find a heart overflowing with false humility pouring out in a torrent of pious-sounding words. True humility is being who God made you to be, nothing more, nothing less. Discover who you are by humbling yourself before God, who loves to raise you up to become who God made you to truly be.

REFLECTION QUESTION: How much do you struggle with self-conceit or false humility?

183

SEPTEMBER 26

*Being found in appearance as a man,
he humbled himself
by becoming obedient to death—
even death on a cross!*

PHILIPPIANS 2:8

The truly humble are down-to-earth, genuine people inside and out, with sincere outward humility expressed in their words and actions originating from their humble hearts. May your outer life and inner life match. Avoid altering your tone of voice to try to sound religious or humble. Don't try to fake being spiritual. Rather, humble yourself before Jesus. Look at how Jesus also humbled himself in becoming human, and in willingly dying on the cross. Jesus will continue to lift you up and strengthen your life from the inside out.

REFLECTION QUESTION: Where do you need God's help in becoming more like Christ?

SEPTEMBER 27

Guard your steps when you go to the house of God. Go near to listen
rather than to offer the sacrifice of fools,
who do not know that they do wrong.
Do not be quick with your mouth,
do not be hasty in your heart
to utter anything before God.
God is in heaven
and you are on earth,
so let your words be few.
A dream comes when there are many cares,
and many words mark the speech of a fool.

ECCLESIASTES 5:1–3

184

When you open your mouth, learn to speak genuinely and simply with the voice God gave you, speaking from your heart. There is no point in trying to act humble in your speech or actions if humility has not yet taken hold of your heart. What more needs to be said of this sickness of the soul? Unless a person willingly receives God's grace like an antidote, they will not find healing from the disease of hypocrisy, but will continue to sink further and further into a life of deception, drowning themselves in their own self-made misery. With God's grace, received spoonful by spoonful, a person will recover from this soul sickness over time, and begin to be transformed into a beautiful new Creation from the inside out.

REFLECTION QUESTION: What has helped you become a better listener?

SEPTEMBER 28

Rid yourselves of all malice and all deceit, hypocrisy, envy, and slander of every kind. Like newborn babies, crave pure spiritual milk, so that by it you may grow up in your salvation, now that you have tasted that the Lord is good.

1 PETER 2:1–3

The spiritual life is not about following religious laws, or judging people. The spiritual life is about loving God and loving people. There are religious-looking people who think they are following God's holy way by judging others. Enflamed with passion to keep God's laws, they love to point out the faults of others who try to live for God. On the outside they appear very spiritual, keeping as busy as priests by trying to cure souls. They take it upon themselves to try to straighten other people out, thinking they are pleasing God by telling people what is wrong with their lives. They claim to be passionate about God and believe they are filled with God's love in their hearts. In truth, their minds and hearts are filled with fiery condemnation, not with love. God did not send Jesus into the world to condemn us, but to rescue us from such self-deceptions, and lead us into a life of love.

REFLECTION QUESTION: How much do you struggle with judging others?

SEPTEMBER 29

Keep your servant also from willful sins;
may they not rule over me.
Then I will be blameless,
innocent of great transgression.

PSALM 19:13

Some people allow their hearts and minds to be filled with so much criticism and condemnation that this toxic spirituality spills over in their words and actions in the way they regularly condemn others who do not measure up to perfection. They lack discernment and humility, condemning others for little pebble faults while they are blind to their own mountain of arrogance. A person who has allowed the gift of God's grace to transform both heart and mind begins humbly to see his or her own selfish conceits and unseen faults. Those who meditate upon

God's Word begin to discern between good and evil, between bad and worst, and between what is good and what is best.

REFLECTION QUESTION: With what do you fill your heart and mind?

SEPTEMBER 30

By their fruit you will recognize them. Do people pick grapes from thorn bushes, or figs from thistles?

MATTHEW 7:16

There are some people who think they've rejected hypocrisy, yet who still wander off on their hypocritical way through arrogance, intellectual pride, and misguided reason. By relying too much on their own brains and the praise of people, they leave behind the eternal wisdom and counsel of Scripture, and neglect life together in accountability with Christ's people, the church. They do not humbly root their lives in the good earth of God's love, and thus their lives do not produce the good fruit of good living. Instead, their lives produce bad-tasting fruit of a life marked by phoniness and pretense, grown in darkness by delusions. Others will surprise you, because though they do not seem to be religious, their lives produce good-tasting fruit of a life marked by humility and goodness, fruit grown in the radiance of God's love. Learn to recognize people by the fruit they produce in their lives.

REFLECTION QUESTION: What spiritual fruit is growing in your life?

Body and Soul

OCTOBER 1

I urge . . . that petitions, prayers, intercession and thanksgiving be made for all people—for kings and all those in authority, that we may live peaceful and quiet lives in all godliness and holiness. This is good, and pleases God our Savior.

1 TIMOTHY 2:1–3

There are highly cultured and articulate people who have plenty of education and hold positions of power, but who have never grown their inner life and thus remain spiritually immature. Some such people, including those in positions of leadership and power, will erupt in verbal rants, revealing a heart filled with impiety, cynicism, and sarcasm, as they condemn what is holy, putting down religion, saints, sacraments, and sacred ways of living with God. Some brilliant nonbelievers and skeptics who are excellent communicators gain a following, leading others to reject the wisdom of the Scriptures and the counsel of the church. Do not spend much time worrying about such people or railing against them. It is better to simply pray, offering such people up in intercession before God's throne of grace.

REFLECTION QUESTION: Who are you praying for?

OCTOBER 2

When you ask, you must believe and not doubt, because the one who doubts is like a wave of the sea, blown and tossed by the wind. That person should not expect to receive anything from the Lord. Such a person is double-minded and unstable in all they do.

JAMES 1:6–8

Like children playing in the ocean, followers of skeptics or agnostics put their confidence in worldly wisdom, allowing their minds and souls to be tossed around by waves of worldly passion or by empty and deceptive ways. Too often, these immature thinkers are swept away by tides of empty philosophies. They prefer to be buffeted by what is ever-changing and uncertain rather than rooted and resting their lives in what is unchanging and eternal. When you ask God to be with others, simply believe God is at work in their lives, confident that God loves to hear our prayers and answer us when we call.

REFLECTION QUESTION: How healthy is your prayer life?

OCTOBER 3

Prepare the way for the Lord,
make straight paths for him.
Every valley shall be filled in,
every mountain and hill made low.
The crooked roads shall become straight,
the rough ways smooth.

LUKE 3:4–5

There are people who refuse to enter by the little gate of humility and poverty of spirit, and who reject the small path that leads to life. Oddly, people who abandon the gate of Jesus and speak ill of the Christian faith will at the same time promote diversity as the highest virtue, and embrace every other spiritual way as acceptable. Yet, all paths do not lead to the same destination. In reality, many such roads lead to destructive ways of thinking and unhealthy ways of living. Every person needs to consider for themselves what is the wisest way, the highest truth, and the life-giving path to follow. As you consider what path to follow, also consider what burdens will be laid upon your soul along that way.

REFLECTION QUESTION: What path are you following?

OCTOBER 4

In the way of righteousness there is life;
along that path is immortality.

PROVERBS 12:28

Many paths seem to offer personal freedom, but provide no relief, rest, peace, or forgiveness for already heavy-laden souls. Some skeptics and intellectuals who promote such paths may be found parading in costumes of civility, compassion, and tolerance. Inwardly, their hearts wallow in troughs of self-indulgence, cynicism, and disgust toward all who disagree with their views and visions. As you learn to walk along the pathway of life with God, your inward life will flow genuinely and gracefully into your outward life, so that what people see on the outside is who you truly are on the inside.

REFLECTION QUESTION: How do you stay on the pathway?

OCTOBER 5

I no longer call you servants, because a servant does not know his master's business. Instead, I have called you friends, for everything that I learned from my Father I have made known to you.

JOHN 15:15

When people are filled with hubris, they allow their minds to be misled by hollow ways of thinking, and they easily misunderstand the high, upward way. Some are misled by what they read, others by what they hear. Spiritual gurus abound who preach and publish platitudes on how to transcend the limitations of mere mortality, and become one with the cosmos. Some gurus spend their lives staring at the stars as if the created universe unveiled in the night sky is the surest way to spiritual enlightenment, the easiest way to hear the angels of heaven sing. Stargazers have always sought to pierce the mysteries of the night sky, hoping to find pattern in the darkness above to make sense of the darkness within. Some have spent their whole lives making gods in their own image, dressing them with inflated human attributes, setting them upon exalted thrones among the constellations to be worshiped. Others believe there is no higher reality than the cosmos, and the highest movement of the human soul is to dissolve into the great cosmic mind. God overlooks such limited ways of thinking and invites us to step out by childlike faith and become a friend of God.

REFLECTION QUESTION: How is your friendship with God?

OCTOBER 6

They exchanged the truth about God for a lie, and worshiped and served created things rather than the Creator—who is forever praised. Amen.

ROMANS 1:25

Humans often diminish God's glory. We mistake our own imagination and mental confusions with the voices of angels or the voice of God. Unable to see our inner befuddlement, we focus on the passions pulsing within our spirit, believing we are listening to angelic messages. Sometimes we adjust our lives around these inner voices, including our diet and daily way of life, opening our minds to listen to self-made angels, eating only what someone tells us to eat, and only going where someone tells us to go. We believe we are following high ways of devotion, but our empty souls and confused minds unveil the darkness and deceit to which they've fallen prey. Don't allow your inner life to overflow with self-centeredness and dishonesty. May you learn to become God's friend, and your life will overflow with God's goodness and grace.

REFLECTION QUESTION: In the past, how have you become befuddled in your spiritual life?

OCTOBER 7

When they landed, they saw a fire of burning coals there with fish on it, and some bread.
Jesus said to them, "Bring some of the fish you have just caught."
JOHN 21:9–10

There are people who follow after visionaries of every kind, thinking saints and mystics are speaking to them from the heavenly places, guiding them to lift their eyes and hands to the skies. They tell everyone they meet to also lift their souls up, though they themselves have only been looking down into the darkness of their own self-made confusion. You are wise, instead, to lift up your eyes and hands to God, allowing your spirit to be moved by the Holy Spirit, like a fire kindled at a beach. Gather with Christ around this fire. Ultimately, the true direction of the spiritual life is not east or west, north or south, up or down, left or right, as though it is merely related to your physical body within physical space. The true direction of the spiritual life is toward friendship with God and toward others in the direction of God's fire of love.

REFLECTION QUESTION: How is the fire burning in your soul?

OCTOBER 8

I needed clothes and you clothed me, I was sick and you looked after me, I was in prison and you came to visit me.

MATTHEW 25:36

Consider the life of Martin of Tours. He saw visions of God's beauty and glory, visions given to strengthen his spiritual life. As a young soldier, Martin met an ill-dressed beggar man in winter. Moved with compassion, Martin tore his military cloak in two, giving half of the warm garment to the beggar, wrapping his own body in the other half. That night, Martin dreamed he saw the Son of God wearing the half-cloak that he'd given to the beggar. He heard the Son of God say to the angels, "This is Martin who, though still a youth, gave his cloak to me to show compassion for the poor."[38] Of course, Martin never physically gave his cloak to Jesus, for Jesus has no need of a cloak for protection from the cold. But without knowing what he was doing, Martin gave his cloak to Jesus by giving it to a beggar. Martin was leading others toward God, and that night he was given a vision in a dream to help him better understand the intimacy between heaven and earth in every compassionate action.

REFLECTION QUESTION: How have you reached out with compassion for the poor?

OCTOBER 9

The King will reply, "Truly I tell you, whatever you did for one of the least of these brothers and sisters of mine, you did for me."

MATTHEW 25:40

W hen you offer compassion to a poor person, no matter how small, you do this act of kindness for God. Every compassionate person is rewarded for their acts of kindness as if they acted physically for Jesus. Whoever shares their clothes with the poor, visits the sick, welcomes the stranger, offers food for the hungry, or does any good deed for the love of God does it for Christ, even if they are not aware of this.[39] They shall be rewarded as though they had done this action for Christ Jesus while he lived in the body.

REFLECTION QUESTION: What act of kindness for the poor will you do this week?

OCTOBER 10

The god of this age has blinded the minds of unbelievers, so that they cannot see the light of the gospel that displays the glory of Christ, who is the image of God.

2 CORINTHIANS 4:4

When Martin of Tours offered his clothing to a poor beggar man that winter's day, he was doing it for Jesus, though he did not know it at the time. Only after the dream in which he saw Jesus wearing Martin's cloak did he more fully understand the intimate relationship between earth and heaven. Dreams and visions often point beyond this earthly life into the mysteries of heaven and the spiritual way of living. Those who look on what is unseen and eternal recognize the spiritual meanings of such visions of glory, even when they appear in physical form. Therefore, learn to peel away the rough, outer skin of mortality, in order to feast upon the sweet, inner fruit of eternity. Let the light of the glory of Christ to shine into your life to guide you along the way.

REFLECTION QUESTION: When has the light of God's glory been revealed to you?

OCTOBER 11

Remain in me, as I also remain in you. No branch can bear fruit by itself; it must remain in the vine. Neither can you bear fruit unless you remain in me.

JOHN 15:4

Consider a cup of wine as a beautiful picture of our spiritual life in Christ. Wine is made from grapes, and grapes come from the vine. Abide in Christ the Vine, as Christ abides in you, and you will bear much fruit. This is a tangible miracle, God's presence expressed in physical form, through a vineyard and a chalice of wine. There are some who willfully destroy this beautiful picture by getting drunk on wine, losing self-control, and indulging themselves in gross behaviors. Just as a vine bears much fruit when it is rooted in good earth, so let your life bear much fruit by being rooted in the good earth of humility. It is better to be filled with the Spirit of God than to be drunk on the fruit of the vine. Celebrate the gift of wine; but even more, celebrate the wine of God's Spirit in your life, filling you to overflowing. Let God lift you out of every kind of self-indulgence, into the Cloud of Unknowing, and into the mystery of life with Christ where your soul is filled to overflowing with the wine of God's presence.

REFLECTION QUESTION: How are you seeking to live to the fullest?

OCTOBER 12

*Then he took a cup, and when he had given thanks, he gave it
to them, saying, "Drink from it, all of you. This is my blood of
the covenant, which is poured out for many for the forgiveness of sins."*

MATTHEW 26:27–28

The vine and the cup are intimately connected, not only in the visible realm of vineyards, grapes, and wine, but also in the invisible realm of the Spirit within the Cloud of Unknowing. For the making and drinking of wine calls the soul deeper into the mystery and miracle of Christ's passion and compassion poured out for the forgiveness of all people. When Jesus prayed in Gethsemane, he asked for the cup to be taken away from him, yet surrendered his life to God, praying "may your will be done" (Matthew 26:42). The cup Jesus spoke of was the cross where he was crucified. When Jesus died on the cross, his blood was poured out for the forgiveness of our sins. Anyone who drinks of the cup of the new covenant drinks of Christ's great love poured out for our forgiveness.

REFLECTION QUESTION: What goes on within you when you receive Communion?

195

OCTOBER 13

*I tell you, I will not drink from this fruit of the vine from now on until
that day when I drink it new with you in my Father's kingdom.*

MATTHEW 26:29

Whenever you drink of this cup, you look backward by faith, recalling the story of Jesus's death. You look forward by hope, reflecting on Christ's return. You look outward by love into the world, retelling the story of Jesus's love witnessed in his death and resurrection. Though Jesus ascended into the clouds as witnessed by his earliest followers, you do not need to look up to pray. There are many ways to drink from the fruit of God's vine. There are many ways to look with the eyes of the heart: backward and forward, inward and outward, as well as upward. God is nearer than you imagine. "Come near to God and he will come near to you" (James 4:8).

OCTOBER 14

While they were stoning him, Stephen prayed, "Lord Jesus, receive my spirit." Then he fell on his knees and cried out, "Lord, do not hold this sin against them." When he had said this, he fell asleep.

ACTS 7:59–60

Consider Stephen, the first martyr among Jesus's followers. He looked up and saw heavenly visions as he was being stoned to death. As Stephen looked with his heart, he saw Jesus standing in eternal glory ready to help him. Yet, we say, there is no need to look up when you pray. There is also no need to wonder why the Lord was standing rather than sitting or lying down. It is enough to see a heavenly vision of holy God and be encouraged to face whatever trials may come. The more your body is in tune with your spirit, the more your physical eyes will see beyond this physical world and begin to perceive spiritual truths in the Cloud of Unknowing. In the same way, the more your life is united with God's life, the more Christ's love and light will fill your eyes and your soul.

REFLECTION QUESTION: Have you ever prayed, "Lord Jesus, receive my spirit"?

OCTOBER 15

Stand firm. Let nothing move you. Always give yourselves fully to the work of the Lord, because you know that your labor in the Lord is not in vain.

1 CORINTHIANS 15:58

Just as Jesus stood by Stephen as he was being put to death, Jesus is standing by you, ready to help you as one friend helps another. When you enter the trials or conflicts you are facing today, Jesus is there by your side to encourage you. Be strengthened, friend, with stillness in your soul, standing firm in your faith. Just as Stephen was encouraged by the vision he received of Jesus standing near him as he was being stoned to death by angry people, so you will be strengthened as you look to Christ in times of trial and conflict. To see the Lord, you do not need to look up into the skies, beyond the stars. Jesus is with you, by your side, ready to help you in your time of need. Therefore, stand firm in faith, not letting anything unsettle your soul, as you continue to give yourself fully to the soul labor of loving God and loving others. Your labor for Christ's sake is never in vain.

REFLECTION QUESTION: How firm do you stand in your faith in the face of troubles?

OCTOBER 16

But Stephen, full of the Holy Spirit, looked up to heaven and saw the glory of God, and Jesus standing at the right hand of God. "Look," he said, "I see heaven open and the Son of Man standing at the right hand of God."

ACTS 7:55–56

The goal of the spiritual life is unity with God in body and soul. Just before St. Stephen was stoned to death, he looked up to heaven and saw a glorious vision of the unity of God. In the same way, many eyewitnesses looked up into the heavens at the time of Jesus's ascension. Because the early followers of Jesus looked up into the sky at Jesus's ascension, and St. Stephen looked up into heaven at death, must we look upward to be united with God? Not at all. Jesus reveals to us the fullness of God, wherever we look. We enter into unity with God in our body and soul by entering into life with Jesus. Just as Jesus ascended into the clouds, so we also can ascend into the Cloud of Unknowing, where we may enjoy unity with God in body and soul.

REFLECTION QUESTION: Do you rely more upon your body or your soul?

OCTOBER 17

Since we have a great high priest who has ascended into heaven, Jesus the Son of God, let us hold firmly to the faith we profess.

HEBREWS 4:14

St. Stephen's vision revealed Jesus standing bodily at the right hand of God. The Scriptures tell us that Jesus was raised from the dead in a physical body. Jesus ascended into heaven in body and soul. All who enter into unity with God through Jesus will be raised to fullness of life on the final day, in body and soul. The faith we profess teaches us that our bodies matter to God just as our souls matter to God. Jesus stands by us, as a friend stands by a friend, to support us and defend us in times of trouble. Keep holding on to the faith you profess, faith in Jesus, the Son of God, who lived fully in a human body, was raised bodily, and ascended into heaven in body and soul. Your body is a gift from God. Your soul is a gift from God. God has made you body and soul to become like Jesus. Just as Jesus triumphed over mortality, death, and the grave, so Jesus invites you to have life to the fullest in body and soul.

REFLECTION QUESTION: How do you view your body?

OCTOBER 18

For you created my inmost being;
you knit me together in my mother's womb.
I praise you because I am fearfully and wonderfully made;
your works are wonderful,
I know that full well.

PSALM 139:13–14

On the final day, as you cross over the threshold into eternity, you will look back on your mortal life on earth and marvel how wonderfully your life has been knit together, an interweaving of body and soul beginning in your mother's womb. With such a vision of the inner unity of body and soul, physical directions become less significant. It matters less what is up or down, side to side, behind or before. It matters more to grow in love with God and with others. While on earth, you are not able to come to heaven physically, but only spiritually. Though you may describe your spiritual experiences as up or down, side to side, behind or before, this movement is less about your body and more about your soul.

REFLECTION QUESTION: What most influences the way you think about your body?

OCTOBER 19

Where can I go from your Spirit?
Where can I flee from your presence?
If I go up to the heavens, you are there;
if I make my bed in the depths, you are there.

PSALM 139:7–8

Pay attention when someone writes or talks about the spiritual life. Whenever they speak about being "lifted up" or "going in," they are describing the journey of the soul, not of the body. Though body and soul are intimately woven together, the movement of the spiritual life is not primarily about doing something physical such as moving your body up or down, in or out, ahead or behind. No matter how high you go, nor how low your life gets, God is present with you, to encourage and strengthen you with God's Spirit.

REFLECTION QUESTION: How has God encouraged you in a low time?

OCTOBER 20

Truly my soul finds rest in God;
my salvation comes from him.

PSALM 62:1

Even the beautiful experience of rest is not primarily about closing your eyes, laying your head upon a pillow on a bed, and going to sleep. May your soul find rest in God alone. All who believe are invited by God to rest our lives in God. This soul rest may come in the middle of physical work just as surely as while your body rests while you dream upon your bed in the middle of the night. The gift of rest comes to all who seek their rest in God alone, a gift that refreshes both body and soul. Enter that rest.

REFLECTION QUESTION: How hard is it for you to rest in God?

OCTOBER 21

My soul yearns, even faints,
for the courts of the LORD;
my heart and my flesh cry out
for the living God.
Even the sparrow has found a home,
and the swallow a nest for herself,
where she may have her young—
a place near your altar,
LORD Almighty, my King and my God.

PSALM 84:2–3

There will come times in your life when a spark of love is ignited in you. When this fire is kindled, physical coordinates such as time and place become less significant; however, spiritual signposts such as love and grace become more significant. The experience is happening within your body and within your soul. You hear your body and soul crying out for the living God. When a vision of heaven opens up before your eyes, body posture and the exact time on the clock are less important than the beautiful truth that you are finding your way back home to God.

REFLECTION QUESTION: How are you helping someone else find their way back home?

OCTOBER 22

[Jacob] stopped for the night because the sun had set. Taking one of
the stones there, he put it under his head and lay down to sleep. He
had a dream in which he saw a stairway resting on the earth, with its
top reaching to heaven, and the angels of God were ascending and
descending on it.

GENESIS 28:11–12

While body posture has some value, such as kneeling prayer, or lifting up your hands, more important is that your soul is kindled with flames of love for God and others. Jacob encountered God while dreaming during the middle of the night as he was lying out in nature with his head on a stone pillow. In his dream, he heard God speak to him as though from the top of a stairway reaching from earth to heaven, speaking these promises: "I am with you and will watch over you wherever you go, and I will bring you back to this land. I will not leave you until I have done what I have promised you" (Genesis 28:15). God is with you and does not leave you, even when it seems as though God is far, far away. Even if you could climb beyond the moon and the stars, you still would find yourself the same distance from heaven as when you took your first step up the stairway into heaven.

REFLECTION QUESTION: How near or far does God seem to you?

OCTOBER 23

He knows the way that I take;
when he has tested me, I will come forth as gold.
My feet have closely followed his steps;
I have kept to his way without turning aside.

JOB 23:10–11

You cannot climb to heaven alone. Even the finest athletes are unable to run or climb or jump or fly high enough to attain to God's eternal glory. Everyone falls short. There has never been anyone who has ever climbed up into heaven except the one who first climbed down out of heaven. Only by Jesus's side, only with Jesus walking by your side, can you make this ascent. Come with Christ and walk alongside him in body and in soul, in this life, and in the life to come, upward into the Cloud of Unknowing.

REFLECTION QUESTION: How have you sought to follow in Jesus's steps?

OCTOBER 24

"For my thoughts are not your thoughts,
neither are your ways my ways,"
declares the LORD.
"As the heavens are higher than the earth,
so are my ways higher than your ways
and my thoughts than your thoughts."

ISAIAH 55:8–9

You may be wondering why most people think of heaven as above. After all, the direction Jesus ascended into heaven was upward, and the Holy Spirit descends from above, downward upon humans, as seen at Jesus's baptism in the Jordan River, when the Holy Spirit descended in bodily form like a dove. Why not then direct your attention in an upward direction when praying or meditating upon God? The answer may surprise you. People tend to try to understand eternal matters from a mortal perspective. To help you understand, seek to look upon what is unseen, from an eternal perspective. For God's thoughts are not like our thoughts; nor are our ways God's ways.

REFLECTION QUESTION: How might God's ways become more your ways?

OCTOBER 25

The Holy Spirit descended on him in bodily form like a dove. And a
voice came from heaven: "You are my Son, whom I love;
with you I am well pleased."

LUKE 3:22

So often, the language used in the Bible is used to help humans make sense of what is a mystery. It makes more sense to mortal minds that Jesus went up and the Holy Spirit came down. Up and down makes more sense to the imagination than saying the movement is from within, beneath, behind, before, alongside, or some other direction. But from an eternal perspective, direction is less important than devotion. The distance is all the same when measured by love. It is something like getting out your measuring tape and trying to measure love. It will make as much sense trying to do this as trying to understand up or down, behind or before, from a spiritual point of view.

REFLECTION QUESTION: What measure do you most often use to assess your life?

OCTOBER 26

Jesus replied, "The coming of the kingdom of God is not something that can be observed, nor will people say, 'Here it is,' or 'There it is,' because the kingdom of God is in your midst."

LUKE 17:20–21

Heaven is as near to you in the depths of your soul as it is in the heights of your soul. Heaven is both behind you and before you, as well as on either side. Just as the air you breath is all around and within you, so heaven is all around you, above and below, behind and before, by your side and in your midst. Anyone who truly yearns to be in heaven may be surprised to discover they have already entered and tasted of heaven's joys. The pathway to heaven is not measured by miles and feet, but by love. Set your heart on love and you'll find you've set your heart on a heavenly pilgrimage.

REFLECTION QUESTION: In what way is your life a pilgrimage?

OCTOBER 27

We know and rely on the love God has for us.

1 JOHN 4:16

The surest and quickest way to heaven is to set your heart to love God and love others. As St. Paul declares, "Christ's love compels us" (2 Corinthians 5:14). So many other forces will try to take first place and become the main motive in your life. Although we live physically here on earth, our true life and love are with God in heaven. Loving and being loved is what matters most in life. Get to know God's love personally and rely on the love that God has for you. Whatever your soul loves most reveals whether your soul is living or dying. Live in love and God's love will live in you.

REFLECTION QUESTION: What are some of the main forces that motivate your life?

OCTOBER 28

This is love: that we walk in obedience to his commands. As you have heard from the beginning, his command is that you walk in love.

2 JOHN 6

To get to heaven, you do not need to break a sweat or strain yourself with physical exertion. You do not need to starve yourself to death or crawl up mountains on your knees or bloody yourself with whips or freeze your body by lying in the snow. God does not ask for any heroics. Simply live in love. "God is love. Whoever lives in love lives in God, and God in them" (1 John 4:16b).[40] Heaven is not discovered by looking above or below, outside or inside, behind or before, up or down. Heaven is discovered by following God along the path of love.

REFLECTION QUESTION: How goes your walk with God?

OCTOBER 29

By day the LORD went ahead of them in a pillar of cloud to guide them on their way and by night in a pillar of fire to give them light, so that they could travel by day or night.

EXODUS 13:21

As you walk the path of love on your way heavenward, you'll find it worthwhile to look to the sky. You will discover many around you who look down much of the time, who have faces that are downcast. There are many burdens and weights that can come upon the soul, and cause us to look down rather than look up. Try looking up. By day, look up at the clouds illuminated by the light of the sun. By night, look up at the night sky, at the moon and the stars stretching out across the dark canopy of space. Just as ancient Israel was guided by a cloud by day and a pillar of fire by night, look up to God, and to God's Creation in the clouds by day and fiery stars by night.

REFLECTION QUESTION: In your spiritual life, do you tend to look down or look up?

OCTOBER 30

The Son is the image of the invisible God, the firstborn over all creation. For in him all things were created: things in heaven and on earth, visible and invisible, whether thrones or powers or rulers or authorities; all things have been created through him and for him. He is before all things, and in him all things hold together.

COLOSSIANS 1:15–17

Allow God ample space to work in your soul, as these reflections on Creation inspire your spirit. As David wrote long ago, "The heavens declare the glory of God; the skies proclaim the work of his hands. Day after day they pour forth speech; night after night they reveal knowledge" (Psalm 19:1–2). All Creation, from the smallest particle to the grandest galaxy, pulsates with God's power and glory. Through God's voice, all things were created. In Christ, all things hold together. Everything in the whole universe is held together by God. Spiritual life empowers and energizes physical life.

REFLECTION QUESTION: How is your life held together by Christ?

OCTOBER 31

In your relationships with one another, have the same mindset as Christ Jesus:
Who, being in very nature God,
did not consider equality with God something to be used to his own advantage;
rather, he made himself nothing
by taking the very nature of a servant,
being made in human likeness.

PHILIPPIANS 2:5–7

Look at the way Jesus came to earth and the way Jesus departed from earth. In his birth, Jesus descended out of eternity into time, coming down from glory to begin life on earth as a baby in a lowly place, humbling himself to be born into human flesh taking on "the very nature of a servant." Years later, as a fully grown adult, just after he said his final words of blessing to the people gathered, Jesus was taken up into heaven while the people looked upward. His body was taken up and they watched him ascend until a cloud hid him from their sight. Jesus's destination was not some physical place among the clouds or the stars but a reunion with God in eternal glory.

REFLECTION QUESTION: How can you live more in the mindset of Christ Jesus?

November

Soul Powers

NOVEMBER 1

We know that if the earthly tent we live in is destroyed, we have a building from God, an eternal house in heaven, not built by human hands. Meanwhile we groan, longing to be clothed instead with our heavenly dwelling, because when we are clothed, we will not be found naked.

2 CORINTHIANS 5:1–3

In his departing, Jesus ascended into eternity, going up into heaven to be reunited with God in glory, exalted in body and spirit. Those first followers watched his body going up into the clouds so that they would better understand that mortal human bodies are intended for immortality. While you are still in your physical body, you are never far from pain and suffering because of the burden of mortality that weighs you down. Consider the lives of the saints who have gone before us, facing suffering and death, yet pressing on by faith, fixing their eyes on what is unseen and eternal. All who follow Jesus will be clothed one day with a new body, our new eternal dwelling, so "what is mortal may be swallowed up by life" (2 Corinthians 5:4).

REFLECTION QUESTION: Which of the saints have most influenced your life?

NOVEMBER 2

We all, who with unveiled faces contemplate the Lord's glory, are being transformed into his image with ever-increasing glory, which comes from the Lord, who is the Spirit.

2 CORINTHIANS 3:18

Yield your body and spirit to God's Spirit. That is what is at the heart of this book you are reading. The more you allow yourself to live in this way of love, the more your body and spirit will be invigorated by this great purpose and passion. At first, you discovered that your body and spirit were often directed in a mortal direction, toward perishable bodily passions, hungers, fears, frustrations, and darkness. By virtue of the Holy Spirit at work within your spirit, you began to turn your attention heavenward, toward the Cloud of Unknowing. You discovered with delight that you could see anew and live in a new way. Keep looking with love into God's face, and you'll discover that you are being transformed into God's beautiful image from one degree of glory to the next.

NOVEMBER 3

God saw all that he had made, and it was very good. And there was evening, and there was morning—the sixth day.

GENESIS 1:31

Of all the beautiful creatures made by God, humans are the loveliest since we are made in God's own image. God made us to walk with two feet, not upon all fours with our heads to the ground as most other animals. With our two feet upon the earth, our eyes are able to gaze upward into the heavens. Our bodies express the design of God for our soul. God desires for us to stand and walk upright in our spiritual life, just as we learned to stand and walk upright when we were babies. God also desires for us to learn to look with our soul upon heaven. Keep looking up to your heavenly Father, who reaches out with loving arms to receive you as you walk in this way of love.

REFLECTION QUESTION: Upon what do you base your self-image?

NOVEMBER 4

See to it that no one takes you captive through hollow and deceptive philosophy, which depends on human tradition and the elemental spiritual forces of this world rather than on Christ. For in Christ all the fullness of the Deity lives in bodily form, and in Christ you have been brought to fullness.

COLOSSIANS 2:8–10

Be attentive to words and their meanings. Jesus was a master at using earthly pictures to help us understand heavenly principles. Your ears may hear physical words, but your heart may hear spiritual truths. Though people often use physical directions for spiritual guidance, the spiritual life is much more than up or down, behind or before, left or right. Just as we rely upon our physical tongues to speak about spiritual truths, we also need to rely upon God's Spirit to help us discern God's instructions and follow in God's way. As mortals, we easily misunderstand immortality. Our spiritual life is much more than reading words on a page, looking into the night sky with our eyes, or following directions on a compass. We begin to comprehend the mystery and fullness of spiritual life with God when we enter the Cloud of Unknowing and learn to listen to Christ.

REFLECTION QUESTION: Where do you look to see God?

NOVEMBER 5

The body that is sown is perishable, it is raised imperishable; it is sown in dishonor, it is raised in glory; it is sown in weakness, it is raised in power; it is sown a natural body, it is raised a spiritual body. If there is a natural body, there is also a spiritual body.

1 CORINTHIANS 15:42–44

That we may better understand the spiritual wonders and workings beyond human senses, Scripture often uses word pictures of ordinary physical life and labor. There are many kinds of bodies. Some are mortal, some immortal. Though God made the physical body, the physical body is perishable. God wants you to understand in a spiritual way when considering what is beneath you, what is within you, and what is above you. Physical things are "beneath" spiritual things. Your physical body is "beneath" your soul, at least in the truest nature of understanding. We are wise to focus our lives upon what will never perish.

REFLECTION QUESTION: How do you view your body?

NOVEMBER 6

There are also heavenly bodies and there are earthly bodies; but the splendor of the heavenly bodies is one kind, and the splendor of the earthly bodies is another. The sun has one kind of splendor, the moon another and the stars another; and star differs from star in splendor.

1 CORINTHIANS 15:40–41

Even though the sun and moon along with all the stars are above your head in the sky, they too are "beneath" your soul in their form and nature. God made the heavenly bodies, including the moon, sun, and all the stars. All these differ in their glory, some with reflected glory such as the moon, and others with radiant glory. All heavenly bodies, all angels, and all heavenly messengers, though created with beauty, excellence, and purity, are alongside you in their true form and nature, as part of the whole symphony of Creation, playing God's heavenly music to encourage you in your spiritual life and journey.

REFLECTION QUESTION: How does Creation help you in your spiritual life?

NOVEMBER 7

Hear, O Israel: The LORD our God, the LORD is one. Love the LORD your God with all your heart and with all your soul and with all your strength.

DEUTERONOMY 6:4–5

In the days ahead, we will consider the unique powers of the soul. The primary aspects of the soul include our reason and our will. The secondary powers of the soul include our imagination and our senses. Each of these are within you as part of our true form and nature. Each of these unique parts of our soul are given to us as gifts to lead us closer to God, who is above us in nature. God is above everything. God is above all Creation and far beyond our soul. God is also closer to us than our breath is to our body. God is One, and there is no other like God. God loves to give gifts to us, and God loves to empower our soul.

REFLECTION QUESTION: Which soul power best leads you closer to God?

NOVEMBER 8

Jesus answered, "Everyone who drinks this water will be thirsty again, but whoever drinks the water I give them will never thirst. Indeed, the water I give them will become in them a spring of water welling up to eternal life."

JOHN 4:13–14

Whenever you read spiritual writings describing the human soul, though they are written with metaphors using bodily language, the meaning points beyond what can be known by your body, your senses, or your intelligence alone. Jesus often spoke in pictures, describing eternal life as a spring of water welling up within the human soul, or as a seed planted in a field. There is a realm above and beyond the physical and material universe, a realm of eternal radiance and delight within the Cloud of Unknowing that the soul may penetrate only with help from God. The more we focus our attention upon what is of eternal worth, and upon what lies beyond mortality, the more we will know and truly understand what is beneath us, what is within us, and what is above.

REFLECTION QUESTION: How do you picture eternal life?

NOVEMBER 9

With minds that are alert and fully sober, set your hope on the grace to be brought to you when Jesus Christ is revealed at his coming. As obedient children, do not conform to the evil desires you had when you lived in ignorance.

1 PETER 1:13–14

Your mind is a gift from God, designed by the mind of God. You've been given power in your soul, including your mind, expressed through reason, will, imagination, and senses. These powers are held within your soul to help you live more fully in God's presence. These soul powers are given to help you comprehend the mysteries of God and treasure them. Some of these soul powers are leaders and some are supporters. Your soul is not divided up into different compartments but functions in different ways. In light of each of these, some are primary and some secondary, just as spiritual matters are primary and physical matters are secondary. We are wise when we admit our ignorance regarding the mysteries of the human soul. Seek to grow in understanding of how God has made your body and soul.

REFLECTION QUESTION: What confuses you about your mind or your soul?

NOVEMBER 10

Since the day we heard about you, we have not stopped praying for you. We continually ask God to fill you with the knowledge of his will through all the wisdom and understanding that the Spirit gives.

COLOSSIANS 1:9

Let's consider how the unique powers of the soul are meant to work. Learn to focus your mind through your reason, and your will to live more fully in God's presence, and they will begin to find their purpose and place within your life. God loves to fill our minds with spiritual understanding and empower our will to do God's will. Your imagination and your senses are more intimately connected to your physical life and bodily awareness, though they primarily are soul powers. Left to themselves, without the help of your reason and will, your imagination and your senses will not be of much help in discovering and developing your spiritual life with God. We need all our soul powers to best comprehend and understand the purpose of human life among all Creation, within the vastness and wonder of the cosmos.

REFLECTION QUESTION: What place do reason and will have in your life?

NOVEMBER 11

Make every effort to add to your faith goodness; and to goodness, knowledge; and to knowledge, self-control; and to self-control, perseverance; and to perseverance, godliness; and to godliness, mutual affection; and to mutual affection, love.

2 PETER 1:5–7

Your reason and will are primary powers of the soul, intended to lead you closer to God. They work in accord with your spirit and God's Spirit, with fewer distractions from the physical and sensual realms. Your imagination and senses are secondary powers. They work within the physical realms, helping your body learn to live in harmony with your soul and with the Holy Spirit. We all have choices to make about how best to grow in our spiritual life. Choose today to use the powers God has given you to grow your life with God. As St. Peter encourages us, "make every effort to add to your faith." With God's grace active in your soul, learn to use your God-given powers of reason and will to add to your faith and grow spiritual fruit of goodness, knowledge, self-control, perseverance, godliness, mutual affection, and love.

REFLECTION QUESTION: How have you sought to better understand God's thoughts and ways?

NOVEMBER 12

The heart of the discerning acquires knowledge,
for the ears of the wise seek it out.

PROVERBS 18:15

God gave us the soul power of our reason to help us turn away from evil and turn toward good. Use reason to discern between good and evil in your daily life. But also learn to use your reason to discern what is good, better, and best. Every day, we make many choices between what is evil or good, what is bad or worst, what is better or best. When sin enters into human life, our reason is blinded. When we are blinded in our reason, we are unable to distinguish good from evil, or what is worst from what is best. Ask God to heal your blindness. Illumined by God's grace we can be healed of this blindness. God gave us the power of reason to draw us closer to God. With God's grace shining in your soul, keep turning away from evil and continue turning toward good. By God's illuminating grace, learn to use reason and will to choose what is good, better, and best.

REFLECTION QUESTION: How have you learned to discern between what is good, better, and best?

NOVEMBER 13

God, who said, "Let light shine out of darkness," made his light shine in
our hearts to give us the light of the knowledge of God's glory displayed
in the face of Christ.

2 CORINTHIANS 4:6

If your reason is blinded by the idols of this age, you will not be able to see the light of God's good news displayed in the glory of Christ, who is the very image of God. God's very first words recorded in Scripture were, "Let there be light" (Genesis 1:3). The Creator of light continues to shine into human hearts and minds to give you the light of the knowledge of God's glory. Your reason and your will live in the dark until you open the blinds, allowing your soul to be illuminated by God's grace as you look into Christ's face.

REFLECTION QUESTION: What idols of this age have blinded you?

NOVEMBER 14

If serving the Lord seems undesirable to you, then choose for yourselves this day whom you will serve. . . . But as for me and my household, we will serve the Lord.

JOSHUA 24:15

Another soul power is our will. With our will, we have power not merely to understand good and evil, but to choose between good and evil. Ask God to awaken and empower your will with grace. By God's grace at work within our will, we are empowered to choose what is good, better, and best. With our will, we learn to love what is good. With our will, we choose whom we will serve, how to lay down our lives in this loving service. Daily choose what is loving and good. Decide what will bring rest to your soul, what will bring joy to your life, and what will help the lives of others. Learn to actively choose God's goodwill among the many choices before you each day. Then you will find rest for your soul in God's goodness, with fullness of delight and contentment.

216

REFLECTION QUESTION: What choices do you make each day that reflect whom you serve?

NOVEMBER 15

*Taste and see that the Lord is good;
blessed is the one who takes refuge in him.*

PSALM 34:8

We were made by God to naturally chose what is good and pleasing to God. God placed within us an inner ability to choose goodness. But because of the infection of sin, our will has been corrupted by dark desires. Too often, people seek what is evil and dishonoring to God. Let God's grace renew your reason and will. Begin to truly taste God's goodness at work within your soul. Look for evidence of God's goodness in everyday life. Take time daily to savor God's presence in ordinary moments. "Then you will be able to test and approve what God's will is—his good, pleasing and perfect will" (Romans 12:2).

REFLECTION QUESTION: In what ways today will you taste God's goodness?

NOVEMBER 16

Let the wise listen and add to their learning,
and let the discerning get guidance.

PROVERBS 1:5

Like getting an infection in your body, so often, people can become sickened or unhealthy in their mind, including in their reason and will. Just as a sick body loses appetite and taste for healthy food, so with an infection of the soul, you are unable to taste what is good for the soul. People get confused, thinking a thing is good when it is full of corruption, simply because has the appearance of being good. We are often attracted to what looks good and even feels good, but is actually harmful or destructive. Learn to use your reason and your will to grow closer to God. Whenever unhealthy distractions take your focus off of God, pray using a single word or phrase to break through into the Cloud of Unknowing, where you are surrounded once again by what is true and good. As St. Paul wrote, "Whatever is true, whatever is noble, whatever is right, whatever is pure, whatever is lovely, whatever is admirable—if anything is excellent or praiseworthy—think about such things" (Philippians 4:8).

REFLECTION QUESTION: Where do you go for spiritual guidance?

NOVEMBER 17

To him who is able to do immeasurably more than all we ask or
imagine, according to his power that is at work within us, to him be
glory in the church and in Christ Jesus throughout all generations, for
ever and ever! Amen.

EPHESIANS 3:20–21

Let us consider the gift of the imagination. At this moment, very likely, there are several images forming in your mind, sparked by what you've been reading, or by some other influence. Your imagination is a wonderful gift from God, the power to envision physical and spiritual entities, including things tangible and intangible. Human imagination is intended by God to serve reason as a servant serves a good master. With our imagination, we are able to bring God-honoring images, pictures, and stories to life, to help us and others live more fully for God. With our imagination, we may ascend into the heights of heaven, to perceive anew what lies beyond words in the mysterious Cloud of Unknowing. With our imagination, we discover God doing immeasurably more with our life than we asked for or dreamed possible.

REFLECTION QUESTION: What do you imagine God may do in your life?

NOVEMBER 18

Watch out for those who cause divisions and put obstacles in your way that are contrary to the teaching you have learned. Keep away from them. For such people are not serving our Lord Christ, but their own appetites. By smooth talk and flattery they deceive the minds of naive people. Everyone has heard about your obedience, so I rejoice because of you; but I want you to be wise about what is good, and innocent about what is evil.

ROMANS 16:17–19

Without the guiding power and radiance of divine grace flooding your imagination, your mind will work overtime, day and night, producing myriads of images of fantasies and wild stories that have little or nothing to do with God. Some of these images are spiritual ideas masquerading as attractive bodies, while others are bodily seductions parading through your mind as spiritual truths. How easy it is today to be led astray by such deceits and falsehoods. Keep looking to Christ, who began your soul's journey and who will be there when you complete your journey home.

REFLECTION QUESTION: How has your imagination confused you in the past?

NOVEMBER 19

Do not offer any part of yourself to sin as an instrument of wickedness, but rather offer yourselves to God as those who have been brought from death to life; and offer every part of yourself to him as an instrument of righteousness.

ROMANS 6:13

Too often, today, human imagination has not yet been yielded to God, nor subjected to human reason. People who are new to walking in the spiritual way of contemplative prayer with God can easily be led astray by their imaginations, unless their reason is brought under the guidance of the light of God's grace. Offer your imagination to God to be trained and restrained by the habit of meditating on spiritual truths, such as your own weakness of spirit, or the strength and compassion of Christ's passion and cross. Bring every darkened thought into the brilliance of God's light.

REFLECTION QUESTION: What are you offering to God today?

NOVEMBER 20

The weapons we fight with are not the weapons of the world. On the contrary, they have divine power to demolish strongholds. We demolish arguments and every pretension that sets itself up against the knowledge of God, and we take captive every thought to make it obedient to Christ.

2 CORINTHIANS 10:4–5

Some people refuse to train their imagination. Instead of bringing every thought captive to Christ, they expose themselves to many unnecessary sorrows and miss out on many joys and delights. You will find yourself tossed and spun around by many fruitless fantasies, some of which may seem truly wonderful at first, but have little substance to feed you or to bring about true transformation of all that you are. As thoughts come into your mind, bring them before Christ, who declared himself to be "the way and the truth and the life" (John 14:6). With Christ's grace and power at work in our reason, will, and imagination, we are able to demolish strongholds of deception and pretension. As one who knows God and loves God, be willing to walk through doors of humility and compassion into the lives of people who have been held captive to help them discover the truth that can set them free.

REFLECTION QUESTION: How have you yielded your thought life to Christ?

NOVEMBER 21

*The life appeared; we have seen it and testify to it, and we proclaim to you the
eternal life, which was with the Father and has appeared to us. We proclaim to
you what we have seen and heard, so that you also may have fellowship with us.
And our fellowship is with the Father and with his Son, Jesus Christ.*

1 JOHN 1:2–3

Your senses also are gifts from God, empowering your soul to
connect with the natural world through your mind. Through
touch, taste, smell, sight, and sound, you gain understanding of
the physical universe. What you touch is sometimes soft and sometimes
abrasive. Some foods taste sweet and some sour. Some smells are
fragrant and others are odious. Some sights are beautiful and others
are unattractive to your eyes. Not all sounds you hear are melodious.
Through our senses, we encounter a wide variety of experiences, both
pleasing and unpleasing, harmful and edifying.

REFLECTION QUESTION: How do your senses bring you closer to Christ?

NOVEMBER 22

*The woman said to him, "Sir, give me this water so that I won't get
thirsty and have to keep coming here to draw water."*

JOHN 4:15

Your senses act in two distinct ways. Either they support your
basic physical needs, or they indulge your sensual lusts. Learn
to discern the difference between what you need and what you
lust after. With your senses, you know when your body is hungry, thirsty,
or tired. Senses help you stay healthy with basic life-giving practices
of eating, drinking, and sleeping. With your senses, sometimes your
appetites are overindulged, causing you to eat too much, drink too much,
or sleep too much, giving in to vices of gluttony, drunkenness, or sloth.
By God's grace, we may use our senses to grow the spiritual fruit of self-
control, offering our life to God more completely when we are thirsty,
hungry, blind, tired, or out of touch.

REFLECTION QUESTION: How has your thirst, hunger, or tiredness help
you come closer to God?

NOVEMBER 23

Very early in the morning, while it was still dark, Jesus got up, left the house and went off to a solitary place, where he prayed.

MARK 1:35

With your senses, your body sometimes feels pain when lacking basic needs, and sometimes feels pleasure when these basic needs have been met. There are times when your senses cause you to feel pain in the company of people, especially those who are undesirable; and other times when your senses cause you to experience pleasure in solitude. Your senses and the influence they have upon your life are aspects of your soul at work, helping you live more fully for God. Learn to use your five senses to draw your life closer to God in prayer.

REFLECTION QUESTION: How has some form of sensory deprivation helped you?

NOVEMBER 24

Train yourself to be godly. For physical training is of some value, but godliness has value for all things, holding promise for both the present life and the life to come.

1 TIMOTHY 4:7–8

Senses were designed by God to keep us in tune with God, eagerly serving the goodwill of God without any grumbling, hypocrisy, or spiritual seductions. But senses can be corrupted or misused, making it much more difficult for your senses to simply serve the goodwill of God. Unless you yield your senses to God's grace and God's goodwill, they will often lead you astray. Humbly accept some discipline and training of your senses. This is part of what it means to be human. Learn how to fast. Learn to live without some basic life comforts, and be willing to put up with some discomfort through spiritual disciplines for the purpose of coming closer to God.

REFLECTION QUESTION: In what ways do you discipline your bodily appetites?

NOVEMBER 25

Anyone who lives on milk, being still an infant, is not acquainted with the teaching about righteousness. But solid food is for the mature, who by constant use have trained themselves to distinguish good from evil.

HEBREWS 5:13–14

Allow physical suffering or discomfort to teach you, as you learn to restrain from indulging in physical pleasures that are destructive. Without such restraint, you will wallow as a pig in the muck of self-indulgent lusts, including the lusts of the body, the lust for wealth, and the lust for power.[41] We were not made to lust. We were made to love, to love God, to love ourselves, and to love others. We are designed by God to rise above lower ways of lust, to become fully human, as our soul is made new in God's grace. Be willing to be trained and to grow up into maturity in Christ.

REFLECTION QUESTION: When did you first begin eating solid food in your spiritual growth?

NOVEMBER 26

As I have often told you before and now tell you again even with tears, many live as enemies of the cross of Christ. Their destiny is destruction, their god is their stomach, and their glory is in their shame. Their mind is set on earthly things.

PHILIPPIANS 3:18–19

How is a soul made new? God desires to be with you as a spiritual friend, hoping that you will better understand how your life may be transformed from the inside out. There are many misconceptions about this mystery. This should come as no surprise. People often walk in darkness, blinded to spiritual truths and practices. This is especially true concerning the unique abilities of the soul and the ways the soul grows. When your mind is focused upon physical or bodily things, you are engaging in what is transitory, not in what is eternal. You are created for eternity. Though you live in time and must daily engage in earthly things, learn to set your mind and heart on things above, in life with God.

REFLECTION QUESTION: How is your spiritual life being transformed by God?

NOVEMBER 27

Make every effort to enter through the narrow door, because many,
I tell you, will try to enter and will not be able to.

LUKE 13:24

Occupy your attention with the amazing powers of your soul and with spiritual practices that will transform you. Seek to better understand the live-giving way of virtue and the destructive way of vice. Both of these ways are within you at any given moment. Learn to know yourself better, becoming aware of the destructive ways at work in your life. "Make every effort to enter through the narrow door," as our Lord instructs us, entering into the way of spiritual maturity. Live more for the soul than the body. In this way, body and soul will mature, helping you become more and more who you truly are with Christ. When you set your heart on what is above rather than on your body or soul, you will discover life being more and more transformed into God's beautiful character and image. You will begin to live less for yourself, and more for God.

REFLECTION QUESTION: What effort are you making to enter the narrow way of life with Christ?

NOVEMBER 28

I have given them the glory that you gave me that they may be one as
we are one—I in them and you in me—so that they may be brought to
complete unity. Then the world will know that you sent me and have
loved them even as you have loved me.

JOHN 17:22–23

The more you live fully for God, the more God's grace will flow into your life, transforming your soul in a way that is impossible by mere human effort. In this way, you will be united with Christ, a union in spirit, love, and will. Of course, God's thoughts will always be higher than our thoughts, and God's ways higher than our ways. Even when your soul enjoys union with God, you will always be human and God will always be God. Even though Scripture speaks of your life becoming one with God, this oneness is the union of a love relationship between two loving beings, not the dissolving of your soul into the ocean of God.

REFLECTION QUESTION: How would you describe the unity you have with Christ?

NOVEMBER 29

I am the LORD, and there is no other;
apart from me there is no God.

ISAIAH 45:5

God alone is God. We will never become God. Though people in every age will try to persuade others that they can become fully divine as God is fully divine, know the truth of who you are and who God is. As the Lord declared through the prophet Isaiah, "apart from me there is no God" (Isaiah 45:5). Even when you feel so united to God that you are caught up into Christ's presence, losing all sense of time and space, in union with God's eternal love, you are still human and not God. Why is this? Because God is God, by nature without beginning and without end. Our days are numbered. But from everlasting to everlasting, God is God.

REFLECTION QUESTION: When have you been closely united to God?

NOVEMBER 30

Suppose one of you has a hundred sheep and loses one of them. Doesn't
he leave the ninety-nine in the open country and go after the lost
sheep until he finds it? And when he finds it, he joyfully puts it on his
shoulders and goes home.

LUKE 15:4–6

By God's creative power and love, we came into being, and were born into this world. By our own choice, we wander away from God, causing distance and disruption in our relationship with God, making our life worse and worse. By God's grace and mercy, we are brought back to God. The Good Shepherd finds us, joyfully puts us upon his shoulders, and carries us home. As we find our way back to God, we unite our souls with God in a union that began in time on earth but will continue without interruption with unending joy in heaven. So, though we are far beneath God in our nature, by God's grace may we come to know union with God in the perfect unity of love.

REFLECTION QUESTION: How is your relationship with God right now?

December

Longing for Paradise

DECEMBER 1

You will call on me and come and pray to me, and I will listen to you.
You will seek me and find me when you seek me with all your heart.

JEREMIAH 29:12–13

As a spiritual friend of God, may you see glimpses of the mystery of life with God. Those who do not know the creative power within their own soul and the spiritual patterns for soul-making easily get confused or deceived in trying to understand such spiritual instructions as have been written in these pages. Therefore, play those childlike games such as hide-and-seek. The more we seek God by dying to our selfish ways, hiding our life with Christ in God, the more God's life will appear in our lives, and so we will appear with Christ in eternal glory.

REFLECTION QUESTION: In what ways are you seeking God at this time?

DECEMBER 2

We are confident, I say, and would prefer to be away from the body and
at home with the Lord. So we make it our goal to please him, whether
we are at home in the body or away from it.

2 CORINTHIANS 5:8–9

Some will encourage you to gather all the powers of your mind and soul, and move further inward to worship God within your heart. Such people speak with wisdom and truth, for God loves to make his home within human hearts. Understand what is being said and do not be misled by such instruction, worshiping your heart rather than God. Consider another way of thinking. In seeking to live more fully in God's presence, do not look within yourself or outside yourself. Do not look above you or behind you, to one side or the other. Perhaps you are asking, *Where then is the best place to look for God?* Perhaps it seems to you that the answer is *Look nowhere!* You are right. That is the place to look: *nowhere.* Why is this so? Because God does not primarily dwell in physical spaces, but in spiritual relationships. *Nowhere* physically is everywhere spiritually. Where you are is where God longs to be.

REFLECTION QUESTION: How do you make your heart a home for God?

DECEMBER 3

If . . . you seek the LORD your God, you will find him if you seek him
with all your heart and with all your soul.

DEUTERONOMY 4:29

When you seek God, no physical place is better or worse than any other, because God lives beyond time and space. Seek to live more fully in Christ's presence in the Cloud of Unknowing by focusing your attention less upon some place on earth and more upon being with God. Treasure God above any place, including places of worship. Keep making deposits into your heavenly account where thieves cannot break in to steal away your treasure. "Where your treasure is, there your heart will be also" (Matthew 6:21).

REFLECTION QUESTION: What do you treasure most?

DECEMBER 4

By day the LORD directs his love,
at night his song is with me—
a prayer to the God of my life.

PSALM 42:8

At first, you may find it difficult to get your bearings with no physical directions to guide your search for God. It may seem like you are doing nothing, and your prayer life is going nowhere. You are right in thinking this way. Prayer is not mainly what you do or what you say, nor it is where you go. Prayer is being with God. Enter into the Cloud of Unknowing. Lay aside what you think is prayer, and simply be with God in prayer, without needing to use words, thoughts, or knowledge. God is love. Prayer is loving: loving God and being loved by God. Keep emptying yourself of the need to be in control, the need to know all, and the need to manage God. Keep doing nothing in your prayer life, but do it for the love of God. Keep going nowhere as you pray, but go nowhere to be with God for the love of God.

REFLECTION QUESTION: When have you experienced God's love in times of prayer?

DECEMBER 5

Then Jesus told his disciples a parable to show them that they should always pray and not give up.

LUKE 18:1

Do not give up on prayer just because it seems as if nothing happens. Rather, keep praying and do not give up. Even though you may not know how to pray or when to pray or where to pray, may God become your heart's greatest desire, as you use your will to seek Christ in greater fullness. Imagine yourself nowhere, as though completely lost, blind, and disoriented in time and space, completely unsure of who you are, yet close to God. For you to be in such a state of life would be preferable to God than for you to become some powerful lord living in a great ornate palace someplace important, in complete control of your realm, yet without any love for God. Develop the habit of prayer, regardless of how you feel.

REFLECTION QUESTION: When does it seem as if nothing is happening when you pray?

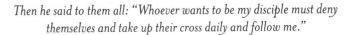

DECEMBER 6

Then he said to them all: "Whoever wants to be my disciple must deny themselves and take up their cross daily and follow me."

LUKE 9:23

In your relationship with Jesus, and in your relationships with others, follow Christ's way of living. Be willing to empty yourself of *everywhere* and *everything* this world has to offer to you. Be willing to become *nothing* for Jesus's sake, and be willing to go *nowhere* for the love of God. As St. Paul taught, "In your relationships with one another, have the same mindset as Christ Jesus: Who, being in very nature God, did not consider equality with God something to be used to his own advantage; rather, he made himself nothing by taking the very nature of a servant, being made in human likeness" (Philippians 2:5–7). Don't worry if this doesn't make any sense to your intellect. Love has its own reasons that our reason cannot comprehend. There are mysteries worthy of our attention that our reason will never understand.

REFLECTION QUESTION: In what ways are you emptying yourself for God?

DECEMBER 7

As he neared Damascus on his journey, suddenly a light from heaven flashed around him. He fell to the ground and heard a voice say to him, "Saul, Saul, why do you persecute me?"
"Who are you, Lord?" Saul asked.
"I am Jesus, whom you are persecuting," he replied. "Now get up and go into the city, and you will be told what you must do."
The men traveling with Saul stood there speechless; they heard the sound but did not see anyone. Saul got up from the ground, but when he opened his eyes he could see nothing. So they led him by the hand into Damascus.

ACTS 9:3–8

H ow does a person become *nothing* for God's sake? This *nothingness* is easier to experience than to explain. For those who are new to life with God, it will seem as if you are walking blind in a misty, unknowable way. As Saul was blinded along the road to Damascus, our lives may be blinded by the presence of Jesus. Truly, our soul is blinded along this way not because there is a lack of light, but because the abundance of divine radiance hides God's presence from our eyes, like looking up at the sun. Who is it that considers this way *nothing*? Your outer self sees little worth in such a way. We may stand there speechless like Saul's companions, unable to understand what is happening, looking around but seeing *nothing*. Our innermost self considers this way everything. The more we surrender our life for God's sake and become *nothing* for the love of God, even though we have never studied or understood the many realms of Creation, we will begin to understand the essence of everything in Creation, whether physical or spiritual.

REFLECTION QUESTION: When have you experienced light from heaven in your life?

DECEMBER 8

He parted the heavens and came down;
dark clouds were under his feet.
He mounted the cherubim and flew;
he soared on the wings of the wind.

He made darkness his covering, his canopy around him—
the dark rain clouds of the sky.
Out of the brightness of his presence clouds advanced,
with hailstones and bolts of lightning.

PSALM 18:9–12

The more you become *nothing* and are willing to go *nowhere*, the more you will experience God's gift of wonder deep within your innermost being. God's presence is often hidden from us until we become *nothing* by admitting we are in the dark about God. How do you begin to become *nothing*? Look inside your soul. See the *nothingness* that lives there. Look upon the dark and secret canvases hanging in the gallery of your soul where you've been painting since you were very young, including paintings in thoughts, words, and deeds. No matter how you hang these inner images, they will keep reappearing before your eyes, until the time comes, after intense and sometimes painful spiritual labor, with groaning and tears, you discover these canvases have all been washed clean by God's grace at work within your soul. Then the brightness of God's presence will advance in your life.

REFLECTION QUESTION: How much are you in the dark about God?

DECEMBER 9

I am the vine; you are the branches. If you remain in me and I in you,
you will bear much fruit; apart from me you can do nothing.

JOHN 15:5

Sometimes, during times of sorrow or inner spiritual turmoil, you may fear that you've been plunged into the dark abyss. You may discover your soul filled with despair from the pain, anxious that you will never again experience light, contentment, and rest. You feel far from God and your life is as *nothing*. For some people, this is as far as they are willing to journey into *nothingness* and *nowhere*. Because of the intensity of the pain and the lack of inner comfort, they turn back to the familiar experiences of *something* or *somewhere*. Lacking in spiritual maturity that may only be discovered through loss or hardship, they turn back to the comforts they've known in the past, filling their lives with short-term pleasures and numbing distractions. When you remain with

Christ, he will remain with you even when you feel your life is *nowhere*. Christ will remain with you through loss of comfort, through absence of pleasure, through the darkness, and beyond.

REFLECTION QUESTION: In what way do you remain in Christ and Christ in you?

DECEMBER 10

Praise be to the God and Father of our Lord Jesus Christ, the Father of compassion and the God of all comfort, who comforts us in all our troubles, so that we can comfort those in any trouble with the comfort we ourselves receive from God. For just as we share abundantly in the sufferings of Christ, so also our comfort abounds through Christ.

2 CORINTHIANS 1:3–5

All who learn to remain in Christ experience his comforting presence and have some hope that you are growing in spiritual maturity. As you rest your soul in Jesus, remaining with him in the face of suffering and pain, you'll discover those ugly paintings of foul thoughts, words, and deeds painted on the wall of your soul are being washed clean by the help of God's grace. This does not mean that you will feel no pain. But at least you will have hope in the face of your suffering that it will soon end and that it is producing the good result of maturing your soul.

REFLECTION QUESTION: How has Christ comforted you in times of trouble?

DECEMBER 11

Consider it pure joy . . . whenever you face trials of many kinds, because you know that the testing of your faith produces perseverance. Let perseverance finish its work so that you may be mature and complete, not lacking anything.

JAMES 1:2–4

Press on into this strange realm of *nothingness* and this mysterious journey toward *nowhere*. As you journey onward, you are being purified through the trials and troubles you face along the way.

Sometimes, you will discover no specific offenses in your soul, but rather find your soul in a bland or drab condition of malaise, a state of spiritual sleepiness, a deep inner sense of desolation where you experience a great distance between your soul and God. You may wonder what this is all about, and realize you too share in the great human catastrophe that separates us from God, that ancient malady brought to every human by our first ancestors. Such trials can bring great joy, knowing that God is allowing your faith to be tested and refined, building God's character within you, helping you grow into full maturity.

REFLECTION QUESTION: How have trials or troubles helped you grow spiritually?

DECEMBER 12

I do not want you to be ignorant of the fact . . . that our ancestors were all under the cloud and that they all passed through the sea. They were all baptized into Moses in the cloud and in the sea. They all ate the same spiritual food and drank the same spiritual drink; for they drank from the spiritual rock that accompanied them, and that rock was Christ.

1 CORINTHIANS 10:1–4

In your journey with Christ, there will be times when you will wonder if you haven't already entered paradise for the wide assortment of sweet wonders and consolations, for the joys and delightful wildflowers of virtues you discover along the way. Then there are those most blessed times in your pilgrimage when your soul is filled with such peace and inner rest that you'll think you've entered the very heart of God. You will have your fill of spiritual food and drink from the spiritual rock of Christ's presence. Yes, you will find yourself thinking many wonderful thoughts about this mysterious realm. But know in truth that your experience of this journey, beginning with the acceptance of being *nothing* and *nowhere*, is the experience of entering the Cloud of Unknowing between your soul and God.

REFLECTION QUESTION: Where are you in your spiritual journey with God this season?

DECEMBER 13

The twelve gates were twelve pearls, each gate made of a single pearl.
The great street of the city was of gold, as pure as transparent glass.
I did not see a temple in the city, because the Lord God Almighty and
the Lamb are its temple. The city does not need the sun or the moon to
shine on it, for the glory of God gives it light, and the Lamb is its lamp.

REVELATION 21:21–23

Actively strive to empty yourself before God, willing to become *nothing* for God's sake and to go *nowhere* in the name of Jesus. Be willing to lay aside your natural ways of learning through your mind and senses. You can try to comprehend physical Creation through them, but the whole spiritual realm of heaven is well out of your reach through your senses. For your physical eyes are limited to perceiving physical objects, their dimensions, whether they are long or narrow, small or large, round or square, far or near, as well as their many colors. But have you seen the color of golden luminescence within the streets of the heavenly city? God gave us eyes to look upon what is unseen. God made our eyes to be the lamp of our whole body and to be filled with the glory of heaven.

REFLECTION QUESTION: In what ways are you filling your eyes with heaven's glory?

DECEMBER 14

Faith comes from hearing the message, and the message is heard through
the word about Christ.
ROMANS 10:17

With our ears, we are able to hear all kinds of noises, words, and songs. With our ears, we hear the message of good news spoken to us by faithful messengers of God. God gave us the sense of hearing for a holy purpose. As St. Paul wrote, "How can they believe in the one of whom they have not heard? And how can they hear without someone preaching to them" (Romans 10:14)? If faith comes from hearing, we are wise to attune our ears to listen to the voice of heaven spoken through God's many messengers, including Creation. As the psalmist reminds us, all Creation declares God's glory, pouring forth

God's speech and unveiling God's knowledge. Even though "they have no speech, they use no words; no sound is heard from them," God's voice goes "out into all the earth" and God's Word "to the ends of the world" (Psalm 19:3–4). As God asks Job, "Where were you . . . while the morning stars sang together and all the angels shouted for joy?" (Job 38:4, 7).

REFLECTION QUESTION: How are you at listening to the voice of heaven?

DECEMBER 15

Thanks be to God, who always leads us as captives in Christ's triumphal procession and uses us to spread the aroma of the knowledge of him everywhere. For we are to God the pleasing aroma of Christ among those who are being saved and those who are perishing. To the one we are an aroma that brings death; to the other, an aroma that brings life.

2 CORINTHIANS 2:14–16

With our nose, we smell whether something has a foul smell, or a beautiful fragrance. God gave us the sense of smell for a holy purpose to discern between life and death, between what is pleasing to God and what is displeasing to God. Our lives are to become a fragrance that is pleasing to God, leading others into life with God. The angels of God offer up fragrant incense on the golden altar before the throne of God, a pleasing aroma joining together with the prayers of all God's people, rising up before God as a fragrant offering.[42]

REFLECTION QUESTION: What in your life is a pleasing and fragrant offering to God?

DECEMBER 16

And he said to me, "Son of man, eat what is before you, eat this scroll; then go and speak to the people of Israel." So I opened my mouth, and he gave me the scroll to eat.
Then he said to me, "Son of man, eat this scroll I am giving you and fill your stomach with it." So I ate it, and it tasted as sweet as honey in my mouth.
He then said to me: "Son of man, go now to the people of Israel and speak my words to them.

EZEKIEL 3:1–4

With your tongue, you know a wide palette of tastes, including what is sour or sweet, salt or savory, bitter or bland. God gave us the sense of taste for a holy purpose to experience the sweetness of God's Word, the saltiness of Christ's presence, the savor of heavenly wisdom, the blandness of life without God, and the bitterness of human corruption. Take up God's Word and eat it like eating honey straight from the honeycomb. You will find God's love letter sweeter than any honey on earth. As with the prophet Ezekiel, so with St. John in the book of Revelation, where the angel gave John a little scroll of God's revelation. The angel told John, "Take it and eat it. It will turn your stomach sour, but 'in your mouth it will be as sweet as honey'" (Revelation 10:9). John took the scroll of God's revelation and ate it. It tasted just as the angel had promised, sweet as honey in John's mouth but sour in his stomach. Then John was called to go speak out God's truth to "many peoples, nations, languages and kings" (Revelation 10:11). We, too, with our sense of taste are to feed upon God's revelation, and speak God's sweet and savory word to others in our daily way of living and in our speech.

REFLECTION QUESTION: What have you tasted when feeding upon God's Word?

DECEMBER 17

Just then a woman who had been subject to bleeding for twelve years came up behind him and touched the edge of his cloak. She said to herself, "If I only touch his cloak, I will be healed."

MATTHEW 9:20–21

The sense of touch helps you know what is hot or cold, hard or soft, smooth or sharp. But have you ever tried to touch the edge of Christ's cloak and in that touch discover you've been completely healed? Or, have you touched the body of someone recently raised from the dead? These are among the works of God. And God gave us the sense of touch for a holy purpose to reach out beyond the physical realm to touch the face of God. There are spiritual realms beyond your natural senses that your rational mind and bodily senses cannot know, either in quantity or quality.

REFLECTION QUESTION: How do you reach out to touch God?

DECEMBER 18

We live by faith, not by sight.

2 CORINTHIANS 5:7

Discover how to rely less on the limited tools of your five senses for spiritual guidance, by yielding your life more fully to God. When you try to use your bodily senses as the main way to discover spiritual truths, thinking you will be able to hear, smell, see, taste, or feel spiritual things, you will find yourself disappointed and even led astray by your efforts. It is better to learn how life has been designed by God. God designed your reason and your senses to discover and understand physical and bodily things. But you are not able to understand spiritual things by these same tools, because of the way these natural tools work. Humans live more by faith than by sight, taste, feel, smell, or sound.

REFLECTION QUESTION: What role do your senses play in prayer?

DECEMBER 19

The true light that gives light to everyone was coming into the world.
He was in the world, and though the world was made through him, the
world did not recognize him.

JOHN 1:9–10

When your senses and your natural abilities no longer are able to guide you, may you discover more of the spiritual and eternal life, leaving behind what is merely physical and temporal. The whole Creation was made through Christ, yet when he came into the world, we did not recognize him. There will also be times when your spiritual understanding will work hard to know more of God, but you will find yourself falling short. Do not get easily frustrated in such times. We are mere mortals. We are able to learn and know many spiritual truths; but we will never fully comprehend God, who is eternal. When we, like little children, receive Jesus and believe in his name, God welcomes us with open arms and helps us grow up into full maturity of love.

REFLECTION QUESTION: What do you do when you get frustrated in your spiritual life with God?

DECEMBER 20

"Now then," said Joshua, "throw away the foreign gods
that are among you and yield your hearts to the LORD, the God of Israel."
And the people said to Joshua,
"We will serve the LORD our God and obey him."

JOSHUA 24:23–24

By falling short of God's glory, you are once again reminded that you are not God. One of the surest ways of knowing God is through the Cloud of Unknowing, by humbling yourself before God, admitting you really don't know as much about God as you thought you knew. It is better to yield your life to God than to try to analyze God with your mind or senses. There have been many wise writers through the centuries who have spoken these same truths.[43] Living fully for God requires that we do as the ancient Israelites did before Joshua: cast away our false gods and idols and yield our lives completely to the Lord our God in loving service and obedience.

REFLECTION QUESTION: What idols are you are clinging to right now?

DECEMBER 21

My sheep listen to my voice; I know them, and they follow me.
JOHN 10:27

Listen carefully . . . and attend . . . with the ear of your heart."[44] Learn to listen to the voice of Christ calling to you. Follow where Christ leads your heart. The voice of the Lord is heard through Creation, through God's Word, through the church, and through the great cloud of witnesses who have lived by faith in the past. When you read a wise book on the spiritual life written by one of the great heroes of the faith, ask if the writing is supported by God's Word, and by the teachings of wise church leaders from the past. Use discernment to choose what is best. The best books on prayer were written by people who lived with humility before God. In their writings, they did not merely share their own opinions, but rooted their writings in the good earth of God's Word. Jesus invites us to learn to listen. "Whoever has ears, let them hear" (Matthew 11:15). Listen with your heart to what you've read this past year, and may your faith be strengthened as you follow in Christ's path of life.

REFLECTION QUESTION: What is most difficult for you about listening to God?

DECEMBER 22

May the God of peace, who through the blood of the eternal covenant brought back from the dead our Lord Jesus, that great Shepherd of the sheep, equip you with everything good for doing his will, and may he work in us what is pleasing to him, through Jesus Christ, to whom be glory for ever and ever. Amen.

HEBREWS 13:20–21

Some people believe that genuine, spiritual encounters with God are very rare, achieved only through intense human effort or through ecstatic experiences. According to them, when the encounter finally occurs, the soul is completely ravished by God's presence. In reality, every person encounters God uniquely, according to God's good, pleasing, and perfect will. The only way you will ever experience God's presence is by the gift of God's grace active within your soul, working in accord with your unique abilities and personality. May God continue to empower you with everything good for doing God's will. May God work within you what is good and pleasing to God.

REFLECTION QUESTION: How is God equipping your life to better do God's will?

DECEMBER 23

Love the Lord your God with all your heart and with all your soul and with all your strength. These commandments that I give you today are to be on your hearts.

DEUTERONOMY 6:5–6

By God's grace, there are some people who rarely have direct encounters with God, and then only through long periods of intense searching. Through extensive spiritual exercises over months or even years, they finally experience the fruit of their labor, catching a glimpse of eternity that ravishes their soul. By the same wisdom and grace given by God, there are others who welcome God's presence daily into the ordinary times and places of their lives, while they are sitting at home, standing to do a daily chore, walking along the way, or kneeling by their bed. In these everyday encounters with God, they remain fully aware of their surroundings, and continue about their daily tasks. Yet, they keep inviting God to participate in their lives, both physically and spiritually, without needing to exert lots of energy or effort, but humbly practicing the presence of God in ordinary times and places. No matter whether you are the first kind of spiritual person with few life encounters with God, or the second kind of spiritual person with daily, ordinary encounters with God, we are all invited by God to love God with our whole being, in every setting and situation, whether at home, or outside walking along, when we lie down, or when we get up. God is present.

REFLECTION QUESTION: How present is God in your life now?

DECEMBER 24

There were shepherds living out in the fields nearby,
keeping watch over their flocks at night. An angel of the Lord appeared
to them, and the glory of the Lord shone around them, and they were
terrified. But the angel said to them, "Do not be afraid. I bring you
good news that will cause great joy for all the people."

LUKE 2:8–10

There are many examples of encounters with God in the Bible, including the ravishing but rare encounters, and the ordinary daily encounters. Look at the lives of Moses and his brother Aaron. They both spent extensive time with God, Moses on the sacred mountain, and Aaron within the temple. Moses climbed up to the top of the mountain, laboring with many steps to enter the cloud of God's presence, finally encountering God after much effort and many days of waiting. By Moses's example, understand that some people encounter God's presence only after many steps upward in their spiritual journey. After intense effort and many days of waiting, by God's grace, Moses finally heard the voice of God. The shepherds at the time of the birth of Jesus also waited for years, hoping for an encounter with the living God. They were surprised and terrified with the angel of the Lord appeared to them in the night. God's glory shone upon them out of the darkness, declaring joyful news of the birth of Jesus, "good news that will cause great joy for all the people" (Luke 2:10).

REFLECTION QUESTION: When have you been surprised by a God encounter?

DECEMBER 25

Suddenly a great company of the heavenly host appeared with the angel,
praising God and saying,
"Glory to God in the highest heaven,
and on earth peace to those on whom his favor rests."

LUKE 2:13–14

Aaron's calling was different from Moses's spiritual path. God empowered Aaron to go into the sacred temple as often as he wanted to go. Within the temple was the ark of the covenant. Within the ark of the covenant were the sacred objects manifesting God's presence in physical forms, including the tablets of the Ten Commandments that Moses received upon the mountain within the cloud of God's presence. The Cloud of Unknowing filled the sacred temple whenever Aaron went in to commune with God. The grace of being in God's presence was symbolized by the ark of the covenant. The same grace of being in God's presence became most powerfully evident in a manger in the stable where Jesus was born in Bethlehem. May our lives become humble places where Jesus comes to dwell, bringing God's peace and favor.

REFLECTION QUESTION: How does Jesus dwell with you?

DECEMBER 26

Since we have confidence to enter the Most Holy Place by the blood of
Jesus, by a new and living way opened for us through the curtain, that
is, his body, and since we have a great priest over the house of God, let
us draw near to God with a sincere heart and with the full assurance
that faith brings.

HEBREWS 10:19–22

Think of your soul as a living temple of God in which you have an inner ark of the covenant where God loves to dwell. Access into this living temple is through the new and living way Jesus opened through his body and blood. All Christ's sacred virtues expressing God's presence are contained within this inner ark within your soul. Like Aaron, we may return often to the temple of God within our soul where, by the help of God's ravishing grace and with a little dart of love, we may pierce into the Cloud of Unknowing and encounter the living God anytime we want, day or night.

REFLECTION QUESTION: In what way is your life a living temple where God loves to live?

DECEMBER 27

As each of us has one body with many members, and these members do not all have the same function, so in Christ we, though many, form one body, and each member belongs to all the others. We have different gifts, according to the grace given to each of us.

ROMANS 12:4–6

Understand that people come to God in many different ways. One person must not think less of another because of differences in their spiritual life with God. One person may strive long and hard in various spiritual exercises and rarely catch a glimpse of eternal glory. How absurd for such a person to expect that every other person should also be required to labor long and hard before they encounter God. Yet, there are such people who become resentful when others meet with God in daily life as though meeting with a dear friend. There are people who regularly hear God speak to their hearts at any ordinary hour of the day or night. Such people are wise to realize that not everyone has such intimacy with God. How silly for such a person to judge another because they do not yet hear the voice of God speaking personally to them. How equally silly for one person to envy another because that person encounters God daily. According to the grace given to you, offer your life to God, encouraging others as fellow members of Christ's body.

REFLECTION QUESTION: How did you first come to God?

DECEMBER 28

When Moses went up on the mountain, the cloud covered it, and the glory of the LORD settled on Mount Sinai. For six days the cloud covered the mountain.

EXODUS 24:15–16

Consider the life of Moses, who labored hard to climb to the top of the sacred mountain. There he waited patiently for many days and nights on the mountaintop before God spoke. While in the Cloud of Unknowing on the mountain, God gave Moses the pattern for the ark of the covenant. Later, Moses was able to meet with God whenever he wanted by entering the temple of God to sit next to the ark of the covenant, completely enveloped by the Cloud of God's glory. The greatest labor in your life with God is the labor of loving God. This labor may include intense times of climbing, and long periods of waiting on the Lord. The second greatest labor is the labor of loving others. Find this way of living, and you will find God.

REFLECTION QUESTION: How are you at waiting?

DECEMBER 29

I will give you hidden treasures, riches stored in secret places, so that you may know that I am the Lord, the God of Israel, who summons you by name.

ISAIAH 45:3

Imagine your soul is a sacred temple, a place where God loves to dwell. In the most sacred place within your soul rests a beautiful treasure chest, like the ark of the covenant in the time of ancient Israel. In the time of Moses, Bezalel the master artist crafted the ark of the covenant from the design God gave to Moses.[45] This beautifully crafted ark was placed within the temple. Even so, God has crafted a beautiful treasure chest and placed it in the innermost place within your soul where God loves to dwell. As you read earlier in this book, in this life there are many ways God's grace works within the human soul, including through ordinary places, along special paths, and through extraordinary ways. We see these three graces in the lives of Moses, Bezalel, and Aaron. Allow God's grace to work within the treasure chest of your soul, in ordinary, special, and even in extraordinary ways.

REFLECTION QUESTION: What treasures are stored in the beautiful treasure chest of your soul?

DECEMBER 30

On the seventh day the Lord called to Moses from within the cloud. To the Israelites the glory of the Lord looked like a consuming fire on top of the mountain. Then Moses entered the cloud as he went on up the mountain. And he stayed on the mountain forty days and forty nights.

EXODUS 24:16–18

God's extraordinary grace invites you to enter the Cloud of Unknowing into the glory of the Lord, ascending along the paths of prayer up the sacred mountain, in the same way Moses climbed Mount Sinai long ago. Upon the mountain, while enveloped within the Cloud of God's presence, Moses waited many days to hear from God. When God finally spoke, Moses received a vision from God for the design for the ark of the covenant, and instructions about what to place within this sacred chest. Then Moses came down from the mountain, to share the extraordinary grace of God with the people. Sometimes, we are given extraordinary grace from God to ascend and wait and listen within the Cloud of Unknowing to the voice of God. We are given divine guidance on how to craft our life in God's likeness and how to fill our inner treasure chest with God's glorious presence.

REFLECTION QUESTION: What have you learned this year about waiting on God?

DECEMBER 31

The Word became flesh and made his dwelling among us. We have seen his glory, the glory of the one and only Son, who came from the Father, full of grace and truth.

—JOHN 1:14

God's special grace invites us to learn and create. Because we are made in the image of the Master Artist, we're empowered with creativity from God to craft our life and the life of others more in the image of God's beautiful design. Bezalel, a master artist, crafted the ark from the design given by God to Moses. By God's special grace, continue to practice the artistry and craftsmanship on God's treasure chest within your soul. God's ordinary grace invites us to abide with God and love God at any time of day or night. Like Aaron, who went into the sacred place to dwell with God near the ark of the covenant at any time, keep coming into the sacred place where God loves to dwell with you in your inner treasure chest. Friend of God, you'll find it best to welcome God's ordinary grace by abiding with God more and more during the day and night, like Aaron in the temple of God. It is better to continually be with God as Aaron was, than only occasionally to craft special work for God as Bezalel did, or rarely to have a vision of God as Moses had upon the mountain. God loves to come to dwell with us in the everyday places of our lives. In the ordinary times and spaces of daily life, contemplate the fullness of God's grace and truth by abiding more and more with Jesus.

REFLECTION QUESTION: How have you grown closer in your friendship with God during this past year?

God's Way of Friendship

T hroughout *The Cloud of Unknowing*, the anonymous author writes as a friend of God to one other person who is called a friend of God. The other person was likely a younger monastic under the spiritual direction of the author. Such spiritual mentoring was the normal practice in a monastery in the fourteenth century, just as it is the normal practice within monasteries today.

One of the most common expressions found throughout *The Cloud* is the author's way of addressing the reader as friend of God. In the spiritual life, what a comfort to be called a friend of God. Jesus assured us with his final words before he went to the cross: "I no longer call you servants, because a servant does not know his master's business. Instead, I have called you friends, for everything that I learned from my Father I have made known to you" (John 15:15). The following paragraphs are my translation of the epilogue of *The Cloud of Unknowing*, the author's summary of spiritual wisdom.

Friend of God, I pray that you will continue to grow with ordinary grace, learning to practice the presence of God out of an abiding friendship with God. As you abide with Jesus, he will abide with you within your soul, God's treasure chest. Christ will help you grow in your spiritual life with God. If you find that the way of spiritual life with God expressed in this book does not agree with your personality style, for the love of God, lay it aside and pick up another. There's no problem in finding some other wise spiritual counsel to guide your life. The daily devotions above were written in the hope that these words would benefit your life with simple wisdom. If you have found some benefit from these words, I encourage you to read through this book again, day by day, through another year. If at first, you do not understand some sentence or section, when you read it a second or third time, you may discover that passage making more sense and becoming easier to understand as you progress in this way of life.

Anyone already inclined to contemplative prayer will have a quick affinity for this writing, either by reading it themselves, or by hearing it spoken of by others. If you discover that these words have helped you come closer to God as a friend of God, then give thanks to God. As I pray for you, so pray with me and keep drawing near to God, who draws near to you. For the love of God, keep pressing onward in prayer and be willing to share this book and the wisdom you've discovered here with others who also are hungry and thirsty for God. When you give this book to another, encourage them to read slowly, allowing plenty of time for God's Spirit to work within their soul, across the pages of an entire year. There may be some patches of fog along the way, at the beginning or in the middle of the book, causing some confusion or disorientation. Encourage friends of God to press on slowly, and not to jump around by reading a bit here and a bit there, but moving through the book, day by day, month by month, as though walking across a cloudy landscape. At times in this journey, a reader may enter some fog along the way, uncertain what lies ahead. At other times, a reader will ascend to a vista to see God's glory revealed. If there are parts of this book that remain closed to your understanding, ask God for wisdom and insight to assist you.

In the spiritual life, there will always be hawkers and gawkers, flatterers and tattlers, blamers and shamers, and every kind of wheeler and dealer who will not understand what is written here. Such people will not accept these words, and therefore I see little value in passing such a book on to them, for they will merely meddle with what is written here or peddle these truths for profit. This book was not primarily written for curiosity-seekers, academics, or intellectuals. Although they may seek to live good lives, this book will not be of much help to cultural or spiritual fad-followers who read merely out of casual curiosity.

If someone picks up this book who is living an active way of life, but also experiences inner longings for the contemplative spiritual way of life, though many of God's ways are hidden and secret, such a person will be given grace upon grace, even though they may not be seeking God as contemplatives. Now and then, through the mists of naiveté, they will perceive the heights of mountains of glory, through times of prayer and meditation. Even an occasional glimpse of these heights, by the grace of God's presence, will provide great comfort and encouragement.[46] May you also know Christ's comfort and encouragement as you journey onward into fullness of life with God. May you "have power, together with all the Lord's holy people, to grasp how wide and long and high and deep is the love of Christ, and to know this love that surpasses knowledge—that you may be filled to the measure of all the fullness of God" (Ephesians 3:18–19).

Not everyone who reads this book is ready to enter into such a contemplative life with God. There will be some who hear about this book or read a portion of it who like what they hear and think this writing wise, yet are not yet really that interested in living fully for God. Some sparks of interest may come from their curious nature or inquisitive mind, but they still have yet to open their hearts to God's grace. They may first need to assess where they are in their life with God. I urge you, as you read and reflect upon this book, as St. Paul declares,

> *In view of God's mercy, to offer your bodies as a living sacrifice, holy*
> *and pleasing to God—this is your true and proper worship.*
> *Do not conform to the pattern of this world, but be transformed by the*
> *renewing of your mind. Then you will be able to test and approve what*
> *God's will is—his good, pleasing and perfect will. (Romans 12:1–2)*

If your soul needs to be washed clean, then offer your confession to God with guidance from a spiritual mentor, pastor, or priest. Receive forgiveness of all your sins, and purification from all ungodliness. Seek out a wise spiritual mentor who can guide you in this, and who will discern with you the next steps in your spiritual journey.

The spiritual life is not a brief encounter or a short-lived experience, but a lifelong journey with God. Look into your soul to discover how much or how little you hunger and thirst for God. If you lack a desire for God, ask God to whet your appetite for spiritual food. Evaluate your way of living, including your physical and spiritual life, listening to the voice of your conscience, to learn how the fire of God's love is burning within your soul, as expressed in the way you are living your daily life.

If God's little flame of love is burning, warming you in body, mind, and spirit, this is a wonderful gift from God. This is also a sign that you are being called by God along the way of friendship with God. The spiritual life is not always warm, radiant, and full of good feelings. Friendships never are. On the contrary, early in your spiritual life with God, you will find times when you wonder if God still exists. There will be times when it seems as though God has completely withdrawn from your life. This experience comes for a variety of reasons. For some, the reason for God's apparent absence is to keep you from taking God's presence for granted. All who neglect God or take God for granted end up living a spiritual life of ingratitude or indifference.

You cannot control or manipulate God. All who try to do so are motivated more by insecurity or arrogance than by love, deluding themselves with self-worship. When pride fills the soul, there is no room for God's grace. In such souls, a person will too often turn against God, thinking God is an enemy rather than your truest friend. For others, God seems absent due to their negligence. Neglect tending the fire of the soul, and the coals burn down to ashes. When the fire goes out, it seems God has ceased to exist. When you discover this state within your soul, you feel a cold pain, a longing for the warm embrace of love you once knew.

At other times, God's presence seems to be withdrawn to cause a soul to yearn all the more for the gift of grace, and be grateful for this gift when the experience of grace is once again felt and known. If you find yourself overcome with gratitude for knowing God's nearness, you can be sure you are living more fully in God's presence, especially after a time of separation from God. Some people wander in dry lands of the soul for months or even years, wondering when they will once again drink deeply from the wells of God's presence. The joy in finding God is near once again overcomes all the sorrow of losing touch with God. Finding God and being found by God is life's greatest joy, not something to be squandered or easily tossed aside. Once found, you may be sure you will keep being found and brought home again and again. For God looks at you with loving eyes, seeing you not as you are at this moment, nor as you were in the past, but as you are becoming.

Laying aside what is in the past, keep reaching out toward your future with God, journeying onward into the fullness of life toward which God is calling you. As a wise sage from the ancient past wrote, "All holy desires grow by delays: and if they wane by delays, they were never holy desires."[47] As you grow in your friendship with God, you will discover your appetite for old natural desires diminishing more and more, and you will realize they never were sacred desires in the first place.

Traveling mercies, friend of God. Go with God's blessings and mine. I pray for you before the God's throne of grace, asking your life to be filled with God's gifts of peace, wisdom, and encouragement with an abundance of God's grace. Christ will be with you always and with all lovers of God on earth. Amen.

ACKNOWLEDGMENTS

After my first two years of full-time pastoral ministry, I was burned out. I was twenty-nine years old, married with two children and a third child on the way. My boss, the senior pastor at the church where I served had asked me to leave by the end of that year, not because I had done anything wrong, but because he didn't believe I belonged in ministry. I felt angry, depressed, fearful, and ready to quit. That was in October 1986, the month I made my first contemplative retreat to a monastery. I got away to Our Lady of Guadalupe Trappist Abbey, located less than an hour's drive from Portland, Oregon. I met with Father Peter McCarthy, then guest master, now serving as abbot.

On the first day of that weeklong retreat, Father Peter sat with me to listen as I described to him the state of my soul. At the end of an hour, he asked me if I was interested in finding my way back into God's presence. He introduced me to an ancient pattern of contemplative prayer called centering prayer. He gave me a couple of books to read on centering prayer, and encouraged me to try this approach to prayer as a simple way into God's presence. I am grateful for Father Peter's mentoring me at the trailhead of my contemplative journey back to God.

Along the way, I've met many wise trail guides, both living and dead, including the author of *The Cloud of Unknowing*, who, like Father Peter, also encouraged me to try contemplative prayer as a way back into God's intimate presence. Over the past decades, the anonymous author of the *Cloud of Unknowing* has been a trail guide in my spiritual journey, gently leading me out of my head, into my heart, into the beautiful presence of Christ waiting within. Again and again, I enter into what St. Paul declares as "the glorious riches of this mystery, which is Christ in you, the hope of glory" (Colossians 1:27).

I am grateful for the spiritual direction I have received from the monks of Mount Angel Abbey, where I have been refreshed and renewed in my contemplative journey as an Benedictine Oblate. I am grateful for the people of Cannon Beach Community Church who faithfully pray for me and support me as their pastor. Thanks to Dr. MaryKate Morse, Professor of Leadership and Spiritual Formation at Portland Seminary, for her encouragement in the contemplative way of spiritual formation.

Thanks also to Jon Sweeney, Robert Edmonson, and the staff of Paraclete Press for bringing ancient and medieval contemplative voices of wisdom into the twenty-first century to guide us into God's presence. They provided excellent editorial work on this book, for which I am grateful.

In translating and paraphrasing *The Cloud of Unknowing*, I worked from a Middle English edition based on the British Library Harlein manuscript 674. I am indebted to several modern English-language editions, including translations by Carmen Acevedo Butcher, William Johnston, and James Walsh.

I am grateful for Trina, my wife and life companion in our spiritual journey in Christ, for her support in my life as a pastor and writer, and for her passionate pursuit of God.

Finally, I give thanks for all the women who have faithfully nurtured my spiritual life with God, including my mom, Berta Robinson, who was the first person to teach me to pray; and my wife's Danish mom, Sigrid Hudson (1923–2019), who loved to pray.

APPENDIX A
Praying with the Author of *The Cloud of Unknowing*[48]

Dear God,
open my heart and teach me to listen.
Nothing is hidden from You.
Cleanse the intent of my heart
with the unspeakable gift of Your grace,
that I may more perfectly love You,
more fully live in your presence,
and more worthily praise You. Amen.[49]

The Cloud of Unknowing opens with this beautiful prayer from the eighth century. At the time *The Cloud* was written, this prayer had been prayed by countless souls across five centuries. In our time, this prayer spans twelve centuries, with a cloud of witnesses lifting up their souls to God. This short, ancient prayer contains three requests. The third request contains a threefold petition. First, this prayer invites us to open our hearts, become teachable, and learn to listen to God. Second, since nothing is hidden from God including the condition of our hearts, this prayer asks God to wash our hearts with "the unspeakable gift of grace." With hearts washed anew, we pray a threefold request: to better love God, to live more fully in God's presence, and to more worthily praise God.

The author of *The Cloud* loved to pray, including praying centuries-old written prayers. Through seventy-three short chapters, together with a prologue and epilogue, this anonymous author calls us deeper into a life of prayer. I offer below fifty-two practical ways of prayer drawn from *The Cloud of Unknowing*. Chapter references below refer to the original text of *The Cloud of Unknowing*. I hope this list of prayer patterns will provide personal ways to enter into God's presence through a full year of weeks, as you learn to live more fully with God.

52 Ways to Pray with the Author of *The Cloud*

1. Come near to God through ordinary ways and places by walking in love.
   (CHAPTER 1)

2. Wake up and drink deeply of God's love.
   (CHAPTER 2)

3. Learn to pray naked.
   (CHAPTERS 3, 53)

4. Encounter God in the present moment.
   (CHAPTER 4)

5. Put a Cloud of Forgetting between you and everything that will pass away.
   (CHAPTER 5)

6. Keep aiming upward into the Cloud of Unknowing with the sharp dart of love.
   (CHAPTER 6)

7. Pray short prayers such as the ancient prayer, "Lord, have mercy."
   (CHAPTER 7)

8. Let your soul be filled with Mary-like wonder by sitting in Christ's presence.
   (CHAPTER 8)

9. Push distractions away and keep pressing into the Cloud of Unknowing.
   (CHAPTER 9)

10. Weed out temptations when they first arise, and root your life in Christ.
    (CHAPTERS 10, 11)

11. Never cease in your intent to pray.
    (CHAPTER 12)

12. Let humility grow in your soul as you allow God to work within.
    (CHAPTERS 13, 14, 51, 55)

13. Quietly press on with great love for God in the way of true lovers.
    (CHAPTER 16)

14. Learn to live with contentment.
    (CHAPTERS 17, 50)

15. Allow your soul to be stirred by God's grace and by wise counsel.
    (CHAPTER 18)

16. Pray by the golden rule, giving grace to others who pray in a differently way.
    (CHAPTER 19)

17. Know the one thing necessary in life, which is to fully love God.
    (CHAPTER 20)

18. Discover what is good, what is better, and what is best in prayer.
    (CHAPTERS 21, 22)

19. Gaze more and more upon God's beauty and worth, and glare less and less at your own shortcomings.
    (CHAPTER 23)

20. See Christ's face in the face of everyone you meet.
    (CHAPTERS 24, 25)

21. Practice the presence of God in the everyday places of your soul.
    (CHAPTERS 26, 27)

22. Allow your soul to be washed clean and clothe yourself daily with Christ's new clothes.
    (CHAPTER 28)

23. Press on with perseverance through the darkness, eager for the eternal light of Christ's dawning glory.
    (CHAPTER 29)

24. Let your soul be ignited by God's Spirit to help warm the soul of another.
    (CHAPTER 30)

25. Turn away from what lies behind, and press on toward what is ahead.
    (CHAPTERS 31, 33)

26. Seek what is higher and more glorious, like opening the curtains and the window in a mountain chalet to enjoy a view of the mountains.
    (CHAPTERS 32, 36)

27. Let God's grace and goodwill be your guides as you pray.
    (CHAPTER 34)

28. Make reading the Bible, meditating on the Bible, and praying the Bible part of your daily life.
    (CHAPTERS 35, 52)

29. Let your meditations and prayers fly up to heaven likes sparks from a campfire.
    (CHAPTER 37)

30. Pray single word prayers such as *Help, Thanks,* and *Wow.*
    (CHAPTERS 38, 39, 40)

31. Learn to pray continually.
    (CHAPTER 41)

32. Love God with complete abandonment.
    (CHAPTERS 42, 43)

33. In prayer, as in living, be gentle with yourself and attentive to your need for good self-care.
    (CHAPTERS 44, 45)

34. Pray playfully, and play prayerfully.
    (CHAPTERS 46, 47)

35. As you pray, let your soul be filled with wonder, sweetness, and delight.
    (CHAPTER 48)

36. Go grace-hunting, letting God's goodness be your guide to prayer.
    (CHAPTER 49)

37. Incline your whole heart to the unseen movement of God's love within you.
    (CHAPTER 52)

38. Through prayer, allow your life to be transformed from the inside out, into the beautiful new creation God intends you to be.
    (CHAPTER 54)

39. As you pray, walk along the pathway of life and love, filled with joy in God's presence.
    (CHAPTERS 56, 60)

40. Lift up your eyes and hands to God, allowing your spirit to be moved by God's spirit upward like sparks from a fire in a woodstove.
    (CHAPTERS 57, 58)

41. Find rest in body and soul in God alone.
    (CHAPTER 59)

42. Go outside by day or by night and look into the sky as you pray to God.
    (CHAPTER 61)

43. Pray to God, who is far above you, far beyond you, yet within you and closer to you than your breath is to your body.
    (CHAPTER 62)

44. Pray with all the powers of your soul, including your reason, your will, your imagination, and your five senses.
    (CHAPTERS 63, 64, 65, 66)

45. Set your heart on what is above rather than upon either your body or your soul, and so discover your life being more and more transformed into God's beautiful character and image.
    (CHAPTER 67)

46. Keep praying and do not give up, even when it seems as though nothing happens when you pray.
    (CHAPTER 68)

47. When praying, be willing to become *nothing* and go *nowhere*.
    (CHAPTER 69)

48. As you pray, rely less upon your senses, and yield your life more fully to God.
    (CHAPTER 70)

49. By the help of God's ravishing grace, with a little dart of love, pierce into the Cloud of Unknowing and encounter the living God anytime you want, day or night.
    (CHAPTER 71)

50. Discover as you pray that the greatest labor in your life with God is found in loving others.
    (CHAPTER 72)

51. In the ordinary times and places of daily life, abide with Christ in God's treasure chest hidden within your innermost being.
    (CHAPTER 73)

52. Laying aside what is in the past, keep reaching out toward your future with God, journeying onward toward the fullness of friendship with God.
    (CHAPTERS 74, 75)

APPENDIX B
The Author of *The Cloud of Unknowing*

Fourteenth-century Europe was troubled with many forms of darkness, including widespread famine, illiteracy, violence, poverty, and pandemic disease. Millions across the European continent died during the Great Famine of 1315–1317. The Hundred Years' War began in 1337. The plague known as the Black Death entered Europe in 1346, decimating the population. In less than a decade, this pandemic claimed more than 100 million lives, nearly half the population of Europe. Because of fear of contracting the disease, this plague destroyed not only lives, but also the impulses of love and charity.

In the darkness of the fourteenth century, many souls were enlightened by brilliant mystics who radiated God's heavenly light, entering into intimate communion with Jesus through contemplative spiritual practices. The Rhineland German mystics were led by Meister John Eckhart, a Dominican monk. He mentored others, including Henry Suso and Johannes Tauler. One of the greatest of the Italian mystics, Catherine of Siena, invested her prayers and labors in seeking to heal the schism of the papacy. The Flemish mystics of that century include John of Ruysbroeck, Geert Groote, and Thomas à Kempis, author of the enduring spiritual classic *The Imitation of Christ*. England also knew an abundance of mystics, both men and women. Richard Rolle left us such devotional works as *The Fire of Love*, *Mending of Life*, and *Meditations on the Passion*. Walter Hilton wrote *The Scale of Perfection*. Living during the same half century as Hilton was the anchoress of East Anglia Julian of Norwich, who wrote *Revelations of Divine Love*.

In the fourteenth century we discover another bright light shining in the darkness, the anonymous author of *The Cloud of Unknowing*. Though we have no dates, parentage, place of birth, educational history, and almost no historic information on this writer, we do have the bright lamp of a devotional guide to prayer known as *The Cloud of Unknowing*. Who was this author of one of the most enduring and beloved spiritual classics from the medieval period? Nobody knows for certain. What linguists are able to discern from the literary style of this person's writing is that the author lived sometime in the middle to second half of the century, someplace in the middle of England, perhaps near Nottingham.

Though scholars have traditionally assumed the author was a man, I believe the author was just as likely a woman, a female monastic, offering advice to a younger monastic. The evidence in the writing intuitively points to a woman author. For example, one of the major reasons this work was written anonymously may simply have been due to the author's gender. Without the support of a well-known male mentor during her life such as Julian of Norwich knew in the same century, or Hildegard knew two centuries earlier along the Rhine River in Germany, a female author had no possibility of being heard or respected. Though several fourteenth-century female mystics are known and some of their writings are still read today, including Julian of Norwich, England in the 1300s was most certainly a male-dominated world.

The life of the anonymous author of *The Cloud of Unknowing* is enshrouded in mystery. Some who argue for male authorship will cite a later treatise by the same author, *The Letter of Private Direction*, where the writer states, "I make no secret, as you see, of the fact that I want to be your spiritual father; indeed I do, and intend to be so."[50] Why would a woman write of wanting to be someone's spiritual father? In his letter to the Thessalonian church, Paul writes of himself as a nursing mother, so it should not seem odd that a woman would write of being a "spiritual father," spiritually acting as a wise parent to a younger disciple or mentee.[51] Following my hunch that this remarkable author was a woman, let's examine the evidence within the writing, to fill out a general picture of her character and personality.

One of the first things that stands out about our author is that the original language is not Latin. *The Cloud of Unknowing* was written in Middle English. Other English mystic writers in her time wrote both in Latin and in Middle English, including Richard Rolle and Walter Hilton. The author of *The Cloud* chose to write in the language of the people, not the language of the academy or the church. As a woman, she did not have the opportunity to formally learn Latin or attend classes in Oxford, where Rolle studied, the famous university near her home. She wrote in Middle English because that was the only language she knew well enough to write such a work. *The Cloud* is one of the earliest devotional books written in English, written in the language of the commoner, describing an intimate, personal, nonsystematic approach to prayer and the spiritual life. If the author was indeed a woman, this work also is the first published work in the English language written by a woman. That honor is normally given to Julian of Norwich, who wrote *Revelations of Divine Love* around

1395. *The Cloud* is dated from the mid-fourteenth century, five decades prior to Julian's writing.

The Cloud is deeply rooted in Scripture, with allusions to Scripture woven into this work like a woman weaving at a loom. The author writes of four women from the New Testament, including the woman who anoints Jesus's feet with oil at the house of Simon; Mary and Martha, the sisters of Lazarus; and Mary the mother of Jesus. In each of these stories, the lives of women are lifted up to instruct the reader of how to draw near to God. She closes the work with a benediction imbued with grace and love, such as is found in the writings of Paul:

> *Go with God's blessings and mine. I pray for you before God's throne of grace, asking your life to be filled with God's gifts of peace, wisdom, and encouragement with an abundance of God's grace. Christ will be with you always and with all lovers of God on earth. Amen.*[52]

There are no scriptural citations in Latin in *The Cloud*. The reason for this may simply be that the academic learning of author was rudimentary. Instead, she always offers Scripture quotations in Middle English, in readable vernacular to better help her reader understand. *The Cloud* was not translated into Latin until the late fifteenth century, over a century after it was originally written in Middle English.

Our author expresses herself as a moderate, gentle, nurturing mother writing to a grown child, offering loving encouragement. The voice of *The Cloud* is temperate and relational. She warns her reader against straining herself with heroic efforts of spiritual discipline. There is very little competitive or combative element in her writing. *The Cloud* is written in the form of a lengthy, personal letter to a younger reader. The tone is intimate and personal. The language is simple and direct, with such easily understood phrases as "you only need a naked intent for God," and "select a little word of one syllable. Fasten it to your heart."

She writes in the dialect of the Midlands of England, possibly in Nottinghamshire or Lincolnshire. I enjoyed a year of university studies in the Midlands, in southern Lincolnshire, in 1976–1977. I feel connected to the voice of this author from this region, a down-to-earth voice of common sense, humility, encouragement, and rural grace while speaking of the lofty mysteries of the contemplative life. She seems to draw from a variety of influences, including ideas and themes gleaned from such writers as Bernard of Clairvaux, Hugo of St. Victor, Richard of St. Victor, Pseudo-Dionysius, Hugo de Balma, Guigo II, the Rhineland mystics such as Henry Suso, the Frenchman Thomas Gallus, Walter Hilton, and Richard Rolle—the last two of whom were her contemporaries in England. Since we do not know who served as her confessor and spiritual director, we have no way of knowing who mentored her, helping to shape her spiritual life through such sources of wisdom. Two other female writers, including St. Hildegard of Bingen and St. Teresa of Ávila, were both influenced by male spiritual directors. It was a common practice in medieval times for men to provide spiritual direction to women, especially among monastics.

One of the easily overlooked clues to her affiliation lies in the length she chose for her book. *The Cloud of Unknowing* consists of a prologue, seventy-three chapters, followed by a two-chapter epilogue. Those two chapters function as an epilogue because she repeats themes and even word-for-word sections from the prologue in these chapters, and concludes the entire manuscript with a benediction. Like *The Rule of St. Benedict*, *The Cloud* has seventy-three short chapters woven through with scriptural quotations and allusions. Why seventy-three chapters? The author was most likely a Benedictine nun who lived daily according to *The Rule of St. Benedict*, a spiritual guidebook written by Benedict in the early sixth century. As a Benedictine oblate, I read medieval Christian classics through the eyes of Benedict and found *The Cloud* to resonate deeply with Benedictine spirituality, including such themes as humility, Christ-centered devotion, and moderation in the practice of the spiritual life.

Benedict's Rule consists of a prologue and seventy-three short chapters. The author of *The Cloud* also followed Benedict's style of writing with numerous scriptural quotations and allusions, as I've noted throughout the text. I've also sought to trace the Benedictine spiritual roots and influences within the text of *The Cloud*, as can be discovered in the notes. As the proverb goes, "Imitation is the sincerest form of flattery." A Benedictine monastic would design her writing to emulate the great classic of early medieval monasticism, *The Rule of St. Benedict*. There were numerous Benedictine monasteries in the Midlands of England in the mid-1300s, including such a spiritual house as Wallingwells Priory, a small Benedictine monastery founded around 1140 with land donated by Ralph de Chevrolcourt in Wallingwells, near the town of Carlton-in-Lindrick, located thirty miles north of Nottingham, England.

Finally, the author of *The Cloud* speaks with a feminine voice, writing organically and holistically, connecting body and soul as a united whole. She welcomes our natural powers as God-given assistants in our spiritual journey. *The Cloud of Unknowing* is bathed in grace. In the fourteenth century, England was in a time of turbulent theological and political controversy, with such people as John Wycliffe challenging the status quo. Yet, very little of that intense, conflictive voice is heard across these pages. Instead, we find restraint, humility, wisdom, and moderation as would be found in the heart of a Benedictine cloistered sister.

Regardless of whether you agree or disagree with my thesis regarding the gender the author of *The Cloud*, I think we can agree that the author was a mature spiritual director offering wise, practical, down-to-earth instructions to lovers of God, to both men and women, no matter if they lived six centuries ago or are living today. This remarkable author continues to speak quietly and persuasively today, offering wisdom and encouragement for the spiritual journey into the Cloud of Unknowing. Anyone desiring to live more fully in God's presence will find this enduring classic to be a bright light for the steps ahead on our spiritual journey through a dark world.

NOTES

1 See Genesis 9; Exodus 13–14, 16, 19–20, 40; 1 Kings 8:10–11; Psalm 18:6–13, 104:3; Ezekiel 10:4; Daniel 7:13; Matthew 17:5, 24:30; Mark 13:26; and Luke 21:27.

2 In her chapter on English medieval mystics in *The Mystics of the Church,* Evelyn Underhill writes of Richard Rolle, Julian of Norwich, and the author of *The Cloud of Unknowing*: "All wrote in the vernacular, and were indeed among the first so to do, for Latin was still the literary tongue. They did this in order to widen their circle of appeal. . . . They addressed themselves . . . to the middle class, lay and religious, and especially to the country population, always the home of our peculiar English earnestness." Evelyn Underhill, *The Mystics of the Church* (New York: Schocken, 1964), 110–11.

3 The phrase "the Cloud of Unknowing," the title of this classic, comes up early in this text, and will be used nearly 100 times through the year. This phrase is always used in capital letters in this edition to highlight the original author's intent.The "Cloud of Unknowing" is contrasted with the "Cloud of Forgetting," which often refers to human frailty, limited ways of human thinking, and human mortality.

4 The phrase "pray naked" refers to unadorned prayer, prayer without pretense, or natural, childlike prayer.

5 In Latin, *Kyrie Eleison.* This ancient prayer is found several times in the Bible, such as in Luke 18:13, 38–39. In the original text of *The Cloud,* the author includes two short words for prayerful meditation in this section: "sin" and "God." The author adds that the reader may choose any short word or phrase that leads us closer to God.

6 James 1:19–20.

7 Proverbs 14:30; Ecclesiastes 4:4; Titus 3:3; 1 Peter 2:1.

8 Proverbs 16:18; 1 Peter 5:5.

9 Hebrews 13:5.

10 Matthew 6:25; Matthew 11:19; 1 Corinthians 10:31.

11 Galatians 5:16.

12 See Luke 7:36–50.

13 See Matthew 7:12.

14 Luke 10:42 (NASB).

15 "The best part" is found in the Latin Bible used by the church at the time of the writing of *The Cloud of Unknowing.*

16 The anonymous writer of *The Cloud of Unknowing* has Mary of Bethany as all three of these women.

17 St. Bernard of Clairvaux (1090–1153) lived thee centuries before the author of *The Cloud.* The author of *The Cloud* does not quote Bernard directly, but shares Bernard's understanding of degrees of love. These four degrees of love are from St. Bernard of Clairvaux, *On Loving God,* ed. Hugh Martin (London: SCM Press Ltd, 1959), 61–62.

18 See Matthew 25:35.

19 This in no way condones abuse. Those who have suffered any form of abuse, including physical, emotional, sexual, or spiritual abuse, need support and protection from ongoing abuse.

20 1 Corinthians 11:28.

21 See the book I've written on this subject, *Soul Mentoring: Discover the Ancient Art of Caring for Others* (Eugene, OR: Cascade, 2015). This book is based upon Gregory the

Great's book *Pastoral Care*. For the most recent translation of this ancient text, see George E. Demacopoulos, *The Book of Pastoral Rule* (Crestwood, NY: St. Vladimir's Seminary Press, 2007).

22 See 2 Timothy 1:6. "For this reason I remind you to fan into flame the gift of God, which is in you through the laying on of my hands." Also, see James's warning against thoughtless use of words, in James 3:5–6. "Consider what a great forest is set on fire by a small spark. The tongue also is a fire, a world of evil among the parts of the body. It corrupts the whole body, sets the whole course of one's life on fire, and is itself set on fire by hell."

23 Chapter 32 of *The Cloud* compares spiritual attacks to being attacked by wild boars or bears. In our twenty years of backpacking in national parks, we have frequently come upon bears, including black bears and grizzly bears. Though actual bear attacks are very rare, we have learned basic practices to protect ourselves from such bear attacks, such as proper food storage, hiking together, and being aware of our surroundings while hiking. What is written in this devotion is based upon the last defense when actually being attacked by a bear.

24 Historically, these three spiritual disciplines are part of the four stages of the ancient spiritual discipline of *Lectio Divina* or Sacred Reading: *Lectio, Meditatio, Oratio, Contemplatio*, or Reading, Meditating, Praying, Contemplating. These four stages are first found in a twelfth-century treatise by Guigo II, *The Ladder of Monks and Twelve Meditations*, in which these four movements are described as rungs on a ladder connecting earth to heaven, where humans are united with God through the contemplative discipline of *Lectio Divina*.

25 These three prayers are the title of Anne Lamott's book, *Help, Thanks, Wow: The Three Essential Prayers* (New York: Riverhead, 2012).

26 These three short prayers are from Anne Lamott's book, *Help, Thanks, Wow*. Though these one-word prayers are not found in the original text, the author of *The Cloud* encourages readers to pray by using any short prayer we choose, including a one-syllable word as prayer that will help us come near to God.

27 This short prayer is part of Jonah's longer prayer he prayed while in the belly of the great fish. Jonah's prayer is found in Jonah 2:1–9, a prayer made up of quotations from the Old Testament, mostly from the Psalms, including quotations from Psalms 3:8; 11:4; 18:6; 30:3; 31:22; 42:7; 50:14; 50:23; 69:1–2; 77:11–12; 86:13; 88:6; 116:14; 120:1.

28 This list, found in chapter 40 of *The Cloud*, seems to be a combination of two of Paul's lists of virtues in the New Testament, including his list of spiritual fruit in Galatians 5:22–23 (love, joy, peace, forbearance, kindness, goodness, faithfulness, gentleness, self-control), and his list of Christian virtues in Colossians 3:12–14 (compassion, kindness, humility, gentleness, patience, forgiveness, love).

29 This phrase is similar to that used by another fourteenth-century English devotional writer, Julian of Norwich, who recorded the words she heard from Jesus: "It is true that sin is the cause of all this pain, but all shall be well, and all shall be well, and all manner of thing shall be well." See Julian of Norwich, *Revelations of Divine Love* (Brewster, MA: Paraclete Press, 2011), 65.

30 In this section, based upon chapter 42 of *The Cloud*, the author clearly draws upon The Rule of St. Benedict, one of the foundational texts of medieval Christian spirituality. Benedict wrote, "all things are to be done with moderation." See Timothy Fry, ed., *RB 1980: The Rule of St. Benedict in English* (Collegeville, MN: Liturgical Press, 1981), 69.

31 The author of *The Cloud* uses the image of "treading" upon lower things, a picture of feet trampling a piece of dirt underfoot. We are encouraged to "tread down under

the Cloud of Forgetting" anything of lesser value that hinders us from coming closer to God.

32 Romans 12:2; Colossians 2:2–3.

33 See Psalm 15:1–2: "Lord, who may dwell in your sacred tent? Who may live on your holy mountain? The one whose walk is blameless, who does what is righteous." See Psalm 24:3–4: "Who may ascend the mountain of the Lord? Who may stand in his holy place? The one who has clean hands and a pure heart, who does not trust in an idol or swear by a false god." Also, see Isaiah 56:6b–7a: "All who keep the Sabbath without desecrating it and who hold fast to my covenant—these I will bring to my holy mountain and give them joy in my house of prayer." Finally, see Ezekiel 36:26: "I will give you a new heart and put a new spirit in you; I will remove from you your heart of stone and give you a heart of flesh."

34 As James writes, "Submit yourselves, then, to God. Resist the devil, and he will flee from you. Come near to God and he will come near to you." See James 4:7–8.

35 See *The Rule of St. Benedict* 20:3–4. "We must know that God regards our purity of heart and tears of compunction, not our many words. Prayer should therefore be short and pure, unless perhaps it is prolonged under the inspiration of divine grace." Quoted from Fry, *The Rule of St. Benedict*, 48.

36 The section was likely influenced by St. Benedict. The opening words of *The Rule of St. Benedict,* in Latin: *Obsculta, o fili, præcepta magistri, et inclina aurem cordis.* "Listen carefully, my son, to the master's instructions, and attend to them with the ear of your heart." See Timothy Fry, ed. *The Rule of St. Benedict in Latin and English with Notes* (Collegeville, MN: Liturgical Press, 1981), 156–57.

37 Benedict called such people *gyrovagues,* "who spend their entire lives drifting from region to region, staying at guests for three or four days in different monasteries. Always on the move, they never settle down, and are slaves to their own wills and gross appetites." Benedict also pioneered the vow of stability to overcome this malaise of being always on the move.

38 The original quote is, "Martin, who is still but a catechumen, clothed me with this robe." (Sulpicius, ch. 2.) See http://www.catholic.org/saints/saint.php?saint_id=81.

39 See Matthew 25:34–40.

40 In Leo Tolstoy's short story "What Men Live By," the fallen angel Michael discovers what humans live by: "I have now understood that though it seems to men that they live by care for themselves, in truth it is love alone by which they live. He who has love, is in God, and God is in him, for God is love."

41 See the three temptations Jesus faced as recorded in Matthew 4:1–11 and Luke 4:1–13.

42 See Revelation 8:3–4. "Another angel, who had a golden censer, came and stood at the altar. He was given much incense to offer, with the prayers of all God's people, on the golden altar in front of the throne. The smoke of the incense, together with the prayers of God's people, went up before God from the angel's hand."

43 The author of *The Cloud* refers to Dionysius in this chapter. *The Cloud* may also have been influenced by such medieval writers as Benedict of Nursia, Bernard of Clairvaux, Hugo of St. Victor, Richard of St. Victor, Hugo de Balma, Guigo II, Henry Suso, Thomas Gallus, Walter Hilton, and Richard Rolle.

44 Fry, *The Rule of St. Benedict*, 15.

45 Bezalel is mentioned in Exodus 31, 36, and 39. See Exodus 31:1–5: "Then the Lord said to Moses, 'See, I have chosen Bezalel son of Uri, the son of Hur, of the tribe of Judah, and I have filled him with the Spirit of God, with wisdom, with understanding, with knowledge and with all kinds of skills—to make artistic designs for work in gold, silver and bronze, to cut and set stones, to work in wood, and to engage in all kinds of crafts.'"

46 These same words of warning and encouragement are also found in the earliest parts of *The Cloud*.

47 This quote is from St. Gregory the Great (540–604) from *Homilia in Evangelia* 2., 25 (PL 76,1190). The original is written thus: "All holy desires grow by delays: and if they wane by delays, they were they never holy desires." See James Walsh, sj, ed. and trans., *The Cloud of Unknowing*: The Classics of Western Spirituality (Mahwah, NJ: Paulist Press, 1981), 265.

48 This appendix is inspired by Joan M. Nuth's book *God's Lovers in an Age of Anxiety: The Medieval English Mystics* (Maryknoll, NY: Orbis, 2001), 152–155.

49 This prayer is found as the frontispiece.

50 Quoted in the introduction by Walsh, *The Cloud of Unknowing*, 11.

51 See 1 Thessalonians 2:7–8: "Just as a nursing mother cares for her children, so we cared for you. Because we loved you so much, we were delighted to share with you not only the gospel of God but our lives as well."

52 See the final paragraph of the epilogue.

SELECTED BIBLIOGRAPHY

Armstrong, Karen. *Visions of God: Four Medieval Mystics and Their Writings*. New York: Bantam, 1994.

Baker, Father Augustine, OSB. *The Cloud of Unknowing and Other Treatises*. London: Burns Oates and Washbourne, 1924.

Bernard of Clairvaux. Edited by Hugh Martin. *On Loving God*. London: SCM Press, 1959.

Bullett, Gerald. *The English Mystics*. London: Michael Joseph, 1950.

Butcher, Carmen Acevedo. *The Cloud of Unknowing with the Book of Privy Counsel*. Boston: Shambhala, 2009.

Calhoun, Adele Ahlberg, Doug Calhoun, Clare Loughrige, and Scott Loughrige. *Spiritual Rhythms for the Enneagram: A Handbook for Harmony and Transformation*. Downers Grove, IL: IVP, 2019.

Colledge, Eric. *The Medieval Mystics of England*. New York: Charles Scribner's Sons, 1961.

Cowan, Douglas E. *A Nakid Entent Unto God: A Source/Commentary on The Cloud of Unknowing*. Wakefield, NH: Longwood Academic, 1991.

Cox, Michael. *Handbook of Christian Spirituality*. San Francisco: Harper & Row, 1983.

Fanous, Samuel, and Vincent Gillespie, eds. *The Cambridge Companion to Medieval English Mysticism*. Cambridge: Cambridge University Press, 2011.

Foster, Richard, and Gayle Beebe. *Longing for God: Seven Paths of Christian Devotion*. Downers Grove, IL: IVP, 2009.

Fry, Timothy, OSB, ed. *RB 1980: The Rule of St. Benedict in Latin and English with Notes*. Collegeville, MN: The Liturgical Press, 1981.

Fry, Timothy, OSB, ed. *RB 1980: The Rule of St. Benedict in English*. Collegeville, MN: The Liturgical Press, 1982.

Gallacher, Patrick, ed. *The Cloud of Unknowing*. Kalamazoo, MI: Western Michigan University Medieval Institute Publications; TEAMS Middle English Texts Series, 1997.

Gatta, Julia. *Three Spiritual Directors for our Time: Julian of Norwich, The Cloud of Unknowing, Walter Hilton*. Cambridge, MA: Cowley, 1986.

Gregory the Great. Translated by George E. Demacopoulos. *The Book of Pastoral Rule*. Crestwood, NY: St. Vladimir's Seminary Press, 2007.

Hansen, Gary Neal. *Kneeling With Giants: Learning to Pray with History's Best Teachers.* Downers Grove, IL: IVP, 2012.

Hodgson, Phyllis, ed. *The Cloud of Unknowing: And The Book of Privy Counseling.* Early English Text Society. Oxford: Oxford University Press, 1944.

Hort, Greta. *Sense and Thought: A Study in Mysticism.* London: George Allen & Unwin, 1936.

John-Julian, Father, OJN. *The Complete Cloud of Unknowing with Letters of Privy Counsel.* Brewster, MA: Paraclete Press, 2015.

Johnston, William, ed. *The Cloud of Unknowing and the Book of Privy Counseling.* New York: Image, 1973.

Johnston, William. *The Mysticism of the Cloud of Unknowing.* New York: Fordham University Press, 2000.

Julian of Norwich. *Revelations of Divine Love.* Brewster, MA: Paraclete Press, 2011.

Kirvan, John J. *Where Only Love Can Go: A Journey of the Soul Into the Cloud of Unknowing.* Notre Dame, IN: Ave Maria Press, 1996.

Knowles, David. *The English Mystical Tradition.* London: Burns & Oates, 1961.

Lawrence, Brother. *The Practice of the Presence of God.* Brewster, MA: Paraclete Press, 2010.

Magill, Frank N., and Ian P. McGreal, eds. *Christian Spirituality: The Essential Guide to the Most Influential Spiritual Writings of the Christian Tradition.* San Francisco: Harper & Row, 1988.

McCann, Dom Justin, ed. *The Cloud of Unknowing and Other Treatises.* Westminster, MD: The Newman Press, 1952.

Meninger, William A. *The Loving Search for God: Contemplative Prayer and The Cloud of Unknowing.* New York: Continuum, 1999.

Michael, Chester P., and Marie C. Norrisey. *Prayer and Temperament: Different Prayer Forms for Different Personality Types.* Charlottesville, VA: The Open Door, 1984.

Miller, Gordon L. *The Way of the English Mystics: An Anthology and Guide for Pilgrims.* Ridgefield, CT: Morehouse, 1996.

Morse, MaryKate. *A Guidebook to Prayer: Twenty-Four Ways to Walk with God.* Downers Grove, IL: IVP, 2013.

Murray, Andrew. *With Christ in the School of Prayer.* New Kensington, PA: Whitaker House, 1981.

Nieva, Constantino Sarmiento. *The Transcending God: The Teaching of the Author of "The Cloud of Unknowing."* London: The Mitre Press, 1971.

Nuth, Joan M. *God's Lovers in an Age of Anxiety: The Medieval English Mystics.* Maryknoll, NY: Orbis, 2001.

Pennington, M. Basil. *Centering Prayer: Renewing an Ancient Christian Prayer Form*. New York: Doubleday, 1980.

Progoff, Ira, trans. *The Cloud of Unknowing*. New York: Dell, 1983.

Robinson, David. *Ancient Paths: Discover Christian Formation the Benedictine Way*. Brewster, MA: Paraclete Press, 2010.

———. *Soul Mentoring: Discover the Ancient Art of Caring for Others*. Eugene, OR: Cascade Books, 2015.

Spearing, A. C., trans. *The Cloud of Unknowing and Other Works*. Penguin Classics. New York: Penguin, 2001.

Szarmach, Paul E., ed. *An Introduction to the Medieval Mystics of Europe*. Albany: State University of New York Press, 1984.

Tobin, Frank, ed. *Henry Suso: The Exemplar with Two German Sermons*. Mahwah, NJ: Paulist Press, 1989.

Underhill, Evelyn. *The Cloud of Unknowing: The Classic of Medieval Mysticism*. Mineola, NY: Dover, 2003.

———. *The Mystics of the Church*. New York: Schocken, 1964.

Walsh, James, ed. and trans. *The Cloud of Unknowing*. The Classics of Western Spirituality. Mahwah, NJ: Paulist Press, 1981.

Watkins, John M., ed. *A Book of Contemplation the which is called The Cloud of Unknowing in which a soul is oned with God*. Public Domain Edition. British Museum MS. Harl. 674, 1934.

Watson, Graeme. *Strike the Cloud: Understanding and Practicing the Teaching of The Cloud of Unknowing*. London: SPCK, 2011.

Woods, Richard J. *Christian Spirituality: God's Presence Through the Ages*. Maryknoll, NY: Orbis, 1970.

Wolters, Clifton. *The Cloud of Unknowing and Other Works*. London: Penguin, 1978.

Young, Sarah. *Jesus Calling: Enjoying Peace in His Presence*. Nashville: Thomas Nelson, 2004.

ABOUT PARACLETE PRESS
Who We Are

As the publishing arm of the Community of Jesus, Paraclete Press presents a full expression of Christian belief and practice—from Catholic to Evangelical, from Protestant to Orthodox, reflecting the ecumenical charism of the Community and its dedication to sacred music, the fine arts, and the written word. We publish books, recordings, sheet music, and video/DVDs that nourish the vibrant life of the church and its people.

What We Are Doing

Books

PARACLETE PRESS BOOKS show the richness and depth of what it means to be Christian. While Benedictine spirituality is at the heart of who we are and all that we do, our books reflect the Christian experience across many cultures, time periods, and houses of worship.

We have many series, including *Paraclete Essentials*; *Paraclete Fiction*; *Paraclete Poetry*; *Paraclete Giants*; and for children and adults, *All God's Creatures*, books about animals and faith; and *San Damiano Books*, focusing on Franciscan spirituality. Others include *Voices from the Monastery* (men and women monastics writing about living a spiritual life today), *Active Prayer*, and new for young readers: *The Pope's Cat*. We also specialize in gift books for children on the occasions of Baptism and First Communion, as well as other important times in a child's life, and books that bring creativity and liveliness to any adult spiritual life.

THE MOUNT TABOR BOOKS series focuses on the arts and literature as well as liturgical worship and spirituality; it was created in conjunction with the Mount Tabor Ecumenical Centre for Art and Spirituality in Barga, Italy.